CAMBRIDGE
UNIVERSITY PRESS

Cambridge Lower Secondary

Global Perspectives

TEACHER'S RESOURCE 8

Keely Laycock and Nancy Budler

CAMBRIDGE
UNIVERSITY PRESS

University Printing House, Cambridge CB2 8BS, United Kingdom

One Liberty Plaza, 20th Floor, New York, NY 10006, USA

477 Williamstown Road, Port Melbourne, VIC 3207, Australia

314–321, 3rd Floor, Plot 3, Splendor Forum, Jasola District Centre, New Delhi – 110025, India

103 Penang Road, #05-06/07, Visioncrest Commercial, Singapore 238467

Cambridge University Press is part of the University of Cambridge.

It furthers the University's mission by disseminating knowledge in the pursuit of education, learning and research at the highest international levels of excellence.

www.cambridge.org
Information on this title: www.cambridge.org/9781009316064

First published 2020
Second edition 2024

20 19 18 17 16 15 14 13 12 11 10 9 8 7 6 5 4 3 2 1

Printed in Great Britain by CPI Group (UK) Ltd, CR0 4YY

A catalogue record for this publication is available from the British Library

ISBN 978-1-009-316064 Teacher's Resource with Digital Access

Additional resources for this publication at www.cambridge.org/go

Endorsement statement

Endorsement indicates that a resource has passed Cambridge International's rigorous quality-assurance process and is suitable to support the delivery of a Cambridge International curriculum framework. However, endorsed resources are not the only suitable materials available to support teaching and learning, and are not essential to be used to achieve the qualification. Resource lists found on the Cambridge International website will include this resource and other endorsed resources.

Any example answers to questions taken from past question papers, practice questions, accompanying marks and mark schemes included in this resource have been written by the authors and are for guidance only. They do not replicate examination papers. In examinations the way marks are awarded may be different. Any references to assessment and/or assessment preparation are the publisher's interpretation of the curriculum framework requirements. Examiners will not use endorsed resources as a source of material for any assessment set by Cambridge International.

While the publishers have made every attempt to ensure that advice on the qualification and its assessment is accurate, the official curriculum framework, specimen assessment materials and any associated assessment guidance materials produced by the awarding body are the only authoritative source of information and should always be referred to for definitive guidance. Cambridge International recommends that teachers consider using a range of teaching and learning resources based on their own professional judgement of their students' needs.

Cambridge International has not paid for the production of this resource, nor does Cambridge International receive any royalties from its sale. For more information about the endorsement process, please visit www.cambridgeinternational.org/endorsed-resources

Third party websites and resources referred to in this publication have not been endorsed by Cambridge Assessment International Education.

Contents

Section 5 Collaboration

Section 6 Communication

Digital resources

The following items are available on Cambridge GO. For more information on how to access and use your digital resource, please see front cover.

> Introduction

Welcome to the new edition of this Teacher's Resource for Cambridge Lower Secondary Global Perspectives Stage 8. We are delighted you have decided to use our resources to deliver this dynamic course. Cambridge Lower Secondary Global Perspectives is a transformational programme designed to help learners develop a range of key skills that will aid them not only in their school and academic life but also in their future career. At the heart of the course is a varied and active learning approach, which inspires learners to explore a wide range of issues and different points of view.

This approach is what we have kept in mind whilst writing and updating the Learner's Skills Book and Teacher's Resource for each stage of lower secondary. Stages 7 and 8 are structured around six skills: research, analysis, evaluation, reflection, collaboration and communication. Stage 9 is structured around five skills (collaboration is not assessed at this stage), and a section dedicated to planning, writing and reviewing the Cambridge Lower Secondary Checkpoint assessment.

Each skills section follows the same approach, beginning with 'Let's start thinking about' to excite your learners about the key skill they are going to work on. Each section then guides learners through a 'Starting with', 'Developing' and 'Getting better at' scaffold, building their awareness of their own progress and encouraging them to take charge of their own learning journey. A range of activities and tasks are included, with plenty of opportunities for peer-to-peer and group work, and to encourage learners to reflect upon their progress, track their actions and achievements and record their next steps. The self-assessment activities build on each other to give learners a clear picture of how they are progressing, and these will help you to support them in their learning journey whilst maintaining an overview of any gaps in knowledge and understanding. Each section ends with 'Showcasing your skills' which gives learners an opportunity to reflect on their work. The Learner's Skills Books are write-in resources, so each learner can create and keep a portfolio of their work and track their progression through each skill and each stage.

The first part of this Teacher's Resource includes useful information about the curriculum framework, a set of mapping grids that show how the resources address the learning objectives, and guidance around teaching techniques and pedagogical approaches, with information and tips about things like Assessment for Learning, Differentiation, Language for Learning and integrating the theme of sustainability. The section titled 'Approaches to teaching Cambridge Lower Secondary Global Perspectives' includes guidance about different ways in which you might want to approach the course, using various combinations of the Cambridge University Press and Cambridge International resources to facilitate your learners' development of the key skills. Cambridge Global Perspectives™ is a subject that gives teachers and learners a great deal of flexibility and you should be guided by your own preferences and interests, as well as the needs of your learners, when selecting an approach to take.

Lesson ideas are designed to help you plan for each stage of your lesson, motivate learners and monitor their progress against learning goals. Downloadables and Worked Examples are included for each lesson to illustrate how to build and teach a skill through a relevant Cambridge Global Perspectives topic, using sample material, exemplars and useful weblinks. This selection of real-life and fictional examples is there to help you plan, but is in no way intended to be a 'correct' way of working through the skills – the ideas are intended to be flexible, and we hope they will assist you in generating ideas to apply to the issue you are studying.

Also included in the digital resources that accompany the Cambridge Lower Secondary Global Perspectives Learner's Skills Books and Teacher's Resources is a set of three projects per stage, each with supporting teaching notes. These projects are designed to give learners opportunities to synthesise the different skills they have been developing and use them in real-world scenarios related to Cambridge Lower Secondary Global Perspectives topics. They also give learners the chance to demonstrate and practise their skills in a way that builds towards the Stage 9 Checkpoint assessment.

By using this scaffolded approach through each skill and each stage, we hope that you will find a solid framework upon which to build, and that it will support you as an effective facilitator of Cambridge Global Perspectives, helping your learners to enjoy exploring ideas in the classroom that they can then apply to their lives outside of school and into the future.

Cambridge Lower Secondary Global Perspectives is one of the most rewarding and exciting programmes you will ever teach. Enjoy!

Keely Laycock and Nancy Budler

How to use this series

This suite of resources supports learners and teachers following the Cambridge Lower Secondary Global Perspectives curriculum framework (1129) from 2022. The components in the series are designed to work together and help learners develop the necessary skills for this subject. With clear language and style, they are designed for international learners.

The Learner's Skills Book is designed for learners to use in class with guidance from the teacher. It offers complete coverage of Cambridge Lower Secondary Global Perspectives. The Learner's Skills Book supports learners in developing the Global Perspectives skills of analysis, collaboration, communication, evaluation, reflection and research through an active learning approach. Each section also provides opportunities to practise the Global Perspectives skills through engaging topics, discussion activities and independent reflection.

A digital version of the Learner's Skills Book is included with the print version and is available separately.

The Teacher's Resource provides everything teachers need to confidently deliver the course. It is packed full of useful teaching notes and lesson plans, with suggestions for differentiation to support and challenge learners, and ideas for formative assessment.

A digital version of the Teacher's Resource is included with the print version. The digital resource contains worked examples, templates for activities and three projects which give learners further opportunities to develop the six Global Perspectives skills through interesting topics.

How to use this Teacher's Resource

This Teacher's Resource contains both general guidance and teaching notes designed to help you to deliver the content in Cambridge Lower Secondary Global Perspectives Stage 8.

There are **teaching notes** for each lesson of the Learner's Skills Book. Each set of teaching notes contains the following features to help you deliver the unit.

At the start of each section there is a **Skills overview**, which summarises the learning objectives within each skill and how these are developed across the lessons within that skill. It also contains ideas for which Challenges or topics can be used, and how you may be able to make links with other skills across the curriculum. Key points cover common misconceptions and tips on how to fill learning gaps. The overview also provides language support, highlighting key terminology needed for that section.

Learning objectives	78Rs.01 Construct relevant research questions. 78Rs.02 Identify and begin to reference a range of print and multimedia sources and use them to locate relevant information and answer research questions. 78Rs.03 Select an appropriate method and conduct research to test predictions and begin to answer a research question. 78Rs.04 Select, organise and record relevant information from a range of sources and findings from primary research, using appropriate methods.
Topic ideas	Migration and urbanisation; Change in culture and communities; Development, trade and aid; Poverty and inequality

The **Learning objectives** and **Learning goals** features take the objectives from the curriculum framework and the goals from the Learner's Skills Book, to help you communicate to learners what is expected of them.

CAMBRIDGE STAGE 8 RESEARCH LEARNING OBJECTIVES

78Rs.03 Select an appropriate method and conduct research to test predictions and begin to answer a research question

78Rs.04 Select, organise and record relevant information from a range of sources and findings from primary research, using appropriate methods

LEARNING GOALS

To get better at:

- understanding how research helps test a prediction
- recording information gained from primary research
- presenting information gained from primary research

Each **How will I know if I reach my goals?** heading contains advice on how learners can interact with the success criteria laid out in the Learner's Skills Book.

> ### How will I know if I reach my goals?
> **Good for:** Learners to give examples of their learning from the lesson. They can complete the table at any point in the lesson, but might do it at the end.

Reflecting the activities in Learner's Skills Book, each lesson consists of advice on how to work through the **Prior learning** activity, **Starter activity**, **Main activity**, **Class discussion** and **Peer feedback**, where appropriate. To help you plan, a recommended amount of time to spend on each lesson is given (please note, this is only a recommendation and may need to be altered depending on the structure of your school day). A list of **resources you will need** has been included with each lesson.

> ### Resources needed
> - Learner's Skills Book 8
> - Downloadable 1.7

The **Prior learning** notes provide advice on where your learners should be in their learning before beginning the activity.

> ### Prior learning (approx. 5–10 mins)
> **Good for:** Building on previous knowledge, learning and understanding. This might be from Cambridge Primary Global Perspectives, Cambridge Global Perspectives Stage 7, from other subject areas or from previous Cambridge Global Perspectives Stage 8 lessons (especially Lessons 5 and 6).

The ideas for the **Starter activity** are designed to grab your learners' attention and create interest and engagement. They include advice on what to listen out for, how to diagnose any issues and how to make decisions about what to do next.

> ### Starter activity (approx. 10 mins)
> **Good for:** Identifying good research questions and some of the features of good research questions.

The **Main activity** ideas give instructions for successful execution of the activity, with differentiation advice, suggestions for feedback and answers where relevant.

> ### Main activity (approx. 20–25 mins)
> **Good for:** Producing good research questions about an issue.
>
> **Activity:** Learners produce a mind map of questions about an issue (it can be any issue).

In each lesson there is also a **Worked Example** for the Starter activity or Main activity, to demonstrate how the activity could work with a relevant topic. This serves as an example of what success looks like, but you do not have to use the issue given in the example.

> ### Worked Example for the Starter activity
> Topic: Values and beliefs
>
> **Sub-topic:** Beliefs about foods
>
> See Downloadable 2.3.
>
> **1** Bar graph showing why people eat the foods they do.

At the end of each lesson there are ideas on how to use the **Independent reflection activity**, **Self-assessments** and **Issue review**, depending on which lesson you are in and if your learners are completing these in the lesson or as homework. These are scaffolded throughout each section.

Independent reflection activity; Self-assessment; Issue review (approx. 15–20 mins)

Good for: Encouraging learners to consider their learning and progression in learning in lessons. Ask them to be as honest as they can.

At the end of each section, there is advice about how to use the Showcasing your skills pages that feature at the end of each Learner's Skills Book section. These passages in the Teacher's Resource also indicate which of the three projects could be used to help learners demonstrate and practise the skills they have developed in each section.

Showcasing your skills: Research

Good for: Showing learners how others felt at the end of the research tasks. These young people have practiced and developed their research skills and learned a lot about how conducting research and asking key questions can make them even better at Cambridge Lower Secondary Global Perspectives. You may intend to have your learners write the Checkpoint Report in Stage 9. Learners should be improving their ability to write a question that will allow them to fulfill all the Assessment Criteria. You can help them by encouraging them to think about issues that have causes and consequences, and that require solutions. Those are the kinds of questions they need to ask!

Supporting resources including worksheets, worked examples and a set of three projects are available on Cambridge GO. For more information on how to access and use your digital resource, please see front cover.

> About the curriculum framework

The information in this section is based on the Cambridge International curriculum framework. You should always refer to the appropriate curriculum framework document for the year of examination to confirm the details and for more information. The curriculum framework document is available on the Cambridge International website at www.cambridgeinternational.org.

Cambridge Lower Secondary Global Perspectives is an interdisciplinary skills-based programme that encourages learners to consider and connect personal, local and global perspectives on global issues and topics. The programme aims to foster independent learning and to help learners make sense of the world around them.

The learning objectives for Cambridge Global Perspectives are divided into six strands that correspond to the six key skills that the course aims to develop:

- Analysis
- Collaboration
- Communication
- Evaluation
- Reflection
- Research

To aid progression, separate sets of learning objectives are provided for Stages 7 and 8, and for Stage 9.

There is no prescribed content for Cambridge Lower Secondary Global Perspectives. Instead, the focus is on developing the six skills listed above. Learners should be given opportunities to develop and practise the skills while exploring personal, local and global perspectives. This is best achieved by focusing on global issues that have an impact in the community served by the school.

It is recommended that learners explore a range of global issues. The curriculum framework suggests that learners might focus on some of the following topics:

- Arts in society
- Change in culture and communities
- Climate change, energy and resources
- Conflict and peace
- Development, trade and aid
- Digital world
- Education for all
- Employment
- Environment, pollution and conservation
- Globalisation

- Health and wellbeing
- Law and criminality
- Media and communication
- Migration and urbanisation
- Political power and action
- Poverty and inequality
- Social identity and inclusion
- Sport and recreation
- Technology, industry and innovation
- Transport, travel and tourism
- Values and beliefs
- Water, food and agriculture

In addition to the Cambridge Lower Secondary Global Perspectives curriculum framework, Cambridge International provides a set of Challenges. These resources provide suggestions for ways in which teachers can help their learners practise their Cambridge Global Perspectives skills. Information about the Cambridge Challenges can be found on the Cambridge Lower Secondary Support Site (https://lowersecondary.cambridgeinternational.org/)

About the assessment

Information about the assessment of the Cambridge Lower Secondary Global Perspectives curriculum framework is available on the Cambridge Assessment International Education website: www.cambridgeinternational.org/lowersecondary

> Curriculum mapping

The information in this section is based on the Cambridge International curriculum framework. You should always refer to the appropriate curriculum framework document for the year of examination to confirm the details and for more information. The curriculum framework document is available on the Cambridge International website at www.cambridgeinternational.org.

The mapping grid below and those on the following pages show how the Learner's Skills Book and accompanying downloadable resources made available with this Teacher's Resource can be used to support your delivery of the Cambridge Lower Secondary Global Perspectives curriculum framework. They show how the lesson learning goals for each lesson in the Learner's Skills Book map to and provide comprehensive coverage of the learning objectives listed in the curriculum framework. They also demonstrate how the lessons in the Learner's Skills Book can be used to support the Cambridge Lower Secondary Global Perspectives Challenges. The key Challenge and topic listed for each skills-based chapter correspond to the Challenge that Cambridge International have identified as primarily supporting that skill. The additional Stage 8 Challenges and Lower Secondary topics listed are those that also relate to the issues explored in that chapter.

1 Research

Challenge(s)	Key: Making a difference in our community	
Curriculum topic(s)	Key: Change in culture and communities Additional: Climate change, energy and resources; Health and wellbeing; Transport, travel and tourism	
Lesson	**Lesson learning goals**	**Curriculum learning objectives**
Lesson 1	Constructing research questions	
	To start to: • explain the term 'research' • recognise a good research question • write a good research question	78Rs.01 Construct relevant research questions.
Lesson 2	Information skills	
	To start to: • select appropriate research methods to begin to answer a research question	78Rs.03 Select an appropriate method and conduct research to test predictions and begin to answer a research question.
	Recording findings	
	To start to: • summarise information from texts into own words	78Rs.04 Select, organise and record relevant information from a range of sources and findings from primary research, using appropriate methods.

Challenge(s)	Key: Making a difference in our community	
Curriculum topic(s)	Key: Change in culture and communities Additional: Climate change, energy and resources; Health and wellbeing; Transport, travel and tourism	
Lesson	**Lesson learning goals**	**Curriculum learning objectives**
Lesson 3	Information skills	
	To start to: • realise the importance of referencing information sources • find relevant information about a topic • reference sources of information accurately	78Rs.02 Identify and begin to reference a range of print and multimedia sources and use them to locate relevant information and answer research questions.
Lesson 4	Constructing research questions	
	To develop knowledge and understanding about: • the features of a good research question • how to write a good research question • how to write sub-questions to help answer research questions	78Rs.01 Construct relevant research questions.
Lesson 5	Constructing research questions	
	To develop knowledge and understanding about: • good questions for a questionnaire/survey • writing questions to gain relevant information	78Rs.01 Construct relevant research questions.
	Conducting research	
	To develop knowledge and understanding about: • different research methods	78Rs.03 Select an appropriate method and conduct research to test predictions and begin to answer a research question.
Lesson 6	Information skills	
	To develop knowledge and understanding about: • referencing sources of information	78Rs.02 Identify and begin to reference a range of print and multimedia sources and use them to locate relevant information and answer research questions.
	Conducting research	
	To develop knowledge and understanding about: • recognising good questions to test predictions • writing questionnaires to gain relevant information	78Rs.03 Select an appropriate method and conduct research to test predictions and begin to answer a research question.

Challenge(s)	Key: Making a difference in our community	
Curriculum topic(s)	Key: Change in culture and communities Additional: Climate change, energy and resources; Health and wellbeing; Transport, travel and tourism	
Lesson	**Lesson learning goals**	**Curriculum learning objectives**
Lesson 6	Recording findings	
	To develop knowledge and understanding about: • selecting information to write questions	78Rs.04 Select, organise and record relevant information from a range of sources and findings from primary research, using appropriate methods.
Lesson 7	Conducting research	
	To get better at: • understanding how research helps test a prediction	78Rs.03 Select an appropriate method and conduct research to test predictions and begin to answer a research question.
	Recording findings	
	To get better at: • recording information gained from primary research • presenting information gained from primary research	78Rs.04 Select, organise and record relevant information from a range of sources and findings from primary research, using appropriate methods
Lesson 8	Information skills	
	To get better at: • doing an internet search to find relevant information	78Rs.02 Identify and begin to reference a range of print and multimedia sources and use them to locate relevant information and answer research questions.
	Conducting research	
	To get better at: • understanding when to use primary and secondary information sources	78Rs.03 Select an appropriate method and conduct research to test predictions and begin to answer a research question
	Recording findings	
	To get better at: • judging the quality of an information source to help answer a research question	78Rs.04 Select, organise and record relevant information from a range of sources and findings from primary research, using appropriate methods.
Lesson 9	Information skills	
	To get better at: • referencing sources of information	78Rs.02 Identify and begin to reference a range of print and multimedia sources and use them to locate relevant information and answer research questions
	Conducting research	
	To get better at: • finding relevant information to answer a research question	78Rs.03 Select an appropriate method and conduct research to test predictions and begin to answer a research question.

Challenge(s)	Key: Making a difference in our community	
Curriculum topic(s)	Key: Change in culture and communities Additional: Climate change, energy and resources; Health and wellbeing; Transport, travel and tourism	
Lesson	**Lesson learning goals**	**Curriculum learning objectives**
Lesson 9	**Recording findings**	
	To get better at: • recording relevant information	78Rs.04 Select, organise and record relevant information from a range of sources and findings from primary research, using appropriate methods.

2 Analysis

Challenge(s)	Key: Beliefs about foods Additional: How can we use resources sustainably?	
Curriculum topic(s)	Key: Values and beliefs Additional: Climate change, energy and resources; Digital world; Education for all	
Lesson	**Lesson learning goals**	**Curriculum learning objectives**
Lesson 1	**Identifying perspectives**	
	To start to: • summarise relevant information	78A.01 Identify ideas and evidence from different perspectives within different sources on a given issue.
Lesson 2	**Identifying perspectives**	
	To start to: • explain what an issue is • explain what a perspective is	78A.01 Identify ideas and evidence from different perspectives within different sources on a given issue.
Lesson 3	**Identifying perspectives**	
	To start to: • understand the difference between an issue, a perspective and a course of action	78A.01 Identify ideas and evidence from different perspectives within different sources on a given issue.
	Interpreting data	
	To start to: • explain how data from a graph can support an argument	78A.02 Explain how graphical or numerical data supports an argument or a perspective.
	Solving problems	
	To start to: • suggest courses of action to make a positive difference to an issue	78A.04 Suggest and justify different actions to make a positive difference to a national or global issue.

Challenge(s)	Key: Beliefs about foods Additional: How can we use resources sustainably?	
Curriculum topic(s)	Key: Values and beliefs Additional: Climate change, energy and resources; Digital world; Education for all	
Lesson	**Lesson learning goals**	**Curriculum learning objectives**
Lesson 4	**Solving problems**	
	To develop knowledge and understanding about: • questions to ask to decide on suitable courses of action to help resolve an issue • taking action to help resolve or make a positive difference to an issue.	78A.04 Suggest and justify different actions to make a positive difference to a national or global issue.
Lesson 5	**Identifying perspectives**	
	To develop knowledge and understanding about: • the difference between a local and a personal perspective	78A.01 Identify ideas and evidence from different perspectives within different sources on a given issue.
	Interpreting data	
	To develop knowledge and understanding about: • how graphs can be used as evidence to support an argument	78A.02 Explain how graphical or numerical data supports an argument or a perspective.
	Making connections	
	To develop knowledge and understanding about: • how to explain the causes and consequences of issues	78A.03 Explain causes of a local or global issue and consequences on others.
Lesson 6	**Identifying perspectives**	
	To develop knowledge and understanding about: • the difference between a global, a national and a personal perspective • identifying and explaining different perspectives from an information source • explaining my own personal perspective	78A.01 Identify ideas and evidence from different perspectives within different sources on a given issue.

Challenge(s)	Key: Beliefs about foods Additional: How can we use resources sustainably?	
Curriculum topic(s)	Key: Values and beliefs Additional: Climate change, energy and resources; Digital world; Education for all	
Lesson	Lesson learning goals	Curriculum learning objectives
Lesson 7	Identifying perspectives	
	To get better at: • understanding Cambridge Global Perspectives key terms • identifying different groups of stakeholders • explaining the perspective of a group of stakeholders	78A.01 Identify ideas and evidence from different perspectives within different sources on a given issue.
Lesson 8	Identifying perspectives	
	To get better at: • giving examples of different groups of stakeholders • finding ideas and evidence from different perspectives	78A.01 Identify ideas and evidence from different perspectives within different sources on a given issue.
	Interpreting data	
	To get better at: • asking questions to gain information from a specific group of people	78A.02 Explain how graphical or numerical data supports an argument or a perspective.
Lesson 9	Interpreting data	
	To get better at: • using data from research into different perspectives on an issue to help support an argument	78A.02 Explain how graphical or numerical data supports an argument or a perspective.
	Making connections	
	To get better at: • explaining consequences of a local or national issue	78A.03 Explain causes of a local or global issue and consequences on others.
	Solving problems	
	To get better at: • suggesting an action to make a positive difference to a local or national issue	78A.04 Suggest and justify different actions to make a positive difference to a national or global issue.

3 Evaluation

Challenge(s)	Key: What are the challenges and opportunities of migration?; Predicting the future	
Curriculum topic(s)	Key: Migration and urbanisation; Digital world	
Lesson	**Lesson learning goals**	**Curriculum learning objectives**
Lesson 1	**Evaluating sources**	
	To start to: • understand what 'fake news' is, why it is created and how to recognise it	78E.01 Evaluate sources, considering the author and purpose, recognising that some sources may be more credible than others
Lesson 2	**Evaluating sources**	
	To start to: • recognise that facts from news stories can be real or fake • understand how to judge if a fact is real or fake	78E.01 Evaluate sources, considering the author and purpose, recognising that some sources may be more credible than others
Lesson 3	**Evaluating sources**	
	To start to: • recognise that some facts in a news story might not be true • identify bias in a source • realise that news stories may contain bias	78E.01 Evaluate sources, considering the author and purpose, recognising that some sources may be more credible than others
	Evaluating perspectives and arguments	
	To start to: • realise that the argument in a source should make sense if it is to be trusted	78E.02 Discuss the effectiveness of an argument, making explicit reference to its structure and use of evidence
Lesson 4	**Evaluating perspectives and arguments**	
	To develop knowledge and understanding about: • the characteristics of an argument in Cambridge Global Perspectives • the features of an effective argument • writing an effective argument.	78E.02 Discuss the effectiveness of an argument, making explicit reference to its structure and use of evidence
Lesson 5	**Evaluating perspectives and arguments**	
	To develop knowledge and understanding about: • identifying claims • identifying reasoning to justify a claim • identifying evidence in support of a claim	78E.02 Discuss the effectiveness of an argument, making explicit reference to its structure and use of evidence

Challenge(s)	Key: What are the challenges and opportunities of migration?; Predicting the future	
Curriculum topic(s)	Key: Migration and urbanisation; Digital world	
Lesson	**Lesson learning goals**	**Curriculum learning objectives**
Lesson 6	**Evaluating sources**	
	To develop knowledge and understanding about: • the meaning of the term 'bias' and judging if a text contains any bias • the purpose of different texts • the audience for different texts	78E.01 Evaluate sources, considering the author and purpose, recognising that some sources may be more credible than others
Lesson 7	**Evaluating sources**	
	To get better at: • understanding the difference between audience and purpose • recognising bias	78E.01 Evaluate sources, considering the author and purpose, recognising that some sources may be more credible than others
	Evaluating perspectives and arguments	
	To get better at: • recognising fact and opinion	78E.02 Discuss the effectiveness of an argument, making explicit reference to its structure and use of evidence

4 Reflection

Challenge(s)	Key: Who am I? Additional: What are the challenges and opportunities of migration?	
Curriculum topic(s)	Key: Change in culture and communities Additional: Migration and urbanisation; Education for all; Law and criminality	
Lesson	**Lesson learning goals**	**Curriculum learning objectives**
Lesson 1	**Personal contribution**	
	To start to: • identify and explain personal strengths	78Rf.01 Explain personal contribution to teamwork and identify targets for improvement
	Personal learning	
	To start to: • identify areas for development	78Rf.04 Identify skills learned or improved during an activity and relate to personal strengths and areas for improvement
Lesson 2	**Personal contribution**	
	To start to: • explain personal contributions to teamwork	78Rf.01 Explain personal contribution to teamwork and identify targets for improvement

Challenge(s)	Key: Who am I? Additional: What are the challenges and opportunities of migration?	
Curriculum topic(s)	Key: Change in culture and communities Additional: Migration and urbanisation; Education for all; Law and criminality	
Lesson	**Lesson learning goals**	**Curriculum learning objectives**
Lesson 2	**Teamwork**	
	To start to: • explain what teamwork is • explain the benefits and challenges of teamwork	78Rf.02 Consider the benefits and challenges of teamwork experienced when working together to achieve a shared outcome
Lesson 3	**Personal contribution**	
	To start to: • explain personal contributions to teamwork • explain areas for improvement in teamwork	78Rf.01 Explain personal contribution to teamwork and identify targets for improvement
	Teamwork	
	To start to: • explain the benefits and challenges of teamwork	78Rf.02 Consider the benefits and challenges of teamwork experienced when working together to achieve a shared outcome
	Personal perspectives	
	To start to: • explore personal perspective on an issue	78Rf.03 Consider ways that personal perspective on an issue may have changed as a result of conducting research or exploring different perspectives
Lesson 4	**Personal contribution**	
	To develop knowledge and understanding about: • my contribution(s) to teamwork • setting targets to improve my contribution(s) to teamwork	78Rf.01 Explain personal contribution to teamwork and identify targets for improvement
Lesson 5	**Personal contribution**	
	To develop knowledge and understanding about: • contributing to teamwork	78Rf.01 Explain personal contribution to teamwork and identify targets for improvement
	Personal learning	
	To develop knowledge and understanding about: • how learning and improving skills adds to personal strengths	78Rf.04 Identify skills learned or improved during an activity and relate to personal strengths and areas for improvement

Challenge(s)	Key: Who am I? Additional: What are the challenges and opportunities of migration?	
Curriculum topic(s)	Key: Change in culture and communities Additional: Migration and urbanisation; Education for all; Law and criminality	
Lesson	Lesson learning goals	Curriculum learning objectives
Lesson 6	Teamwork	
	To develop knowledge and understanding about: • the challenges of teamwork and how to overcome these	78Rf.02 Consider the benefits and challenges of teamwork experienced when working together to achieve a shared outcome
	Personal perspectives	
	To develop knowledge and understanding about: • how a personal perspective can develop or change after research and considering different perspectives	78Rf.03 Consider ways that personal perspective on an issue may have changed as a result of conducting research or exploring different perspectives
Lesson 7	Personal contribution	
	To get better at: • understanding that my personal strengths can benefit teamwork • working with others towards a shared outcome	78Rf.01 Explain personal contribution to teamwork and identify targets for improvement
	Personal learning	
	To get better at: • explaining skills used and improved	78Rf.04 Identify skills learned or improved during an activity and relate to personal strengths and areas for improvement
Lesson 8	Personal contribution	
	To get better at: • explaining my personal contribution(s) to teamwork	78Rf.01 Explain personal contribution to teamwork and identify targets for improvement
	Personal learning	
	To get better at: • explaining the skills that I have learned or improved • explaining areas for improvement	78Rf.04 Identify skills learned or improved during an activity and relate to personal strengths and areas for improvement
Lesson 9	Teamwork	
	To get better at: • explaining the challenges of teamwork • explaining how to overcome the challenges of teamwork	78Rf.02 Consider the benefits and challenges of teamwork experienced when working together to achieve a shared outcome

Challenge(s)	Key: Who am I? Additional: What are the challenges and opportunities of migration?	
Curriculum topic(s)	Key: Change in culture and communities Additional: Migration and urbanisation; Education for all; Law and criminality	
Lesson	Lesson learning goals	Curriculum learning objectives
Lesson 9	Personal perspectives	
	To get better at: • explaining my personal perspective on an issue	78Rf.03 Consider ways that personal perspective on an issue may have changed as a result of conducting research or exploring different perspectives

5 Collaboration

Challenge(s)	Key: What everyone needs: How is aid money spent? Additional: How can we use resources sustainably?	
Curriculum topic(s)	Key: Development, trade and aid Additional: Law and criminality; Climate change, energy and resources; Water, food and agriculture; Environment, pollution and conservation	
Lesson	Lesson learning goals	Curriculum learning objectives
Lesson 1	Working together	
	To start to: • explain the term 'collaboration' • explain how to collaborate in Cambridge Global Perspectives lessons	78Cl.01 Work positively within a team to achieve a shared outcome and improve team work, for example by contributing useful ideas, offering solutions to problems, encouraging other team members to participate and being open to others' ideas.
	Being an effective team	
	To start to: • explain the characteristics that team members need for effective collaboration	78Cl.02 The team assigns roles and divides tasks fairly, considering the skills of team members and the time available, resolves disagreements and works together to achieve a shared outcome.
Lesson 2	Working together	
	To start to: • share relevant ideas with team members • work with a team to plan and produce a shared outcome	78Cl.01 Work positively within a team to achieve a shared outcome and improve team work, for example by contributing useful ideas, offering solutions to problems, encouraging other team members to participate and being open to others' ideas.

Challenge(s)	Key: What everyone needs: How is aid money spent? Additional: How can we use resources sustainably?	
Curriculum topic(s)	Key: Development, trade and aid Additional: Law and criminality; Climate change, energy and resources; Water, food and agriculture; Environment, pollution and conservation	
Lesson	Lesson learning goals	Curriculum learning objectives
Lesson 2	Being an effective team	
	To start to: • explain the strengths of individual team members	78CI.02 The team assigns roles and divides tasks fairly, considering the skills of team members and the time available, resolves disagreements and works together to achieve a shared outcome.
Lesson 3	Working together	
	To start to: • work with a team to review and evaluate a shared outcome	78CI.01 Work positively within a team to achieve a shared outcome and improve team work, for example by contributing useful ideas, offering solutions to problems, encouraging other team members to participate and being open to others' ideas.
	Being an effective team	
	To start to: • explain the strengths of individual team members	78CI.02 The team assigns roles and divides tasks fairly, considering the skills of team members and the time available, resolves disagreements and works together to achieve a shared outcome.
Lesson 4	Working together	
	To develop knowledge and understanding about: • collaboration to achieve shared outcomes	78CI.01 Work positively within a team to achieve a shared outcome and improve team work, for example by contributing useful ideas, offering solutions to problems, encouraging other team members to participate and being open to others' ideas.
	Being an effective team	
	To develop knowledge and understanding about: • resolving conflict during teamwork	78CI.02 The team assigns roles and divides tasks fairly, considering the skills of team members and the time available, resolves disagreements and works together to achieve a shared outcome.
Lesson 5	Working together	
	To develop knowledge and understanding about: • collaborating to produce shared outcomes • contributing ideas to shared outcomes	78CI.01 Work positively within a team to achieve a shared outcome and improve team work, for example by contributing useful ideas, offering solutions to problems, encouraging other team members to participate and being open to others' ideas.

Challenge(s)	Key: What everyone needs: How is aid money spent? Additional: How can we use resources sustainably?	
Curriculum topic(s)	Key: Development, trade and aid Additional: Law and criminality; Climate change, energy and resources; Water, food and agriculture; Environment, pollution and conservation	
Lesson	Lesson learning goals	Curriculum learning objectives
Lesson 6	Working together	
	To develop knowledge and understanding about: • collaborating to produce shared outcomes • how feedback can improve shared outcomes	78Cl.01 Work positively within a team to achieve a shared outcome and improve team work, for example by contributing useful ideas, offering solutions to problems, encouraging other team members to participate and being open to others' ideas
Lesson 7	Working together	
	To get better at: • understanding what effective teamwork is	78Cl.01 Work positively within a team to achieve a shared outcome and improve team work, for example by contributing useful ideas, offering solutions to problems, encouraging other team members to participate and being open to others' ideas.
	Being an effective team	
	To get better at: • reflecting on roles and responsibilities during teamwork • evaluating teamwork	78Cl.02 The team assigns roles and divides tasks fairly, considering the skills of team members and the time available, resolves disagreements and works together to achieve a shared outcome.

6 Communication

Challenge(s)	Key: How can we use resources sustainably?; Improving communication	
Curriculum topic(s)	Key: Climate change, energy and resources; Digital world	
Lesson	Lesson learning goals	Curriculum learning objectives
Lesson 1	Communicating information	
	To start to: • explain how to structure a text	78Cm.01 Present information and arguments clearly with some reasoning, referencing sources where appropriate.
Lesson 2	Communicating information	
	To start to: • explain what helps to make a well-structured argument • create a well-structured argument with a claim, reasoning and supporting evidence	78Cm.01 Present information and arguments clearly with some reasoning, referencing sources where appropriate.

Challenge(s)	Key: How can we use resources sustainably?; Improving communication	
Curriculum topic(s)	Key: Climate change, energy and resources; Digital world	
Lesson	Lesson learning goals	Curriculum learning objectives
Lesson 2	Listening and responding	
	To start to: • contribute ideas to show understanding of an issue	78Cm.02 Listen to ideas and information and offer relevant and well-judged contributions that demonstrate understanding of the issue.
Lesson 3	Communicating information	
	To start to: • explain the features that help to create a well-structured argument • create a well-structured argument with a claim, reasoning and supporting evidence	78Cm.01 Present information and arguments clearly with some reasoning, referencing sources where appropriate.
	Listening and responding	
	To start to: • give and receive feedback to improve an argument	78Cm.02 Listen to ideas and information and offer relevant and well-judged contributions that demonstrate understanding of the issue.
Lesson 4	Listening and responding	
	To develop knowledge and understanding about: • the importance of feedback • listening to and recording ideas and information gained from others	78Cm.02 Listen to ideas and information and offer relevant and well-judged contributions that demonstrate understanding of the issue.
Lesson 5	Communicating information	
	To develop knowledge and understanding about: • presenting information clearly • recording information accurately	78Cm.01 Present information and arguments clearly with some reasoning, referencing sources where appropriate.
	Listening and responding	
	To develop knowledge and understanding about: • listening actively to increase understanding	78Cm.02 Listen to ideas and information and offer relevant and well-judged contributions that demonstrate understanding of the issue.
Lesson 6	Communicating information	
	To develop knowledge and understanding about: • presenting information clearly and with some reasoning	78Cm.01 Present information and arguments clearly with some reasoning, referencing sources where appropriate.

Challenge(s)	Key: How can we use resources sustainably?; Improving communication	
Curriculum topic(s)	Key: Climate change, energy and resources; Digital world	
Lesson	Lesson learning goals	Curriculum learning objectives
Lesson 6	Listening and responding	
	To develop knowledge and understanding about: • improving listening skills to gain information	78Cm.02 Listen to ideas and information and offer relevant and well-judged contributions that demonstrate understanding of the issue.
Lesson 7	Communicating information	
	To get better at: • presenting information with reasoning	78Cm.01 Present information and arguments clearly with some reasoning, referencing sources where appropriate.
	Listening and responding	
	To get better at: • sharing ideas with others	78Cm.02 Listen to ideas and information and offer relevant and well-judged contributions that demonstrate understanding of the issue.

Approaches to teaching Cambridge Lower Secondary Global Perspectives

Alternative approaches to teaching Cambridge Lower Secondary Global Perspectives

As a teacher, or prospective teacher, of Cambridge Lower Secondary Global Perspectives, you will already know that it is a dynamic and innovative programme. It is different to other subjects, in both its content and its delivery. As a result, you may be a bit uncertain as to how you should approach, plan and deliver it.

Cambridge Lower Secondary Global Perspectives is composed of various elements:

- **The six skills** that are taught and assessed: Research, Analysis, Evaluation, Reflection, Communication and Collaboration.
- **The topics** that provide a context for developing these skills. The topics outlined in the Cambridge Lower Secondary Global Perspectives curriculum framework are:
  - Arts in society
  - Change in culture and communities
  - Climate change, energy and resources
  - Conflict and peace
  - Development, trade and aid
  - Digital world
  - Education for all
  - Employment
  - Environment, pollution and conservation
  - Globalisation
  - Health and wellbeing
  - Law and criminality
  - Media and communication
  - Migration and urbanisation
  - Political power and action
  - Poverty and inequality
  - Social identity and inclusion
  - Sport and recreation
  - Technology, industry and innovation
  - Transport, travel and tourism
  - Values and beliefs
  - Water, food and agriculture
- **The Challenges** – a set of optional teaching and learning materials relating to the topics that exemplify how the skills are taught and assessed.

When you teach Cambridge Lower Secondary Global Perspectives, you are helping your learners develop their skills. There is no 'correct' way to teach Cambridge Global Perspectives or to use the Learner's Skills Book. There are several teaching strategies you could follow. Here are some ideas:

1 Follow the Cambridge Lower Secondary Global Perspectives Challenges and structure all your lessons around them. The Challenges are based on the Cambridge Global Perspectives topics. Each of the Challenges focuses on the development of several skills. For example, the Challenge 'Is school the best place to learn?' is based on the topic 'Education for all'. In this Challenge, learners can develop many key skills – for example, researching, analysing and reflecting.

2 Follow the Stage 8 Lower Secondary Learner's Skills Book and use the downloadables provided. Each section of the Learner's Skills Book is focused on one of the six key skills. The skills are developed through a variety of activities based on key Cambridge Lower Secondary Global Perspectives topics. The activities are designed to encourage your learners to develop an understanding of global issues and the different perspectives on them. All the Cambridge Global Perspectives skills are thoroughly covered in the Learner's Skills Books so your learners will be completely prepared for the Cambridge Lower Secondary Checkpoint assessment when they get to the end of Stage 9.

3 Do both! Follow a Cambridge Lower Secondary Global Perspective Challenge and then use the Learner's Skills Book to see how well your learners have understood a key skill. For example, you could teach six lessons based on the Challenge 'Is school the best place to learn?'. Then, at the end of that Challenge, you could provide your learners with the downloadables for Section 1 Research and ask them to complete the activities in Section 1 of their Learner's Skills Book. They could do these as class or homework activities. You could use them for summative assessment to see how well they have understood and can use their research skills.

4 Use a Challenge – for example, 'Is school the best place to learn?' – and the resources that go with it to complete the activities in the Learner's Skills Book. Base your lessons on the eight lesson plans in this Teacher's Resource. You could use the downloadables to further support the activities.

5 Complete the activities in the Learner's Skills Book with resources that you have created. You know your learners best: you know what interests and motivates them and what will engage them. You also know which skills they will find easier to develop and which will require more time and practice. You can use your resources as the basis for all the activities in each section of the Learner's Skills Book. So long as you follow the activities and guidance set out in the Teacher's Resource, you can be confident that you are teaching your learners all the skills they need for Cambridge Lower Secondary Global Perspectives.

Although the only thing you must deliver is the skills, it is recommended that you use the list of topics as a guide. The list has been compiled with the aim of exposing learners to as many important global issues as possible. The issues they explore should be ones on which there are a variety of perspectives. Because global issues change all the time, you may often change the topics you explore with learners and the questions you encourage them to ask. Do not be worried if you teach Cambridge Global Perspectives differently each year. That is OK. In fact, it is great! That flexibility is exactly what Cambridge Global Perspectives is all about. The great thing is that you can choose the Challenges, topics and resources that are the most interesting to you and to your class.

The set of three projects available at cambridge.org/go are stand-alone resources, with each one addressing an issue relating to one of the Cambridge Lower Secondary Global Perspectives topics, and are designed to give learners the opportunity to synthesise the separate skills they have developed in the Learner's Skills Book. Although all three follow a similar project pathway – Preparation, Discovery, Action and Reflection – the learning objectives for each project place an emphasis on just a few of the six skills. Therefore, there is some flexibility in how you choose to integrate these into your teaching. They can either be used together at the end of the year as culminating pieces of work, or attempted at different points throughout the year, whenever you feel your learners have had ample opportunity to develop and practise the focus skills for each project.

Above all, be confident: you can be flexible with your teaching style and your teaching content. The global world is changing all the time. Our aim is to develop learners who have the skills and the confidence to tackle that changing world. However you decide to do it, you will be right!

Teaching Cambridge Lower Secondary Global Perspectives within the wider curriculum

The Cambridge Global Perspectives programme of study is central to the Cambridge Lower Secondary curriculum. The teaching focus is the development of six key skills through the exploration of broad topic areas and specific global issues within them. Inevitably, there are many links between Cambridge Global Perspectives and other subjects, both in terms of skills and content.

The skills developed in Cambridge Global Perspectives are needed by learners in all their wider studies. For example, if learners improve their research or evaluation skills, they will not only become stronger Cambridge Global Perspectives learners, they will also be more proficient in History and Geography. Likewise, when they become better communicators and writers, their performance in English will improve.

The Challenges and topics create scope for cross-curricular links. So, for example, 'Conflict and peace' could be related to History, 'Media and communication' could be related to English, 'Transport, travel and tourism' could be connected to Geography, and so on. To help make these connections, you could talk to colleagues in other departments to try to establish links with curriculum content. Or you could ask learners to identify these kinds of connections themselves.

Integrating the theme of sustainability.

Climate change, sustainability, and the use of energy and resources are some of the most critical issues our young people will encounter. Teaching with a global perspective and teaching about sustainability are inextricably linked. The slogan 'Think globally, act locally' is very apt here.

While much learning will inevitably take place in the classroom, learners' answers to questions about sustainability will be significantly enriched by learning beyond the classroom. The nature and extent of outside learning will vary depending on your school's context. Opportunities to engage with the local environment and community will enhance your learners' awareness of sustainability as an issue and of ways to promote sustainable choices. Giving learners the opportunity to be agents for practical change is a powerful tool for promoting their engagement with the process of learning itself.

The following table suggests enquiry questions for some Cambridge Global Perspective topics centred on the theme of sustainability.

Topics	Questions
Climate change, energy and resources	Is the world running out of water?
Poverty and inequality	How does the climate crisis make some people poorer?
Migration and urbanisation	Is the climate emergency forcing people to move?
Digital world	Can technology make the world greener?
Globalisation	Can globalisation be part of a sustainable world?
Health and wellbeing	Is pollution making us ill?

Both the Teacher's Resource and the Learner's Skills Books include specific ideas about the ways in which Cambridge Lower Secondary Global Perspectives Challenges, topics and issues can be used to further deepen learning about sustainability, integrating those important ideas into the lessons.

Assessment guidance

The purpose of assessment is two-fold. Formative assessment – which aims to determine what learners already know or understand – is often carried out at the start of a lesson or before starting a task. The results are used to inform the planning and delivery of the task or lesson. Once we know what learners know, we can teach them what they don't know.

By contrast, summative assessment – which seeks to determine what learners have understood – is often carried out at the end of a lesson or completion of a task. Cambridge Lower Secondary Global Perspectives is a skills-based course, so summative assessment does not take the form of a test as it might with other subjects. Instead, assessment tasks allow learners to show us what they can do and what new skills they have gained.

Research: The activities in this section will help learners to demonstrate their skills through summative assessment tasks that require them to provide thoughtful explanations for an issue that they have chosen. They will learn to formulate questions that allow for answers that are global, national and local, with clear causes, consequences and solutions. They will be able to demonstrate that they can choose appropriate sources of evidence and record them in a systematic way.

Analysis: The activities in this section will help learners to demonstrate attainment through summative assessment tasks that require them to identify and explain causes and consequences relevant to the issues they are researching. They will learn to clearly link the issues to different global, national and local perspectives. They will be able to demonstrate that they can formulate relevant and effective courses of action, and explain how and why these might help solve the problems/issues.

Evaluation: The activities in this section will help learners to demonstrate attainment through summative assessment tasks that require them to provide clear explanations of the strengths and limitations of actions they have taken. The activities will help them to assess the appropriateness of the course of action they took. They will be able to assess the extent to which they met the goal they initially set themselves. Finally, they will be able to demonstrate that they can explain the credibility of their chosen sources and their usefulness for research.

Reflection: The activities in this section will help learners to demonstrate attainment through summative assessment tasks that require them to reflect on their role in teamwork and their own perspectives. The activities will help them to make connections between their thoughts, behaviour and actions. The activities will enable them to demonstrate that they can provide well-reasoned explanations of how their perspectives on the issue have developed and the reasons for that development.

Collaboration: The activities in this section will help learners to demonstrate attainment through summative assessment tasks that require them to clearly communicate a course of action. They will be able to demonstrate the ways in which they worked effectively as part of a team in order to achieve their goal.

Communication: The activities in this section will help learners to demonstrate attainment through summative assessment tasks that require them to communicate clearly. This may be as part of a team to achieve a project goal or as an individual producing written work. They will be able to demonstrate that they can organise their thoughts and actions, and work in ways that are easily understandable to their audience. They will also provide evidence that their conclusions, reflections and solutions have been supported by their research findings.

The set of three projects available at cambridge.org/go have been designed to prepare learners for the process of the Cambridge Lower Secondary Global Perspectives Checkpoint research report assessment at Stage 9. At Stages 7, 8 and 9, these can be used as scaffolded practice activities working towards Checkpoint, and as a means of assessing learners' progress towards and readiness for the assessment.

Transferring your skills as a teacher

The cross-curricular nature of this programme is what will make you, as a teacher of any other subject, an excellent teacher of Cambridge Lower Secondary Global Perspectives. You do not need to be an 'expert' and are not expected to deliver huge amounts of content. The fluid nature of this interdisciplinary programme means that we are guiding our learners, facilitating the development of their skills and the broadening of their global perspectives.

With its emphasis on active learning, metacognition, reflective learning and integrating real-world local and global issues, Cambridge Lower Secondary Global Perspectives can also help you develop teaching skills that will prove beneficial to your wider teaching practices, to your continued career development, and also to your school and the community it serves. Here are a few ways in which Cambridge Lower Secondary Global Perspectives and the Cambridge University Press resources can positively impact on the teaching and learning practices of you and your learners:

- Engaging with global issues and exploring their relevance locally helps teachers to aim high. Taking action to make a positive change builds trust between learners. Effective teachers will find in Cambridge Lower Secondary Global Perspectives a wealth of opportunities to build self-motivated learners. Tackling visible local issues with a view to making a positive change enables effective teachers to generate enthusiasm for learning. Effective teachers will be alert to local issues that will stimulate and capture their learners' interest. Engagement in global issues with local relevance will provide opportunities for the proactive practitioner to broaden and deepen the contributions their learners make. Growing young global citizens will enhance the life and ethos of the school as well as of the wider community it serves.
- Our resources suggest engaging methods to help learners reflect on their own progress. Colleagues can build on their knowledge of learners' prior attainment across the curriculum. This understanding will be complemented by the regular and systematic progress checks in Cambridge Lower Secondary Global Perspectives skills provided in our resources. The scaffolding that our materials provide ensures that cognitive load is managed appropriately. This will help teachers ensure that over time learners become more independent.

- The high expectations of the Cambridge Lower Secondary Global Perspectives framework, together with the scaffolding in the materials, will help you develop strategies for maintaining a stimulating learning environment. An emphasis is placed on high levels of engagement, collaboration and co-operation through structured group tasks.

There is no better way to make young people into lifelong learners than by showing them that we, too, are always learning and strengthening our understanding of the world around us. As you teach new skills, exploring wider topics and more specific issues with your learners, take a moment to reflect on your own learning and practice. What has gone well? What might you do differently next year? How have your own perspectives changed? We teach our learners that this reflection is an essential part of their learning and developing process – the same is true for us as teachers.

Finally, a global community of Cambridge Lower Secondary Global Perspectives teachers enjoy opportunities to build professional relationships. They welcome opportunities to work collaboratively with international colleagues. A growing number of Cambridge Global Perspectives teachers are taking advantage of opportunities provided by Cambridge International to develop their practice through a wide range of continuing professional development activities and courses. Why not join them?

Approaches to teaching and learning

Active learning

What is active learning?

Active learning is a pedagogical practice that places learner learning at its centre. It focuses on how learners learn, not just on what they learn. We, as teachers, need to encourage learners to 'think hard', rather than passively receive information. Active learning encourages learners to take responsibility for their learning and supports them in becoming independent and confident learners in school and beyond.

Research shows us that it is not possible to transmit understanding to learners by simply telling them what they need to know. Instead, we need to make sure that we challenge learners' thinking and support them in building their own understanding. Active learning encourages more complex thought processes, such as evaluating, analysing and synthesising, which foster a greater number of neural connections in the brain. Although some learners may be able to create their own meaning from information received passively, others will not. Active learning enables all learners to build knowledge and understanding in response to the opportunities we provide.

Why adopt an active learning approach?

We can enrich all areas of the curriculum, at all stages, by embedding an active learning approach.

In active learning, we need to think not only about the content but also about the process. It gives learners greater involvement and control over their learning. This encourages all learners to stay focused on their learning, which will often give them greater enthusiasm for their studies. Active learning is intellectually stimulating and taking this approach encourages a level of academic discussion with our learners that we, as teachers, can also enjoy. Healthy discussion means that learners are engaging with us as a partner in their learning.

Learners will be better able to revise for examinations in the sense that revision really is 're-vision' of the ideas that they already understand.

Active learning develops learners' analytical skills, supporting them to be better problem solvers and more effective in their application of knowledge. They will be prepared to deal with challenging and unexpected situations. As a result, learners are more confident in continuing to learn once they have left school and are better equipped for the transition to higher education and the workplace.

What are the challenges of incorporating active learning?

When people start thinking about putting active learning into practice, they often make the mistake of thinking more about the activity they want to design than about the learning. The most important thing is to put the learner and the learning at the centre of our planning. A task can be quite simple but still get the learner to think critically and independently. Sometimes a complicated task does not actually help to develop the learners' thinking or understanding at all. We need to consider carefully what we want our learners to learn or understand and then shape the task to activate this learning.

Cambridge Lower Secondary Global Perspectives Stage 8 includes many opportunities for active learning such as pair and group work, discussions, working with a variety of texts; written and spoken, and producing a variety of shared outcomes to raise awareness about global issues, like posters, video clips and podcasts.

Assessment for Learning

What is Assessment for Learning?

Assessment for Learning (AfL) is a teaching approach that generates feedback that can be used to improve learners' performance. Learners become more involved in the learning process and, from this, gain confidence in what they are expected to learn and to what standard. We, as teachers, gain insights into a learner's level of understanding of a particular concept or topic, which helps to inform how we support their progression.

We need to understand the meaning and method of giving purposeful feedback to optimise learning. Feedback can be informal, such as oral comments to help learners think through problems, or formal, such as the use of rubrics to help clarify and scaffold learning and assessment objectives.

Why use Assessment for Learning?

By following well-designed approaches to AfL, we can understand better how our learners are learning and use this to plan what we will do next with a class or individual learners (see following diagram). We can help our learners to see what they are aiming for and to understand what they need to do to get there. AfL makes learning visible; it helps learners understand more accurately the nature of the material they are learning and understand themselves as learners. The quality of interactions and feedback between learners and teachers becomes critical to the learning process.

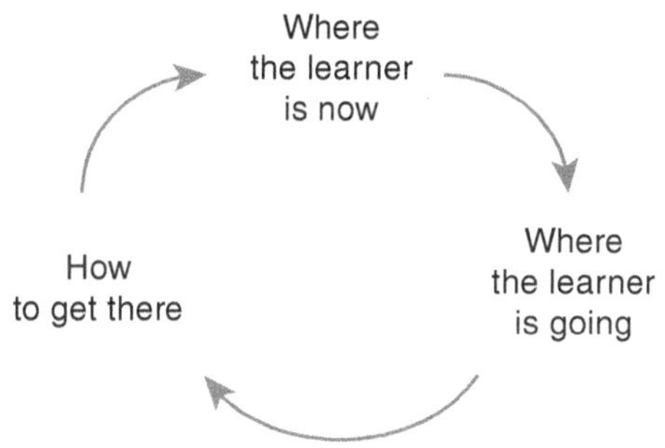

We can use AfL to help our learners focus on specific elements of their learning and to take greater responsibility for how they might move forward. AfL creates a valuable connection between assessment and learning activities, as the clarification of objectives will have a direct impact on how we devise teaching and learning strategies. AfL techniques can support learners in becoming more confident in what they are learning, reflective in how they are learning, more likely to try out new approaches and more engaged in what they are being asked to learn.

What are the challenges of incorporating Assessment for Learning?

The use of AfL does not mean that we need to test learners more frequently. It would be easy to just increase the amount of summative assessment and use this formatively as a regular method of helping us decide what to do next in our teaching. We can judge how much learning has taken place through ways other than testing, including, above all, communicating with our learners in a variety of ways and getting to know them better as individuals.

Cambridge Lower Secondary Global Perspectives Stage 8 provides teachers and learners with opportunities to check learners' progress against learning goals, give peer feedback and improve work after feedback. For example, improving an argument after peer feedback.

Improving learning through questioning

Thinking is driven not by answers but by questions. Learners do best when they are given adequate opportunities to engage with, and respond to questions. As a teacher, you can use questions effectively in the classroom to:

- review learning
- challenge learner thinking
- stimulate interest and motivate learners to become actively involved in the lesson
- cultivate critical thinking skills
- encourage learners to ask their own questions.

There are a number of ways in which you can do this.

Depending on the content and aims of the lesson, it is likely that you will use different types of question. Three types of question are explained and exemplified next.

> **TIP**
>
> You should consider the wording of questions in advance to ensure that they are accessible to all learners. This will be particularly important in contexts where the language of instruction is not the dominant language of learners in you class. For help with language awareness, see the 'Developing learners' language skills' document (available to download from Cambridge GO as part of this Teacher's Resource).

Discussion questions

These facilitate debate and allow teachers to dig deeper into learner reasoning (in some situations, their imagination) by asking probing questions.

Example: Why do you think that?

Activity: could be used in pair, small group or whole-class discussion. Discussion questions do not need to have a 'correct answer' as their value is in helping learners to think through, share and discuss their own response.

Diagnostic questions

These give you a quick insight into whether what you have taught has been learned. Responses may identify parts of the curriculum that warrant re-teaching to clarify misconceptions and fill gaps. They can identify specific gaps in learner understanding while learning is still taking place.

Example: True or false?

Activity: could be a lesson starter (using mini-whiteboards or Post-it notes) or part of a quiz or other form of assessment.

All diagnostic questions must have a clear purpose; you must use the information gathered to help inform your next steps. See below for suggestions on how to use diagnostic results in feedback.

Hinge-point questions

The 'hinge' is the point where you move from one key idea/activity/point on to another. Hinge-point questions are a specific type of diagnostic question that are most useful after a period of learning to help you decide whether to continue, recap or re-teach. It is usually the case that understanding the content that occurs before the hinge is a prerequisite for the next chunk of learning. This is important because moving on is dangerous if key concepts are not fully understood, yet if you get this wrong and re-teach pointlessly then engagement will slip and time will be wasted.

Example: What did we learn today? Why does it matter?

Activity: list of ideas (timed), either individually or in a pair. These could be written on poster paper or shared orally.

For hinge-point questions to be useful, you have to be able to elicit the information from learners immediately and be able to understand and act on it quickly. Dylan Wiliam (2011) suggests that learners should respond within one minute and teachers should be able to view and interpret responses within 15 seconds. Hinge-point questions seek a response in the form of a snapshot, not an essay.

Experienced teachers will use a range of question types in their professional practice, appropriate to the level, subject and learners they are teaching.

Cambridge Lower Secondary Global Perspectives Stage 8 develops learners' ability to not only ask questions like 'what', 'when', 'where' and 'who', but also questions that require more thinking about such as 'how' and 'why'. For example, 'How does the amount of water an individual uses impact the issue of global water shortage?'

Using feedback to optimise teaching and learning

Questions help learners to challenge and explore their understanding of a particular topic. Questions can also help learners identify areas where their knowledge is less secure. This is a valuable part of the learning process. You can help them to move beyond 'struggle zones' in their learning by providing feedback that helps them to fill the gaps in their knowledge, thereby boosting both their competence and their confidence.

Feedback should:

- be oral or written
- be appropriate to the learner
- include information about where to go (which pages in the learner's book, for example) to revise the problematic material.

Once it is clear to learners what must be done to move beyond their current limits of learning, young people often make significant progress. You can facilitate this progress via feedback and help 'close the loop' of learning.

Feedback is powerful: to optimise teaching and learning, you should create an environment in which learners are encouraged to reflect on their learning experiences and identify next steps during the learning process. These next steps may take the form of further questions on the topic, to which the learners might like to research answers, or the next steps may be connected with their experiences of learning (for more information about metacognition, see the document in this introduction).

Self/peer assessment

Rather than always relying on teacher judgement, by assessing their own (and each other's) work, learners independently assess progress with confidence. Learners who can look at their work, and judge the degree by which it reflects explicitly stated goals or criteria, can assess the quality of their work and revise it accordingly. They are actively involved in the learning process and their independence and motivation is improved.

Further reading

Gaunt, A. and Stott, A. (2019) *Transform teaching and learning through talk: the oracy imperative*, Rowman and Littlefield Education, Lanham, MD.

Gershon, M. (2013) *How to use questioning in the classroom: the complete guide*, Amazon Media.

Paul, R.W. and Elder, L. (2000), *Critical thinking: basic theory and instructional structures handbook*, Foundation for Critical Thinking, Tomales, CA.

Wiliam, D. (2011), *Embedded formative assessment*, Solution Tree Press, Bloomington, IN.

Differentiation

What is differentiation?

Differentiation is usually presented as a teaching practice where teachers think of learners as individuals and learning as a personalised process. Although precise definitions can vary, typically the core aim of differentiation is viewed as ensuring that all learners, no matter their interest or context, make progress towards their learning outcomes.

It is about using different approaches and appreciating the differences in learners to help them make progress. Teachers therefore need to be responsive, and willing and able, to adapt their teaching to meet the needs of their learners.

There is no one style teachers should adopt. Teachers do not need to differentiate everything for everyone every day; instead, they should select appropriate moments in the instructional sequence to differentiate. In other words, effective differentiation is part of an experienced teacher's daily lesson plan. It is important that teachers are able to respond to the needs of their learners and use the techniques they deem to be most suitable.

It can be difficult to fit in all the curriculum content and support all learners, keeping them engaged in their learning. This is a challenge for teachers the world over.

Although there is no single formula that creates a differentiated classroom, when differentiation is in place opportunities for innovation and ongoing reflection are created that boost teaching and learning in a way that would not be possible in a 'one size fits all' lesson.

It is clear how much overlap there is between differentiation and Assessment for Learning methodology. Both aim to support all learners to improve their learning, using similar techniques such as questioning, providing feedback and a learner-centred approach. Ongoing assessment in class is fundamental to differentiation; teachers need to see what the learner currently knows or can do, and then work out what the learner needs to know or do next. It is an approach that incorporates a variety of strategies and depends very much on the individual teacher's school and classroom culture to guide practical implementation and outcomes.

Effective differentiation is heavily reliant on teachers being able to respond to each individual and fully understand their needs to best support their next steps. The viability of this will depend on each teacher's specific context, motivation, obstacles to overcome and training.

Role of the learner

Understanding individual learners is vital for successful differentiation. In order to be effective, figuring out what the individual already knows or can do is a vital step in the process.

Getting to know learners is, however, more than just finding out what they know. It is also about a broader understanding of learner difference. Learners and their learning can be different for a number of reasons: they may have different levels of interest in the topic; they may have differences in their levels of motivation, their ability to remember information, their confidence, the accuracy of their handwriting, their levels of vocabulary acquisition.

Having knowledge of the individual helps teachers to plan for learning rather than teaching, and ensures that they are always supporting progress. In a differentiated classroom, teachers and learners collaborate in learning and learners have ownership and responsibility. Offering choice can encourage ownership of individual work and learning, creating a learning environment in which learners 'have no fear' and apply effort.

Techniques

Learning outcomes

Since differentiation aims to support all learners in working towards particular outcomes, it is important to carefully consider what those outcomes are and maintain focus on the overarching learning intention and success criteria. Teachers can then formatively assess against these and gauge learner needs.

A shared concept of quality between the learner and teacher is vital for learner progress. This includes both clarity of learning outcome and the use of examples of good work. If learners are aware of what good work looks like, they are better able to both self- and peer-assess.

Scaffolding

Scaffolding, a metaphor to describe the process of learning support that enables learners to go beyond what they are initially able to do, can be a key component of successful differentiation.

These suggestions include the modelling of work and tasks, use of listening and writing frames, provision of sentence starters and structure guidelines, scaffolded use of questioning and the encouragement of group and pair work.

Feedback

Feedback is a key tool in helping all learners to make progress in their learning. Good feedback can help move learners towards their learning outcomes, provided learners understand, act on and learn from it. Feedback should address any misconceptions that are exposed during learner activities.

Group work

Teachers should employ variety in their classrooms, using a mixture of whole-class instruction, one-to-one work, small group work and peer tutoring. Group work is suggested by many as a good way to differentiate as learners working in groups are able to create knowledge with their peers, help each other to learn, use discussion and apportion tasks based on the relative strengths of the group.

A balance needs to be met between the use of group work and teacher instruction. As John Hattie (2008) argues, direct instruction done properly has a greater impact on learning than group work done incorrectly or inappropriately.

Differentiation support in our materials

Our materials will contain frequent opportunities for ongoing assessment in class to help teachers see what the learner currently knows or can do and then work out what the learner needs to know or do next. This will help to identify misconceptions or misunderstandings and guide actions.

Through the course of the activities in the resources, we will support differentiation predominantly in the following ways:

- differentiation by questioning (embedding questioning strategies to inform better next steps)
- differentiation by grouping (using mixed ability groups)
- differentiation by outcomes (multiple modes of learner output or how learners demonstrate/ show their learning)
- differentiation by task (additional worksheets).

There is no single, optimum way to conduct differentiated teaching. However, we can provide a selection of strategies to help teachers to become more confident in their teaching practice.

Cambridge Lower Secondary Global Perspectives Stage 8 supports differentiation in a number of ways; for example, with each skill section divided into starting with ..., developing... and getting better at... and by offering learners support via their peers, their Skills Book or by using an appropriate Language Support handout.

Language awareness

What is language awareness?

For many learners, English is an additional language. It might be their second or perhaps their third language. Depending on the school context, learners might be learning all or just some of their subjects through English.

For all learners, regardless of whether they are learning through their first language or an additional language, language is a vehicle for learning. It is through language that learners access the learning intentions of the lesson and communicate their ideas. It is our responsibility, as teachers, to ensure that language doesn't present a barrier to learning.

One way to achieve this is to support our colleagues in becoming more language-aware. Language awareness is sensitivity to, and an understanding of, the language demands of our subject and the role these demands play in learning. A language-aware teacher plans strategies and scaffolds the appropriate support to help learners overcome these language demands.

Why is it important for teachers of other subjects to be language-aware?

Many teachers are surprised when they receive a piece of written work that suggests a learner who has no difficulties in everyday communication has had problems understanding the lesson. Issues arise when teachers assume that learners who have attained a high degree of fluency and accuracy in everyday social English therefore have a corresponding level of academic language proficiency. Whether English is a learner's first language or an additional language, learners need time and the appropriate support to become proficient in academic language. This is the language that they are mostly exposed to in school and will be required to reproduce themselves. It will also scaffold their ability to access higher-order thinking skills and improve levels of attainment.

What are the challenges of language awareness?

Many teachers of non-language subjects worry that there is no time to factor language support into their lessons, or that language is something they know little about. Some teachers may think that language support is not their role. However, we need to work with these teachers to create inclusive classrooms where all learners can access the curriculum and where barriers to learning are reduced as much as possible. An increased awareness of the language needs of learners aims to reduce any obstacles that learning through an additional language might present.

This doesn't mean that all teachers need to know the names of grammatical structures or need to be able to use the appropriate linguistic labels. What it does mean is that we all need to understand the challenges our learners face, including their language level, and plan some strategies to help them overcome these challenges. These strategies do not need to take a lot of additional time and should eventually become integral to our process of planning, teaching and reflecting on our practice. We may need to support other teachers so that they are clear about the vocabulary and language that is specific to their subject, and how to teach, reinforce and develop it.

Cambridge Lower Secondary Global Perspectives Stage 8 provides a glossary of terms for use by teachers and learners. Each section in this Teacher Book outlines the subject-specific words and phrases for that section and teachers are encouraged to produce their own Language Support handouts for learners as appropriate.

Metacognition

What is metacognition?

Metacognition describes the processes involved when learners plan, monitor, evaluate and make changes to their own learning behaviours. These processes help learners to think about their own learning more explicitly and ensure that they are able to meet a learning goal that they have identified themselves or that we, as teachers, have set.

Metacognitive learners recognise what they find easy or difficult. They understand the demands of a particular learning task and are able to identify different approaches they could use to tackle a problem. Metacognitive learners are also able to make adjustments to their learning as they monitor their progress towards a particular learning goal. The following diagram shows a helpful way to think about the phases involved in metacognition.

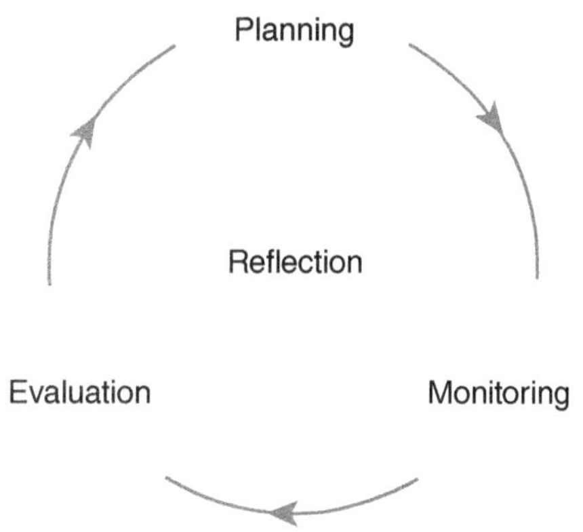

During the planning phase, learners think about the explicit learning goal we have set and what we are asking them to do. As teachers, we need to make clear to learners what success looks like in any given task before they embark on it. Learners build on their prior knowledge, reflect on strategies they have used before and consider how they will approach the new task.

As learners put their plan into action, they are constantly monitoring the progress they are making towards their learning goal. If the strategies they had decided to use are not working, they may decide to try something different.

Once they have completed the task, learners determine how successful the strategy they used was in helping them to achieve their learning goal. During this evaluation phase, learners think about what went well and what didn't go as well to help them decide what they could do differently next time. They may also think about what other types of problem they could solve using the same strategy.

Reflection is a fundamental part of the plan–monitor–evaluate process and there are various ways in which we can support our learners to reflect on their learning process. In order to apply a metacognitive approach, learners need access to a set of strategies that they can use and a classroom environment that encourages them to explore and develop their metacognitive skills.

Why teach metacognitive skills?

Research evidence suggests that the use of metacognitive skills plays an important role in successful learning. Metacognitive practices help learners to monitor their own progress and take control of their learning. Metacognitive learners think about and learn from their mistakes and modify their learning strategies accordingly. Learners who use metacognitive techniques find it improves their academic achievement across subjects, as it helps them transfer what they have learned from one context to another context, or from a previous task to a new task.

What are the challenges of developing learners' metacognitive skills?

For metacognition to be commonplace in the classroom, we need to encourage learners to take time to think about and learn from their mistakes. Many learners are afraid to make mistakes, meaning that they are less likely to take risks, explore new ways of thinking or tackle unfamiliar problems. We, as teachers, are instrumental in shaping the culture of learning in a classroom. For metacognitive practices to thrive, learners need to feel confident enough to make mistakes, to discuss their mistakes and ultimately to view them as valuable, and often necessary, learning opportunities.

Cambridge Lower Secondary Global Perspectives Stage 8 encourages learners to develop their metacognitive skills by providing opportunities for individual reflection at the end of each lesson; for example, by asking learners to consider what helped them learn best in the lesson and what skills they still need to work on.

Skills for Life

How do we prepare learners to succeed in a fast-changing world? To collaborate with people from around the globe? To create innovation as technology increasingly takes over routine work? To use advanced thinking skills in the face of more complex challenges? To show resilience in the face of constant change? At Cambridge, we have been working on how we can help you with this.

The Cambridge Framework for Life Skills

Many frameworks exist that aim to address the skills and competencies learners need to succeed through the levels of their education and on into the world of work for the 21st century. At Cambridge, we are responding to educators who have asked for a way to understand how all these different approaches to life skills and competencies relate to their teaching at all levels and support development of the Cambridge Learner Attributes, and how they can support and evidence the development of these skills by their learners through their learning.

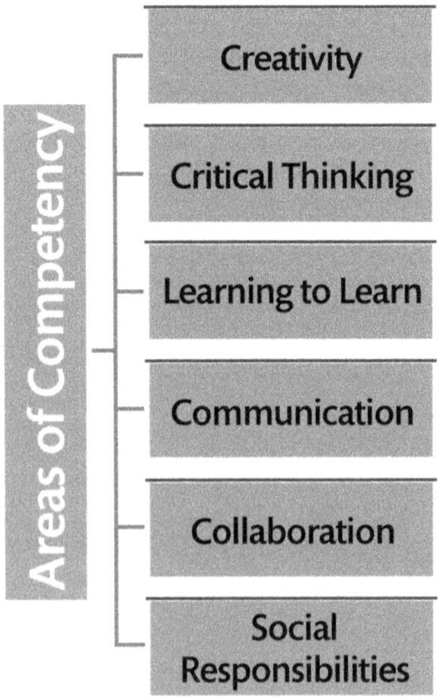

So, we analysed the basic components of these global competencies frameworks and interpreted the different approaches and initiatives to create a common framework of life skills and competencies that can be successfully delivered through teaching at all levels of the Cambridge Pathway.

We have grouped these skills into six main Areas of Competency that can be incorporated into teaching, and have examined the different stages of the learning journey, and how these competencies vary across each stage.

For each of these areas, we have broken down the practical component skills, to help you to understand what each competency involves.

The six key Areas of Competency

The six key skills areas that we will be supporting in our Teacher's Resource and Learner's Skills Book are explained next.

1 Creativity

The ability to generate original and innovative ideas or alternatives that are viewed as being valuable and meaningful. Some attributes of creativity are: divergent thinking, imagination, cognitive flexibility, tolerance for ambiguity or unpredictability and intrinsic motivation. We have identified three key competencies within the area of creativity in an educational context:

- the skills needed to participate in creative activities
- creating new content from one's own ideas or other resources
- discovering and expressing one's personal identity and feelings through creative activities.

2 Collaboration

Collaboration is often described as being a key skill for 21st century education. Some advantages of collaboration over individual problem-solving are effective division of labour, use of information from multiple sources, perspectives and experiences, higher level of creativity and quality of solutions. When people are involved in verbal interaction, they are not simply sharing information but they are supporting each other in collective thinking. This collaborative allows participants to achieve more than they can get alone. We have identified three key competencies within the area of collaboration:

- taking personal responsibility for one's own contribution to a group task
- listening respectfully and responding constructively to others' contributions
- managing the sharing of tasks in a project.

3 Communication

Communication is a vital professional and life skill, involving sharing information, ideas and knowledge between people. It is an active process in which elements such as non-verbal behaviour and individual styles of interpreting and ascribing meaning to events have significant influence. Mastering effective communication is a skill learners need for effective and efficient sharing of information, ideas or knowledge in educational and work settings that can be developed and honed at all levels and stages. We have identified seven key competencies within the area of communication:

- using appropriate language/register for context
- managing conversations
- overcoming one's own language gaps
- participating with appropriate confidence and clarity
- supporting others to communicate successfully
- structuring content
- using language for effect.

4 Critical thinking

The higher levels of thinking that learners need to develop enable them to think effectively and rationally about what they want to do and what they believe is the best action. It consists of identifying links between ideas, analysing points of view and evaluating arguments, supporting evidence, reasoning and conclusions. We have identified six key Critical thinking competencies:

- analysing to understand key points and links between ideas
- evaluating texts, ideas and arguments
- synthesising ideas and information
- identifying and prioritising problems
- evaluating options
- asking effective questions.

5 Learning to learn

It is essential that we continue to learn new skills and knowledge throughout our working lives. The aim of education has to focus as much on the skills of learning as on the outputs of learning. We have identified six key competencies within the area of Learning to learn:

- developing skills for participating in learning
- taking control of one's own learning
- reflecting on and evaluating one's own learning success
- identifying and using effective learning techniques and strategies
- making notes, storing and retrieving information
- managing exam preparation.

6 Social responsibilities

The 'globalised', fast-changing and multicultural world offers clear opportunities for young people to interact with others and to access information across time and space. However, it also brings challenges of a magnitude no other generation has faced. Climate change, war and conflict, refugees, poverty, gender and social inequality demand global action and a new practice and discourse in the education of young people. Social responsibilities refer to the rights and duties that come along with being a citizen of a particular nation or state, as well as of a broader global entity. We have identified six key competencies within the area of Social responsibilities:

- understanding one's personal and social responsibilities as a global citizen
- behaving consistently with one's personal and social responsibilities
- showing leadership skills
- understanding one's own and others' cultures
- understanding and discussing global issues
- understanding and managing career development options and techniques.

Cambridge Lower Secondary Global Perspectives Stage 8 supports all six key areas of competency. Collaboration and communication are the focus of sections 5 and 6 of the Learner's Skills Book. Activities to develop these skills are also contained within other sections of the Learner's Skills Book as are activities to develop creativity, critical thinking, learning to learn and social responsibilities.

> Section 1 Research

Introduction

The learning objectives for research skills for Stage 8 are the same as for Stage 7, and focus on:

- Constructing research questions
- Developing information skills
- Conducting research
- Recording research findings.

However, you might also find opportunities within these lessons to develop some of the other Cambridge Global Perspectives skills. For example, when recording and presenting information, not only will learners be developing their research skills, they will also be developing their communication skills.

The ideas given in Teacher's Resource 8 are suggestions only and the activities can be used with any of the Cambridge Global Perspectives Challenges or topics for Stages 7 to 9. Downloadables and Worked Examples are provided for many learning activities They link to the topic 'Change in culture and communities'. It is hoped that the ideas in Teacher's Resource 8 will help you structure your lessons in an active learning way with input from you as the teacher to help guide and support learners to become more effective and independent researchers.

Research skills overview

Learning objectives	78Rs.01 Construct relevant research questions. 78Rs.02 Identify and begin to reference a range of print and multimedia sources and use them to locate relevant information and answer research questions. 78Rs.03 Select an appropriate method and conduct research to test predictions and begin to answer a research question. 78Rs.04 Select, organise and record relevant information from a range of sources and findings from primary research, using appropriate methods.
Topic ideas	Migration and urbanisation; Change in culture and communities; Development, trade and aid; Poverty and inequality
Key points	• Learners think research is about using a search engine, but often don't know how to use a search engine effectively • Learners copy and paste from information sources rather than making notes and writing in their own words • Research does not just have to be from the internet; learners can use books, newspaper and magazine articles, community newsletters, podcasts, videos; interviews with family, friends, teachers and peers and questionnaires/surveys • Biased and leading questions are questions such as 'Do you agree that migration is beneficial to society?' and 'Why should we not use single-use plastics?' • Questions that only allow for descriptive responses often start with 'How ...?' or 'What ...?' For example, 'What countries do people come from?' and 'How do people earn money to live?'

Language support	• Pre-teach key vocabulary: main ideas; issue-specific words; question; statement; identify; explain; evaluate; evidence; judgement; primary research; secondary research; secondary sources of information; newspaper; article; summarise; sub-heading; title; bias; leading question; prediction; reliable; features; characteristics; data; argument; balance; option; convincing; outdated; perspective; issue; reference. Also include any specific vocabulary for the topics: Migration and urbanisation; Change in culture and communities; Development, trade and aid; Climate change, energy and resources; Poverty and inequality • Handout of question words with some examples from the issues: when, what, which, who, where, why and how
Cross-skills links	**Analysis** 78A.01 Identify ideas and evidence from different perspectives within different sources, on a given issue. **Evaluation** 78E.01 Evaluate sources, considering the author and purpose, recognising that some sources may be more credible than others. 78E.02 Discuss the effectiveness of an argument, making explicit reference to its structure and use of evidence. **Reflection** 78Rf.03 Consider ways that personal perspective on an issue may have changed as a result of conducting research or exploring different perspectives. 78Rf.04 Identify skills learned or improved during an activity and relate to personal strengths and areas for improvement. **Collaboration** 78Cl.01 Work positively within a team to achieve a shared outcome and improve team work, for example by contributing useful ideas, offering solutions to problems, encouraging other team members to participate and being open to others' ideas. 78Cl.02 The team assigns roles and divides tasks fairly, considering the skills of team members and the time available, resolves disagreements and works together to achieve a shared outcome. **Communication** 78Cm.01 Present information and arguments clearly with some reasoning, referencing sources where appropriate. 78Cm.02 Listen to ideas and information and offer relevant and well-judged contributions that demonstrate understanding of the issue.

Let's start thinking about research!

Good for: Enthusing your learners about the skill they are going to work on. The questions give learners ideas about the issues they might explore as they develop their research skills. The first idea suggested is the Challenge 'Making a difference in our community' and the topic 'Change in culture and communities'. The second idea is also based on the topic 'Change in culture and communities'. Although they are not linked to a specific Challenge, the downloadables provide everything your learners need to complete the activities in section 1 and become proficient at research.

Activity: Begin with a quick question and answer session. Ask learners:

- What does 'research' mean?
- What kind of questions could we ask?
- Where might we get our information?
- What issue shall we explore?

Ask learners to each write down one question they have about this section, e.g. on a sticky note. Collate and display their questions so that they are easy to refer to as you work through this section. In that way, learners can see their questions being answered.

Starting with research skills: Lesson 1

Lesson 1 focuses on explaining the term 'research', and recognising and writing good research questions.

CAMBRIDGE STAGE 8 RESEARCH LEARNING OBJECTIVES
78Rs.01 Construct relevant research questions

LEARNING GOALS

To start to:

- explain the term 'research'
- recognise a good research question
- write a good research question

How will I know if I reach my goals?

Good for: Learners to give examples of their learning from the lesson. They can complete the table at any point in the lesson, but might do it at the end.

Resources needed

- Learner's Skills Book 8
- Downloadable 1.1

Prior learning (approx. 5 mins)

Good for: Building on previous knowledge, learning and understanding. This might be from Cambridge Primary Global Perspectives, from other subject areas or from Cambridge Lower Secondary Global Perspectives Stage 7.

Activity: Identify statements to explain what research is.

Differentiation for support: Give learners further options to choose from if they are struggling to come up with their own ideas for task 3. For example: Gaining new knowledge; Using a search engine to find information; Gaining different opinions/viewpoints on an issue; Checking facts/statistics etc.

Suggested answers/ideas: Any reasonable and relevant response. All the suggestions apart from A in task 1 are correct. The intention is to review what research is and stimulate learners' own ideas.

Not issue specific.

Starter activity (approx. 10 mins)

Good for: Identifying good research questions and some of the features of good research questions.

Activity: Give learners a series of research questions related to the issue (including some good and some bad research questions; see Downloadable 1.1 and Worked Example). You can elicit the features of a good research question from the class before referring to the Skills Book to do the activity.

Suggested answers: Good research questions are based on the features in task 2, so point learners to these in their Learner's Skills Book if they are finding this activity a challenge. They should ask themselves:
Is this question interesting? Is it clear what the question is asking for? Is the question too broad? Is it too narrow? Is it too vague? Is it a leading question? Can it be answered?

Worked Example for the Starter activity

Topic: Change in culture and communities

See Downloadable 1.1.

Ideas for good research questions:

A Does economic migration affect communities in a mainly positive or negative way?

B Can people with different cultures and traditions live together in harmony?

C Is technology responsible for changes in communities?

D Is global warming affecting communities in a mainly positive or negative way?

E Does the growth of travel and tourism affect communities in a mainly positive or negative way?

These are all interesting questions from a Cambridge Global Perspectives viewpoint. They are clearly worded, not leading and can be answered after research.

Ideas for bad research questions:

F What are the issues in your community? (not very clear and quite vague)

G Do you agree that litter is an issue in our community? (a leading question and quite narrow)

H What community issues might concern the elderly population? (quite narrow and quite vague)

I How do you think the community is changing? (not very clear (which community?) and quite broad)

J Why do you like living in the community? (quite narrow)

Main activity (approx. 20–25 mins)

Good for: Producing good research questions about an issue.

Activity: Learners produce a mind map of questions about an issue (it can be any issue).

Differentiation: Discuss different types of question word as a starting point: when, what, which, who, where, why and how. Also point to the use of the following as suitable starters for good research questions: 'Is …?'; 'Does …?'; 'Should …?'; 'Can …?' Refer to the good and bad research questions in the Downloadable 1.1 and the Worked Example for Starter activity.

Ways of working: Individually and in pairs, to share ideas and clarify own thinking.

Whole-class discussion based on criteria for a good research question.

Different opinions/perspectives: Also encourage learners to see if their questions allow for different perspectives. For example, the good research questions in Downloadable 1.1 and the Worked Example for the Starter activity will allow for the development of different perspectives, while the bad research questions do not.

Learner response and feedback: Any suggested questions about the issue should be accepted for the mind map activity. Then encourage learners to focus on the features of a good research question to produce their three best questions.

Independent reflection activity (approx. 5–10 mins)

Good for: Encouraging learners to consider what is helping them learn in lessons. Ask them to be as honest as they can. There is no correct response, and they can choose more than one option. Encourage learners to reflect on other skills they have used this lesson as well as research skills. They can choose the examples they think they have used and add further ones as appropriate. This activity can be done in class, at home or in self-study time.

Starting with research skills: Lesson 2

Lesson 2 focuses on being able to select appropriate research methods, explain what texts are about and summarise information from texts in the Learner's own words.

CAMBRIDGE STAGE 8 RESEARCH LEARNING OBJECTIVES

78Rs.03 Select an appropriate method and conduct research to test predictions and begin to answer a research question.

78Rs.04 Select, organise and record relevant information from a range of sources and findings from primary research, using appropriate methods

LEARNING GOALS

To start to:

- select appropriate research methods to begin to answer a research question
- summarise information from texts into own words

How will I know if I reach my goals?

Good for: Learners to give examples of their learning from the lesson. They can complete the table at any point in the lesson, but might do it at the end.

Resources needed

- Learner's Skills Book 8
- Downloadable 1.2

Prior learning (approx. 5 mins)

Good for: Building on previous knowledge, learning and understanding. This might be from Cambridge Primary Global Perspectives, from other subject areas, Cambridge Global Perspectives Stage 7 or from the last Cambridge Global Perspectives Stage 8 lesson.

Activity: Learners choose which they think is the best research question. Encourage them to look at the work they did on research questions in the last lesson and to share their choice and the reasons for this choice with the class.

Differentiation for challenge: Give learners further research questions and ask: 'Is this a good research question? Why/Why not?' You might also recap using the research questions on the topic 'Change in culture and communities' from the last lesson (see Downloadable 1.1).

Suggested answers/ideas: Elicit the features of a good research question from Lesson 1. The best research question is A because it is interesting and neither too broad nor vague. It can be answered after research, and it is not a leading question. It also allows for the development of different perspectives on the impact of urbanisation on biodiversity and ecosystem loss.

It does not need to be issue specific.

Starter activity (approx. 5 mins)

Good for: Identifying the best ways of finding out information.

Activity:

1 Learners list as many ways of finding information as they can.

2 Pair discussion and then whole-class discussion to produce a list on the board and for learners to consider and write down the best ways of finding information to answer the question chosen for the Prior learning activity.

Suggested answers/ideas: Based on the question 'Does urbanisation result in biodiversity and ecosystem loss?': internet websites, environmental organisations specifically concerned with threats to wildlife from building programmes etc., articles from news agencies such as *The Guardian*, *The Hindustani Times* and *The Huffington Post*, local newspapers and newsletters if applicable, interviews with family and friends etc.

Main activity (approx. 25–30 mins)

Good for: Exploring the content of a text and explaining what it is about in the Learner's own words.

Activity: Give learners a text (see Downloadable 1.2 and Worked Example) to read and to give a title to. The text can be on any issue, but it should have no title and should be at least three paragraphs long, so that learners can give a sub-heading for each paragraph and write two sentences in their own words to summarise each paragraph.

1 Learners read through the text; they decide on a title and list all the issue-specific words in the table. They then discuss with their partner and agree on the best title. Next, they share these issue-specific words with their partner to gain further ideas. Class discussion can determine the best title for the text and share all the issue-specific words.

2 Learners discuss the text with a partner. They individually read through each paragraph again and give each paragraph a suitable sub-heading. For each paragraph, learners then write two sentences in their own words to show understanding of the information. Learners discuss their sub-headings and paragraph summaries with a partner and gain peer feedback.

Differentiation: Text lengths can vary. Three paragraphs are suggested, but texts can be shorter or longer according to learners' needs. You might read the text together as a class, perhaps displaying it on the board. You can discuss and model reading comprehension strategies; for example, skimming for the gist and repeated words for clues about the main ideas in the text etc. If learners find producing paragraph summaries a challenge, ask them to write bullet point notes of the key ideas in each paragraph.

Ways of working: Individually, in pairs, and whole class to share ideas and clarify own thinking.

Different opinions/perspectives: Encourage learners to see if there are any different perspectives in the text. For example, for the Downloadable 1.2 and Worked Example, the perspective is very much in favour of having healthy children who spend time outside rather than inside watching television and playing on computers. This text is written from a global perspective, although that is implied rather than explicit as the text refers to children all over the world. It also has a local perspective as local communities feel that it's important to encourage children to play outside.

Learner response and feedback: The summaries of the paragraphs should be in the Learner's own words and should include words/phrases from the table in task 1. Encourage learners to look back at this table to write their paragraph summaries, and to work together and agree on the paragraph summaries.

Suggested answers: These will vary according to the text.

Worked Example for the Main activity

Topic: Change in culture and communities

See Downloadable 1.2.

1 Nowadays, more than ever before, children all over the world are not spending enough time outdoors connecting with nature. Reasons for this include the increasing use of technology for activities on social media and gaming as well as spending free time watching television. School pressures also mean less time is spent outside as children complete homework that mostly requires writing or researching using a computer. Parents don't want their children outside getting dirty and many children are not allowed to play outside for fear of traffic or strangers.

2 Having very little contact with the natural world around them and not connecting enough with nature is having a massive impact, not only on children's physical health but also on their mental health. Increasing obesity among children is the most obvious physical sign of a daily routine of sitting in a classroom and then sitting at home at the computer instead of running around outside. Studies have also shown that mental health is affected, and that children who lack contact with nature are more aggressive than those who get outside for even just five minutes of activity a day.

3 Outdoor activity can improve self-esteem, confidence and emotional well-being, increase happiness and reduce aggressive tendencies. It also helps children to keep a healthy weight. In fact, many local communities are so much in favour of promoting childhood well-being that they are actively encouraging children to enjoy the outdoors. Volunteers supervise outdoor play areas such as parks and outdoor activity centres where children can meet other children and take part in outdoor activities, from climbing trees to studying wildflowers and animals.

Suggested answers:

1 Suggested title: 'Why children need to spend time in nature/outdoors'.

Issue-specific words/phrases: children; nature; outdoors; mental and physical health; parks; activity centres; local communities etc.

2 a Suggested sub-headings: 1. Reasons for not spending time outdoors; 2. Consequences of lack of outdoor activity; 3. Benefits of outdoor activity.

b Suggested paragraph summaries:

1 Children don't spend much time outside because there's a lot of traffic. Parents worry about strangers taking their children. Technology is the main reason why children don't spend time outside.

2 If children don't do physical activity outside, childhood obesity will increase/get worse. Children can also suffer from mental health issues such as lack of confidence and low self-esteem.

3 Being outside has many benefits such as keeping healthy physically and not putting on weight. There are communities where outdoor activity is encouraged and volunteers help supervise children playing in parks.

Independent reflection activity (approx. 5–10 mins)

Good for: Encouraging learners to consider what they found interesting during the lesson. Ask them to be as honest as they can and to choose just one option. There is no correct response. Encourage explanation, but not all learners will be able to do this. Encourage learners to reflect on how they used evaluation skills this lesson; for example, to give feedback on the titles for the text or the paragraph sub-headings. This activity can be done in class, at home or in self-study time.

Starting with research skills: Lesson 3

Lesson 3 focuses on using a search engine to find relevant information and referencing sources of information accurately.

CAMBRIDGE STAGE 8 RESEARCH LEARNING OBJECTIVES

78Rs.02 Identify and begin to reference a range of print and multimedia sources and use them to locate relevant information and answer research questions

LEARNING GOALS

To start to:

- realise the importance of referencing information sources
- find relevant information about an issue
- reference sources of information accurately

How will I know if I reach my goals?

Good for: Learners to give examples of their learning from the lesson. They can complete the table at any point in the lesson, but might do it at the end. At the end of this lesson, learners set their own learning targets before they move on.

Resources needed

- Learner's Skills Book 8
- Downloadable 1.3

Prior learning (approx. 5 mins)

Good for: Building on previous knowledge, learning and understanding. This might be from Cambridge Primary Global Perspectives, from other subject areas, from Cambridge Global Perspectives Stage 7 or from previous Cambridge Global Perspectives Stage 8 lessons.

Activity: Learners choose why it's important to give credit to other people's work by choosing responses from A–D. They can choose as many answers as they like.

Differentiation: Learners can work in pairs and then share with another pair.

Suggested answers/ideas:

1 Any reasonable and relevant response. It is unlikely that learners will choose A. This is not really a reason to give credit to another's work, although authors do sometimes get paid if someone photocopies a page of their book, for example. B, C and D are all relevant. Encourage learners' own ideas.

2 Further ideas might be: because citing another's work gives credibility to your own work; it provides evidence for points you make so that your work is not just assumption or opinion etc.

Not issue specific.

Starter activity (approx. 10–15 mins)

Good for: Evaluating references to see what's missing or inaccurate, and writing own reference accurately.

Activity: Learners look at the reference given (see Downloadable 1.3 and the Worked Example) and identify if anything is missing from it. The whole class could examine the same reference, or you could give different references to different pairs/small groups, but this will make the activity longer. You might want to discuss with the class what needs to be included in a reference before this activity, or you can do it after the activity to see what learners remember from Stage 7.

Can be issue specific.

Worked Example for the Starter activity

Topic: Change in culture and communities

See Downloadable 1.3.

Use the same issue for the Starter and the Main activities.

Ideas for made-up references, although you can use actual references instead.

a Williams. *Humans cause loss of biodiversity.* [Online] Available at: https://www. gardenlife/loss of biodiversity (Accessed 07/06/2022).

b (2021). *Countries need to compete for migrants to strengthen their economy.* [Online] Available at: https://www.conversations/migration (Accessed 02/06/2022).

c Shah, D. (2022). *Women's equal rights in the workplace.* [Online] Available at: https://www.timeshindustani/employment/women.

d Werners, F. *Technology changes society.* [Online] Available at: https://www.technologyandsociety (Accessed 02/06/2022).

e Dela, S. (n.d.). [Online] Available at: https://www.thefuture.com (Accessed 02/06/2022).

f (2021). *The impact of artificial intelligence on society.* [Online] Available at: https://www.watchthisspace (Accessed 03/06/2022).

Suggested answers/ideas:

1 No.

2 a) No date; b) No author; c) No date accessed; d) No date; e) No title of article; f) No author.

3 and **4** Answers will vary. A website reference should include the title of the article, date, author, website address and date accessed.

Main activity (approx. 20–25 mins)

Good for: Enabling learners to do their own research and consider how they reference the articles they find.

Activity: You might start by talking through and showing learners how to conduct research to find the information they are looking for. You can use the 'think aloud' approach using these steps:

- Show learners what you are doing, using your computer attached to the screen and connected to the internet.
- Use a search engine and say for example, 'So, I need to find out about changing communities. Last time I did research, I started by putting the issue into the search engine. So, I'll try that.'
- Do this, then say, 'There are too many results ... wow ... 160 000. I need to narrow my search. I'll change it to "the impact of climate change on communities" to see if I get fewer results. It's also more specific.'
- Then add, 'Wow, there's still a lot of results, but I just want newspaper articles, so I can add that. I'll search for "the impact of climate change on communities" plus "newspaper article" and see what happens.'
- Say, 'That's better – I now have some actual news agencies I've heard of. Right, so I need to ignore sites that have "Ad" – they'll be trying to sell me something, so that's the first two. It leaves a couple that look interesting. I'll try this one.'

Ways of working: Whole class when conducting the 'think aloud' strategy. Individually and in pairs to share ideas, clarify own thinking and give feedback.

Different opinions/perspectives: Encourage learners to find news articles that contain different perspectives and, when researching and skimming articles, to check their relevance to the issue.

Learner response and feedback: Stress that, at the moment, it doesn't matter that learners don't do referencing correctly as this is a skill that can be developed over the next levels (developing … and getting better at …) and Stage 9, but they should try to reference other people's work and keep a list of the sources of information they use. Peer feedback is important so learners can clarify their own understanding and gain ideas from their peers – a valuable part of learning about referencing.

Suggested answers: Will depend on the chosen news articles but all references should include the author, date the article was published or '(n.d.)' if there is no date, title of the article, website address and date accessed by the learner.

Independent reflection activity; Self-assessment; Issue review (approx. 15–20 mins)

Good for: Encouraging learners to consider their learning in lessons. Ask them to be as honest as they can. There is no correct response, and they can choose more than one option. Encourage learners to reflect on how they have used collaboration skills in the lesson, for example, by sharing ideas with a partner or in a small group, or by helping someone else in the lesson.

Learners also complete the self-assessment to set their own learning targets before they move on. Learners think about and shade where they think they have reached at this time in their learning. 'With help' refers to guidance given (pointing a learner in the right direction, although examples should still come from the learner); for example, from the teacher, other learners, previous work done by the learner in the Learner's Skills Book.

For the Issue review, learners explore the issue used in this section to develop research skills.

These activities can be done in class, at home or in self-study time.

Suggested examples:

78Rs.01 *Construct relevant research questions.* Features of a good research question: a question that is interesting; not leading; not too broad, too narrow or too vague; or that allows for information to be found/an answer. An example of a good research question: 'Does economic migration impact communities in a mainly positive or negative way?' An example of a bad research question: 'What is economic migration?'

78Rs.02 *Identify and begin to reference a range of print and multimedia sources and use them to locate relevant information and answer research questions.* To acknowledge/recognise someone else's ideas; give credibility to own ideas etc.

For example, 'Smith, K. (2021). *The impact of artificial intelligence on society*. [Online] Available at: https://www.watchthisspace (Accessed 03/06/2022).'

78Rs.03 *Select an appropriate method and conduct research to test predictions and begin to answer a research question.* Places to get information from: interviews, questionnaires/surveys, internet searches, newspapers, magazines, books. To know what family/friends think: interviews, questionnaires, surveys. To use a search engine, you need to put in specific terms for the information you need to find.

78Rs.04 *Select, organise and record relevant information from a range of sources and findings from primary research, using appropriate methods.* Any relevant example.

Developing research skills: Lesson 4

Lesson 4 focuses on writing a good research question and further questions to help answer this research question. It follows on from work done on research questions in Lesson 1.

CAMBRIDGE STAGE 8 RESEARCH LEARNING OBJECTIVE

78Rs.01 Construct relevant research questions

LEARNING GOALS

To develop knowledge and understanding about:

- the features of a good research question
- how to write a good research question
- how to write sub-questions to help answer a research question

How will I know if I reach my goals?

Good for: Learners to give examples of their learning from the lesson. They can complete the table at any point in the lesson, but might do it at the end.

Resources needed

- Learner's Skills Book 8
- Downloadable 1.4

Prior learning (approx. 5 mins)

Good for: Building on previous knowledge, learning and understanding. This might be from Cambridge Primary Global Perspectives, Cambridge Global Perspectives Stage 7, from other subject areas or from previous Cambridge Global Perspectives Stage 8 lessons (especially Lesson 1).

Activity: Learners write down the features of a good research question: a question that is interesting, not leading, not too broad, too narrow or too vague, and a question that allows for information to be found/an answer.

Differentiation: Allow learners to look back in their Learner's Skills Book to Lesson 1. Some will not need to. Learners work in pairs for support. Each pair can share with another pair for further ideas.

Suggested answers/ideas: Any reasonable and relevant response, but responses will be from Lesson 1 or Cambridge Global Perspectives Stage 7.

Not issue specific.

Starter activity (approx. 10 mins)

Good for: Judging the quality of research questions.

Activity: Learners give reasons why the questions are bad research questions and make them into better research questions.

Ways of working: Individual, pair and perhaps whole-class discussion.

Suggested answers/ideas:

1 a Questions starting with 'What …?' lend themselves to description (rather than analysis and evaluation) and to one answer. This question is not very interesting from a Cambridge Global Perspectives viewpoint; it is too narrow and, although it can be answered, this will only be in a simple, factual way after research. There is no element of argument/debate on which to reach a conclusion. It also does not allow for the development of different perspectives (global or national/local). A better question would be: 'Is global warming causing biodiversity and ecosystem loss?'

b 'Why …?' questions tend to require an answer that is an explanation. They do allow for analysis but not for evaluation. This question is also too narrow as it refers to 'my town' and, while it is interesting, it is not arguable and a conclusion cannot be reached. There is unlikely to be very much information available to answer the question and it might rely on just the opinions of local people. A better question would be: 'Is homelessness an important global issue?'

c This is a leading question as it asks 'Do you agree …' and assumes that tourism is good for a community. The question is too vague, as it's not clear what is meant by 'a community'. It cannot be argued. A better question would be: 'Is tourism mostly beneficial or harmful for communities?'

2 You can ask learners to start each of their 'better' questions with 'Is …?' to see if they can come up with questions that are interesting, and can be argued and answered. You might also do this part of the activity as a whole class after further discussion about the features of a good research question:

- Clear: Does the sentence structure of the question make sense? Is it a question? Would someone else know what you are asking?
- Focused: Is the question too broad, making it hard to answer? Is the question too narrow, making it hard to find enough information?
- Arguable: Does your research question allow you to form an opinion? Does it allow you to support this opinion with evidence?

Main activity (approx. 20–25 mins)

Good for: Gaining further information to help answer a research question.

Activity: Learners choose one of the issues you show/give them (see Downloadable 1.4). They work through the tasks in pairs.

Differentiation: Learners work in pairs for support. You could create a handout with all the features of a good research question on it. (Is it interesting? Is it leading, too broad, narrow or vague? Can it be answered? Is it clear? Is it focused? Is it arguable?) The handout could also include explanations and examples.

Ways of working: In pairs and small groups to share ideas and clarify own thinking.

Different opinions/perspectives: Encourage learners to see if their questions allow for the development of different perspectives at global, local or national levels.

Learner response and feedback: Encourage learners to give feedback to each other based on the features of a good research question.

Suggested answers/questions based on the topic 'Change in culture and communities': Learners are developing their ability to write a good research question (see Worked Example for answers to the different tasks). The sub-questions can be used when doing research using the internet or to ask a visitor to school.

Worked Example for the Main activity

Topic: Change in culture and communities

See Downloadable 1.4.

Issues for learners to choose from: economic migration; gender inequality; global warming; growth of tourism and travel; homelessness; increase in use of the internet and technology; loss of biodiversity; poverty; unemployment; urbanisation.

1 Any relevant response, e.g. There's a lot of construction going on in my city and I'm interested to know more about the reasons for this and the consequences of this.
2 Three questions for the topic 'Urbanisation':
   - What is urbanisation?
   - What is the problem with urbanisation?
   - What can be done about urbanisation?
3 The questions above all start with 'What?' This means that the answers will be descriptive. The questions are too narrow. They are not arguable, making it difficult to reach a conclusion to answer the questions.
4 One possible research question: 'Is urbanisation a problem?'
5 It is interesting; it's not very clear (a problem for whom?); it is arguable.
6 Reworded question: 'Does urbanisation affect communities?'
7 Learners check their questions with you.
8 Reworded after feedback: 'Does urbanisation affect communities in a mainly positive or negative way?'
9 Questions to ask a community leader:
   - Why do you need to build more houses?
   - Is it possible to save space by building upwards rather than outwards?
   - Do you think it's important to have parks where children can play?
   - Does having more houses mean more shops and businesses?
   - Are you going to provide more public transport systems such as trains, buses and trams?
   - Are you going to make the roads better/wider/longer etc.?
   - Is there a sports centre in the building plans?
   - Will there be more schools?
   - How much money will this new development cost?
   - Is this new money or money taken from somewhere else, such as the budget for green spaces?

Independent reflection activity (approx. 5–10 mins)

Good for: Encouraging learners to consider their learning from the lesson. They should apply what they have learned to judge the quality of the question: 'How do young people become unemployed?' The question is not a good research question. It is not very clear what the answer will be; it is not very interesting from a Cambridge Global Perspectives viewpoint; it is too narrow and it is not arguable. It also does not allow for the development of different perspectives. A better question would be: 'Is youth unemployment a global issue?' or 'Does youth unemployment affect communities?' Encourage learners to reflect on their use of communication skills during the lesson; for example, by rewording their questions after feedback. This activity can be done in class, at home or in self-study time.

Developing research skills: Lesson 5

Lesson 5 focuses on different research methods and writing relevant questions to gain information about an issue.

CAMBRIDGE STAGE 8 RESEARCH LEARNING OBJECTIVES

78Rs.01 Construct relevant research questions

78Rs.03 Select an appropriate method and conduct research to test predictions and begin to answer a research question

LEARNING GOALS

To develop knowledge and understanding about:
- different research methods
- good questions for a questionnaire/survey
- writing questions to gain relevant information

How will I know if I reach my goals?

Good for: Learners to give examples of their learning from the lesson. They can complete the table at any point in the lesson, but might do it at the end.

Resources needed

- Learner's Skills Book 8
- Downloadable 1.5

Prior learning (approx. 5–10 mins)

Good for: Building on previous knowledge, learning and understanding. This might be from Cambridge Primary Global Perspectives, Cambridge Global Perspectives Stage 7 lessons, from other subject areas or from other Cambridge Global Perspectives Stage 8 lessons.

Activity: Learners choose which research method(s) is/are most suitable for developing a local perspective about an issue. Encourage learners to explain their choice(s).

Differentiation: Learners can work in pairs and share their ideas with another pair or the whole class.

Suggested answers/ideas: Any reasonable and relevant response.

A A questionnaire allows you to put specific questions to local people (friends, family, people in the community) to gain relevant information about an issue.

B An interview allows you to talk to people to find out what they think about an issue.

C The internet might not be a suitable choice to develop a local perspective, unless a community newsletter or blog is published on the internet.

D A local newspaper might be suitable to find out what local people think about an issue.

E Reasons will vary. If looking to develop a local perspective, primary research methods are more likely to be suitable (asking in school or the community via interviews, surveys, questionnaires) than secondary research methods (internet, books etc.)

Not issue specific.

Starter activity (approx. 10 mins)

Good for: Discussion about how to write good questions for a questionnaire/survey to gain information.

Activity: Learners put the five options in order, starting with the one they think is the most important when writing questions for a questionnaire.

Suggested answers/ideas: All the options are important. Responses will vary. Encourage discussion about what makes a good question.

Not issue specific.

Main activity (approx. 20–25 mins)

Good for: Identifying good and bad questions when writing questionnaires.

Activity: See Downloadable 1.5 and the Worked Example. Discussion about why the questions are good/bad relating to clarity, issue, whether the questionnaire questions contain bias or are leading questions. Learners write another five questions relevant to the issue and check with a partner to see if they are good questions.

Differentiation: Encourage learners to look back at the Starter activity. Individual work as challenge or in pairs for support.

Ways of working: Individually and/or in pairs to share ideas, clarify own thinking. Whole-class discussion about good/bad questions on questionnaires to conduct primary research.

Different opinions/perspectives: Encourage learners to see that the questionnaire questions 2, 4, 6, 9 and 10 in Downloadable 1.5 and the Worked Example are designed to gain their personal perspective (even if some are not very good questions), which might be different from the perspective of their peers.

Learner response and feedback: Encourage learners to discuss the quality of the questionnaire questions in pairs or as a class, once they've had time to answer them.

Suggested answers/questions based on the topic 'Change in culture and communities': Learners are developing their ability to write good questions by evaluating the questions from the Worked Example, so any reasonable response is acceptable. Refer learners back to the Starter activity and to the Tips in their Skills Book.

Questions should:

- be clearly worded so that the researcher gets the information they need
- relate to the issue of the study
- be able to be answered fairly quickly
- be clear in what they are asking
- not be leading or contain bias.

See the Worked Example.

Worked Example for the Main activity

Topic: Change in culture and communities

See Downloadable 1.5.

Primary research questionnaire: To find out how local people feel about the use of cars and public transport.

Name ....

Age ....

1 How often do you use public transport in a week?
0–2 times ☐ 3–5 times ☐ 6– 8 times ☐
9 or more times ☐

2 Do you agree that there are too many cars on the roads?
Yes ☐

3 How often do you walk to school in a week?
Never ☐ A lot ☐

4 Do you think cars are responsible for air pollution?
Yes ☐ No ☐
Why? ....
....

5 How often do you go to the cinema?
Always ☐ Never ☐

6 Do you or do you not like doing the following?
Travelling by car
Using public transport
Walking to school

7 How often do you help the elderly in your community?
Never ☐ 1–2 times per week ☐
more than 3 times per week ☐

8 How often do you suggest that you and your parents travel more by public transport?
Never ☐ 1–2 times per week ☐
3-4 times per week ☐ 5 or more times per week ☐

9 Do you like going everywhere by car?
Yes ☐

10 Do you agree that global warming is responsible for biodiversity and ecosystem loss?
Yes ☐

Thank you for filling in my questionnaire.

Suggested answers:

Name: Probably doesn't need to be included unless you want to follow up with further questions/an interview.

Age: Useful if analysing information gained according to age groups.

1 This is a good question as it is clear, specific and related to issue. It could be broken down further into different types of public transport.

2 This is a leading question with only one option, so it is not a good question.

3 Although related to the issue, this question is not specific (lacking in choices) and is open to interpretation as to what is meant by 'a lot'.

4 This is a fairly good question because of the room to explain. Although some people might not answer the 'why' part, because it would take time to write an answer, the question would still give some information about views on whether cars cause air pollution.

5 This is not relevant to the issue.

6 This is not clear enough as there are two choices in the question.

7 This is not relevant to the issue.

8 This is a good question – clear, specific and related to the purpose and issue.

9 As there is only one option available, this is a leading question.

10 This is a leading question and not relevant to the purpose, which is to find out about the use of cars and public transport.

Independent reflection activity (approx. 5–10 mins)

Good for: Encouraging learners to consider what helped them learn today (e.g. sharing ideas with a partner, evaluating good and bad questions etc.) Encourage learners to reflect on how they have used reflection as well as research skills this lesson (e.g. by considering what has helped them learn best today). This activity can be done in class, at home or in self-study time.

Developing research skills: Lesson 6

Lesson 6 focuses on designing a questionnaire to gain information to help answer a research question. It follows on from Lesson 5, identifying the characteristics of a good question for a questionnaire.

CAMBRIDGE STAGE 8 RESEARCH LEARNING OBJECTIVES

78Rs.02 Identify and begin to reference a range of print and multimedia sources and use them to locate relevant information and answer research questions

78Rs.03 Select an appropriate method and conduct research to test predictions and begin to answer a research question

78Rs.04 Select, organise and record relevant information from a range of sources and findings from primary research, using appropriate methods

LEARNING GOALS

To develop knowledge and understanding about:

- recognising good questions to test predictions
- writing questionnaires to gain relevant information
- selecting information to write questions
- referencing sources of information

How will I know if I reach my goals?

Good for: Learners to give examples of their learning from the lesson. They can complete the table at any point in the lesson, but might do it at the end.

Resources needed

- Learner's Skills Book 8
- Downloadable 1.6

Prior learning (approx. 5–10 mins)

Good for: Building on previous knowledge, learning and understanding. This might be from Cambridge Primary Global Perspectives, Cambridge Global Perspectives Stage 7, other subject areas or from previous Cambridge Global Perspectives Stage 8 lessons.

Activity: Learners decide which of the questions are good questions to test the claim 'Cars are the main source of air pollution in a city'.

Differentiation: Learners can work in pairs for support. Whole-class discussion to clarify which are good questions and why.

Suggested answers/ideas: Any reasonable and relevant response.

A is a leading question with only one choice, so it is not a good question.

B is a good question with two choices but also space for other answers. It is clear, related to the issue and not a leading question or biased. It will also help test the claim.

C is not related to the claim.

D is clear, relates to the claim but only gives two choices, although it does allow for explanation. The question could be improved if it had 'other' as one of the choices for people to complete.

Starter activity (approx. 10–15 mins)

Good for: Revisiting question words in preparation for writing a questionnaire.

Activity: Asking questions to find out more information related to a statement and giving reasons for their choice of their best question. See Downloadable 1.6.

Individual, pair and whole-class discussion.

Suggested answers/ideas: Any reasonable questions, no correct answers. See Worked Example.

Worked Example for the Starter activity

Topic: Change in culture and communities

See Downloadable 1.6.

You can give each pair one of the suggested statements, or show all the statements and ask learners to choose one.

Statement ideas:

- Increasing crime is changing communities.
- Urbanisation is changing communities.
- Poverty causes homelessness.
- Increased population leads to increased traffic.

- Cars cause air pollution.
- Care for the elderly within the community is suffering because of a lack of funding.
- Lack of facilities for young people causes an increase in crime.
- More leisure and entertainment opportunities would result in less crime.
- Urbanisation is causing biodiversity and ecosystem loss.
- Lack of public transport is responsible for air pollution.

Example questions for the statement: 'Cars cause air pollution.'

- When are most cars on the road?
- What else might be causing air pollution?
- Which part of the city is most affected by air pollution?
- Who is responsible for monitoring air pollution in the city?
- Where is air pollution a problem?
- Why are there so many cars on the road at one time?
- How can we prevent the use of cars in the city?

Any reasonable questions; no correct answers.

Main activity (approx. 20–25 mins)

Good for: Creating questions for a primary research questionnaire to gain information related to the issue and referencing sources of information that learners use to write their questions.

Activity: Remind learners of the issue and purpose of their study; for example, testing the claim that cars are responsible for air pollution in cities by asking the question 'Are cars responsible for air pollution in cities?' Should you wish learners to do a different issue, note that they will use the same research question in Lessons 7–9.

Differentiation: Learners can work in pairs for support. Put characteristics of good questions on the board or refer learners back to the Tips in their Skills Book.

Ways of working: Pairs to share ideas, clarify own thinking and as support. Pairs can share with another pair for the questionnaire evaluation in task 3.

Different opinions/perspectives: Encourage learners to write questions to gain different opinions about whether cars are responsible for air pollution in cities.

Learner response and feedback: Encourage learners to give feedback to each other by answering the questions in task 3 in the Learner's Skills Book. If there are any 'No' responses learners should reword their questions.

Suggested answers/questions based on the topic 'Change in culture and communities': Learners are developing their ability to write good questions to conduct primary research, so allow any reasonable questions to do with the issue. Stress the importance of using the characteristics of good questions for primary research when judging the quality of research questions.

Ask learners to give their questionnaire to ten people (family, friends, classmates) to complete before the next lesson. They should collect the completed questionnaires and bring them to the next lesson.

Independent reflection activity; Self-assessment; Issue review (approx. 15–20 mins)

Good for: Encouraging learners to consider their learning and progression in learning during lessons. Ask them to be as honest as they can. For example, they might have found thinking of non-leading questions to be a challenge. They might have asked their partner or you to check some or explain what a leading question is again. Encourage learners to reflect on other skills (analysis, evaluation, reflection, communication, collaboration) they have used this lesson, as well as research skills; for example, using evaluation skills to evaluate another pair's questions.

Learners also complete the self-assessment to set their own learning targets before they move on. Learners think about and shade where they think they have reached at this time in their learning. 'With help' refers to guidance given (pointing a learner in the right direction, although examples should still come from the learner); for example, from the teacher, other learners or previous work done by the learner in the Learner's Skills Book. For the Issue review, learners explore the issue used in this section to develop research skills.

These activities can be done in class, at home or in self-study time.

Suggested examples:

78Rs.01 *Construct relevant research questions.* Features of a good research question: question that is interesting; not too broad, too narrow or too vague; that is not leading and does not contain bias; a question that allows for information to be found/an answer. Examples of good research questions: 'Are cars responsible for air pollution?' and 'Is economic migration good for communities?'

78Rs.02 *Identify and begin to reference a range of print and multimedia sources and use them to locate relevant information and answer research questions.* To acknowledge/

recognise someone else's ideas and give credibility to their own research. Example reference: Grey (2022). *Communities are losing their traditions and culture.* Whatdowethink [Online] Available at: https://www.whatdowethink/ (Accessed 20/06/2022).

78Rs.03 *Select an appropriate method and conduct research to test predictions and begin to answer a research question.* A local newspaper or newsletter, interview, questionnaire (survey), questionnaire. Example question to test prediction: 'Does building more houses cause habitat loss for wildlife?'

78Rs.04 *Select, organise and record relevant information from a range of sources and findings from primary research, using appropriate methods.* Any relevant example.

Getting better at research skills: Lesson 7

Lesson 7 focuses on the use of primary research to gain information, and how to organise and record the information gained from primary research. It follows on from work done in Lessons 5 and 6.

CAMBRIDGE STAGE 8 RESEARCH LEARNING OBJECTIVES

78Rs.03 Select an appropriate method and conduct research to test predictions and begin to answer a research question

78Rs.04 Select, organise and record relevant information from a range of sources and findings from primary research, using appropriate methods

LEARNING GOALS

To get better at:

- understanding how research helps test a prediction
- recording information gained from primary research
- presenting information gained from primary research

How will I know if I reach my goals?

Good for: Learners to give examples of their learning from the lesson. They can complete the table at any point in the lesson, but might do it at the end.

Resources needed

- Learner's Skills Book 8
- Downloadable 1.7

Prior learning (approx. 5–10 mins)

Good for: Building on previous knowledge, learning and understanding. This might be from Cambridge Primary Global Perspectives, Cambridge Global Perspectives Stage 7, from other subject areas or from previous Cambridge Global Perspectives Stage 8 lessons (especially Lessons 5 and 6).

Activity: Review learning about testing predictions from Lesson 6.

Differentiation: Allow learners to look back in their Learner's Skills Book. Some will not need to. Learners can work individually/in pairs and then share ideas with a partner/whole class.

Suggested answers/ideas: Any reasonable and relevant response.

1 **a** A prediction is a statement about what you think will happen or what you think is causing something to happen.

b To test a prediction, you need to ask the right type of question.

2 Research helps test a prediction as you can ask people their views on the prediction, you think you know the answer to.

Not issue specific.

Starter activity (approx. 10–15 mins)

Good for: Discussion about primary sources of information.

Activity: Answering questions about a primary source of information and sharing ideas. See Downloadable 1.7.

Ways of working: Individual, pair and whole-class discussion to clarify thinking and gain new learning.

Suggested answers/ideas: See Worked Example.

Does not have to be issue specific.

Worked Example for the Starter activity

Topic: Change in culture and communities

See Downloadable 1.7.

Starter activity: Bar graph as a primary source of information for learners to answer questions about community issues.

People in a local community were given a list of nine issues (transport; housing; environment; technology; health; crime rate; care homes; sport facilities; shopping) and asked to identify the three they thought were the most important to a community. The results are recorded in the bar graph.

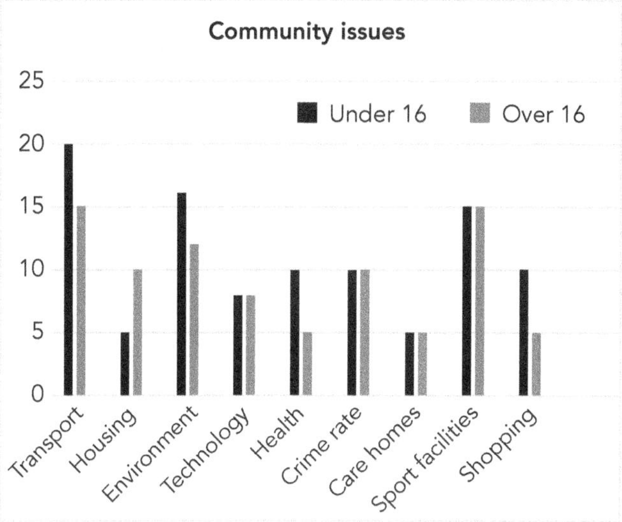

Fig. 1. Community issues. Graph by Eric Holly, '*The Importance of Community Issues.*' (Community Newsletter, 20 June 22).

Suggested answers/ideas:

1 **a** Primary source as a double bar graph in a community newsletter.

b Eric Holly. Nothing else about him is mentioned. However, you might encourage learners to search for the author of a source to verify credentials (this one is made up).

c 20 June 2022.

d Perhaps to get local people's views on what's important to them in a community; to identify the difference/similarity between what those under the age of 16 and over the age of 16 thought important in a community.

e Local community groups, the local council, perhaps the national government when deciding how to allocate funds to communities.

f It's mostly clear but would benefit from having a title for the number of people axis. It might also be useful to see the questionnaire to clarify what the category 'Crime rate' refers to (whether it's increased crime rate or not), as well as what is meant by 'Environment' and 'Technology'. Discussion can emphasise the importance of creating clear sources of information from data in preparation for the main activity.

Main activity (approx. 20–25 mins)

Good for: Analysing and recording information gained from primary research.

Activity: Discussion about ways of recording information gained from primary research.

Differentiation: Learners can work in pairs/small groups for support. You can decide the choice of presentation method or allow learners to choose.

Ways of working: In pairs/small groups for support. Whole-class discussion about ways of recording information from primary research.

Different opinions/perspectives: Stress that primary research methods are a great way of gaining opinions and viewpoints from different groups of people about issues, and can form evidence as part of a perspective. For example, the information gained from neighbours in a community about issues that are important to them can provide evidence for a local perspective that more needs to be done for the community.

Learner response and feedback: Encourage learners to work in pairs/small groups when presenting their information so they can provide continual feedback to each other.

Suggested answers/ideas: Remind learners to consider the purpose and audience for the information they have gathered. Either give them the same presentation method or allow them to choose their own way of presenting the information gained from their questionnaire; for example, poster, leaflet, presentation (set a maximum number of slides), blog, summary, bar graph, pie chart, table.

Independent reflection activity (approx. 5–10 mins)

Good for: Encouraging learners to consider their learning from the lesson, what they think has helped them learn, and how they have helped someone else learn today; for example, by working with a partner, joining in discussions, asking for/giving help/support, helping their partner etc. This activity can be done in class, at home or in self-study time.

Getting better at research skills: Lesson 8

Lesson 8 focuses on the use of secondary information sources to gain information to help answer a research question.

CAMBRIDGE STAGE 8 RESEARCH LEARNING OBJECTIVES

78Rs.02 Identify and begin to reference a range of print and multimedia sources and use them to locate relevant information and answer research questions

78Rs.03 Select an appropriate method and conduct research to test predictions and begin to answer a research question

78Rs.04 Select, organise and record relevant information from a range of sources and findings from primary research, using appropriate methods

LEARNING GOALS

To get better at:

- understanding when to use primary and secondary information sources
- doing an internet search to find relevant information
- judging the quality of an information source to help answer a research question

How will I know if I reach my goals?

Good for: Learners to give examples of their learning from the lesson. They can complete the table at any point in the lesson, but might do it at the end.

Resources needed

- Learner's Skills Book 8
- Downloadable 1.8

Prior learning (approx. 5–10 mins)

Good for: Building on previous knowledge, learning and understanding. This might be from Cambridge Primary Global Perspectives, Cambridge Global Perspectives Stage 7, from other subject areas or from previous Cambridge Global Perspectives Stage 8 lessons (especially Lessons 6 and 7).

Activity: Review learning about primary and secondary sources of information by giving examples and discussing when to use primary and secondary information sources.

Differentiation: Learners work together for this activity.

Suggested answers/ideas:

1 **a** Primary: interview, questionnaire, survey, bar graph or chart – direct and first-hand.

b Secondary: internet, textbooks – indirect, reported, second-hand, existing data.

2 **a** Primary: to develop a local perspective about an issue or gain local information.

b Secondary: to develop a national or global perspective about an issue or gain information from a wider audience.

Not issue specific.

Starter activity (approx. 5–10 mins)

Good for: Reviewing the steps for effective research using a search engine.

Activity: Adding in the missing steps to conduct effective research.

Suggested answers/ideas:

1 Decide what information you need to find.

2 Type in key words (between three and six) into the search engine.

3 Click on a website to open it.

4 Look further down the page beyond the first few results of the search.

5 Skim read the text, asking the following questions: Is it easy to follow? Do I understand it? Might it be useful? If so, bookmark it.

If the internet is available in the lesson, you can model the steps aloud, doing a real search. Example search: 'Increasing numbers of cars are causing air pollution.'

Does not have to be issue specific.

Main activity (approx. 20–25 mins)

Good for: Analysing secondary information sources to gain information to help answer a research question.

Activity: Learners answer questions about a given text (See Downloadable 1.8 and Worked Example).

Differentiation: Learners work in pairs/small groups for support. Give the choice of which questions to answer to some learners. The more challenging questions are f–i. Encourage some learners to answer these questions.

Ways of working: In pairs/small groups for support. Whole-class discussion about secondary sources of information.

Different opinions/perspectives: Stress that secondary research methods are a great way of gaining evidence to support a perspective. For example, for the research question 'Are cars the main cause of air pollution in cities?', there are two clear perspectives:

- Yes, cars are the main cause of air pollution in cities.
- No, cars are not the main cause of air pollution in cities.

Evidence for the 'yes' perspective might come from national evidence/sources of information, and evidence for the 'no' perspective might come from global evidence/sources of information.

Learner response and feedback: Encourage learners to work in pairs/small groups to give feedback to each other on the answers to the questions.

Suggested answers/ideas: See Worked Example.

Worked Example for the Main activity

Topic: Change in culture and communities

See Downloadable 1.8.

Secondary source of information

AIR POLLUTION – A GLOBAL ISSUE?

Jan Feras 14/07/2017

Almost half of all the citizens in America, about 150 million, are reported to live in areas where the air quality is so poor that it is below the government's recommended level. The cause of this air pollution is not the factories and industrial areas but our everyday transport such as cars, taxis, buses and lorries. The consequence of this is dense smog and people who have trouble breathing. This results in the everyday use of masks to help them go about their business.

Cars are the most polluting of all vehicles. They produce carbon monoxide and nitrogen, and the sheer volume of cars in cities is helping to create an atmosphere that most people find difficult to accept. In 2016, more than half of the nitrogen and carbon monoxide in the air came from transportation.

People are suffering from serious health concerns like bronchitis and asthma. Some researchers are even suggesting that air pollution in cities caused by the number of cars is leading to an increased number of people being diagnosed with cancer. This is a life-threatening disease. The increase in air pollution is also helping to cripple our health system as costs to treat these illnesses increase.

And it's not just cities in America that are being affected by increased air pollution. This is a global issue impacting on citizens across the globe. Air pollution is now our biggest global concern and unless we do something about it, more people will become chronically ill. Our wildlife is also affected, and we have a responsibility to protect it as well as our own health and well-being.

Suggested answers/ideas:

a Air pollution – a global issue?

b Jan Feras

c 14/07/2017

d Transportation, mainly cars in cities are the largest source of air pollution. Air pollution is leading to increased illness and loss of wildlife. People are having to protect themselves by wearing masks. It's not just an issue in America, but globally.

e That something needs to be done and we must take responsibility for reducing the amount of air pollution in cities.

f Anecdotal evidence about people suffering from health conditions related to air pollution, although some researchers are mentioned. Statistics about the number of people in America living in areas where the amount of air pollution is unacceptable, but no source is cited or referenced. Also, statistics about the amount of nitrogen and carbon monoxide in the air that have come from transportation, but no source cited or referenced.

g It is fairly convincing as it is logical and the evidence supports the argument made. It would be more convincing if the sources of evidence were cited and referenced and there was evidence to support some of the claims made; for example, 'Cars are the most polluting of all vehicles'.

h It is not very reliable as the author is unknown – their name does not appear in a cross-reference (the author hasn't written anything else). Some of the information is credible but parts are not; for example, citing cars as the most polluting of all vehicles. The source is also outdated and things will have changed since the article was written.

i Examples: 'Is air pollution an important global issue?'; 'Is transportation the major cause of air pollution?'; 'Is air pollution in cities the reason for an increase in chronic health conditions?'

Independent reflection activity (approx. 5–10 mins)

Good for: Encouraging learners to consider their learning from the lesson, what they found challenging and how they addressed this challenge; for example, they needed their partner's help to come up with a research question that the source might help answer. Encourage learners to reflect on how they have used communication skills this lesson; for example, by explaining what the word 'reliable' means to their partner. This activity can be done in class, at home or in self-study time.

Getting better at research skills: Lesson 9

Lesson 9 focuses on gaining information to present an argument for a particular perspective on an important global issue. It follows on from the work done in Lesson 8.

CAMBRIDGE STAGE 8 RESEARCH LEARNING OBJECTIVES

78Rs.02 Identify and begin to reference a range of print and multimedia sources and use them to locate relevant information and answer research questions

78Rs.03 Select an appropriate method and conduct research to test predictions and begin to answer a research question

78Rs.04 Select, organise and record relevant information from a range of sources and findings from primary research, using appropriate methods

LEARNING GOALS

To get better at:

- referencing sources of information
- finding relevant information to answer a research question
- recording relevant information

How will I know if I reach my goals?

Good for: Learners to give examples of their learning from the lesson. They can complete the table at any point in the lesson, but might do it at the end.

Resources needed

- Learner's Skills Book 8
- Downloadables 1.9 and 1.10

Prior learning (approx. 5 mins)

Good for: Building on previous knowledge, learning and understanding. This might be from Cambridge Primary Global Perspectives, Cambridge Global Perspectives

Stage 7, from other subject areas or from previous Cambridge Global Perspectives Stage 8 lessons.

Activity: Review learning about how a search engine is useful for finding information. It is also important that learners know how to use one.

Differentiation: Allow learners to work together for this activity and to look back in their Learner's Skills Book if necessary.

Suggested answers/ideas: A search engine is useful because it enables you to find relevant information to help answer a research question; it helps you to find facts/statistics and evidence to support your own points; it helps you to check information that you might have got from a different source. To know how to use a search engine, you need to:

- decide on the information you need
- type between three and six important key words into the search engine
- look further down the page beyond the first few results of the search
- click on the website to open it
- skim read the text: Is it easy to follow? Do I understand the text? Might it be useful?
- if so, bookmark it.

Further ideas: Keep a list of useful websites; check the credibility of the author by searching for other articles by them; check the reliability of the website (.org; .gov; wiki etc.); can use videos and podcasts as well as written articles.

Not issue specific.

Starter activity (approx. 5–10 mins)

Good for: Reviewing/sharing words, phrases, issues and perspectives for use in the lesson.

Activity: Split the class in half. Give one picture to one half of the class and the other picture to the other half of the class. For example, to gain different ideas for the topic 'Change in culture and communities', you could show the class one picture demonstrating air pollution and one picture demonstrating water pollution (see Downloadable 1.9). This could be a snowball activity (learners share in pairs, then in groups of four and then eights to gain more words and phrases). A snowball activity will take more time.

Suggested answers/ideas: Does not have to be issue specific, but the ideas shared will be useful during the main activity.

Main activity (approx. 20–25 mins)

Good for: Evaluating secondary information sources to gain information to help support a perspective.

Activity: Learners work in groups of four. For each picture from the Starter activity (see Downloadable 1.9), give learners a set of three relevant website addresses (see Downloadable 1.10 and Worked Example) to gain information on their picture/perspective (whether air pollution is a more significant global issue than water pollution or vice versa). They can then use what they know about research to find another information source.

Each team member is responsible for gaining information from one website only. Give a time limit for them to find this information (approx. 10–15 mins).

Teams come together to share their information and discuss the format they might use to persuade the other half of the class of their perspective. If time permits, teams can produce this outcome using the information they have found (podcast, presentation, video clip, leaflet, brochure, board game etc.) and give feedback. Did the information presented persuade them that air or water is the most significant global issue of the two? How might they be better persuaded?

Differentiation: Learners work in groups of four for support and guidance. Select groups to work together or allow free choice. Give the choice of who researches which website address and who finds one of the team's own.

Ways of working: Small groups for support and guidance and to develop team-working skills.

Different opinions/perspectives: Stress that the aim of the two pictures is to give two different perspectives, either:

- Air pollution is a more significant global issue than water pollution, or
- Water pollution is a more significant global issue than air pollution.

One half of the class finds information in small groups to persuade of the first perspective and the other half the second perspective.

Learner response and feedback: Encourage learners to give feedback to each other on the information gained. Ask questions: What did you learn? Were you persuaded by the argument? Did you change your perspective? Why?

Suggested answers/ideas: See Worked Example.

Worked Example for the Main activity

Topic: Change in culture and communities

See Downloadable 1.10.

Main activity: Learners work in groups of four. For each picture, give learners a set of three relevant website addresses (see examples in Downloadable 1.10 and below) to gain information from their perspective, and then each team also finds one other information source. Each team member writes a summary to explain why their type of pollution is a more significant global issue than the other type of pollution.

Picture and website ideas:

- Air pollution is a more significant global issue than water pollution:

  https://www.theguardian.com/environment/2018/nov/05/air-pollution-everything-you-should-know-about-a-public-health-emergency

  https://www.theguardian.com/environment/2021/sep/01/air-pollution-is-slashing-years-off-the-lives-of-billions-report-finds

  https://www.everythingconnects.org/pollution.html

- Water pollution is a more significant global issue than air pollution:

  https://www.water.org.uk/news-item/water-and-nature-cop26/

  https://www.nrdc.org/stories/water-pollution-everything-you-need-know

  https://en.unesco.org/themes/water-security/hydrology/water-scarcity-and-quality

Independent reflection activity; Self-assessment; Issue review (approx. 15–20 mins)

Good for: Encouraging learners to consider their learning and progression in learning during lessons. Learners consider the most important thing that helped them learn in the lesson; for example, class discussion or working with a partner. Encourage learners to reflect on and explain the skills (analysis, evaluation, reflection, communication, collaboration) they have used this lesson, including research skills.

Learners also complete the self-assessment to set their own learning targets. Learners think about and shade where they think they have reached at this time in their learning. 'With help' refers to guidance given (pointing a learner in the right direction, although examples should still come from the learner); for example, from the teacher, other learners and/or previous work done by the learner in the Learner's Skills Book.

For the Issue review, learners explore the issue used in this section to develop research skills.

These activities can be done in class, at home or in self-study time.

Suggested examples:

78Rs.01 *Construct relevant research questions.* Features of a good research question: a question that people care about; a question that is not too broad, too narrow or too vague; a question that allows for information to be found/an answer. Examples of good research questions: 'Is economic migration beneficial to communities?' and 'Does urbanisation benefit communities?

78Rs.02 *Identify and begin to reference a range of print and multimedia sources and use them to locate relevant information and answer research questions.* To acknowledge/recognise someone else's ideas: Avellar, J. (2020) *Car emissions are a major source of pollution.* Lewis & Clark Law School [Online] Available at: https://law.lclark.edu/live/blogs/156-car-emissions-are-a-major-source-of-pollution (Accessed 08/07/22)

78Rs.03 *Select an appropriate method and conduct research to test predictions and begin to answer a research question.* Prediction is a statement about what you think will happen or what you think is causing something to happen; for example, 'Increased traffic will increase levels of air pollution' or 'People living in poverty suffer from poor health'.

Any example steps to do an internet search, as listed in the Prior learning notes previously.

78Rs.04 *Select, organise and record relevant information from a range of sources and findings from primary research, using appropriate methods.* Any relevant example. Learners can use examples from their Skills Book from Lessons 7–9. They can write the source and a sentence or two from it in their own words. Ask them to check that the information:

- is clearly worded
- relates to the issue
- relates to the question
- does not contain words copied from the source.

Showcasing your skills: Research

Good for: Showing learners how others felt at the end of the research tasks. These young people have practised and developed their research skills and learned a lot about how conducting research and asking key questions can make them even better at Cambridge Lower Secondary Global Perspectives. You may intend to have your learners write the Cambridge Lower Secondary Checkpoint Research Report in Stage 9. Learners should be improving their ability to write a question that will allow them to fulfill all the assessment criteria. You can help them by encouraging them to think about issues that have causes and consequences, and that require solutions. Those are the kinds of questions they need to ask!

Activity: This is an opportunity for your learners to reflect on elements of their work in this section that they are particularly pleased with. Read through and discuss the reflections with your class. Then try one these reflection tasks with your learners:

- 'Two stars and a wish' means 'Two things I am pleased with and one thing I want to improve on'. Ask your learners to write their own 'two stars and a wish' on a sticky note and stick it on the board.
- Ask each learner to draw two speech bubbles. In one they write, 'What went well' and in the other they write 'Even better if'. Create a class display of speech bubbles on the classroom wall.

Projects: If learners have had ample opportunities to practise the other skills required, they could also showcase their research skills by attempting any of the three projects available at cambridge.org/go, all three of which have research learning objectives.

Section 2 Analysis

Introduction

The learning objectives for analysis skills for Stage 8 are the same as those for Stage 7 and focus on the following:

- identifying perspectives
- interpreting data
- making connections
- solving problems.

However, you might also find opportunities within these lessons to develop some of the other Cambridge Global Perspectives skills. For example, when identifying ideas and evidence from different perspectives, not only will learners be developing analysis skills, they will also be developing their research skills.

The ideas given in this Teacher's Resource are suggestions only, and the activities can be used with any of the Cambridge Global Perspectives Challenges or topics for Stages 7 to 9. Downloadables and Worked Examples are provided for many learning activities. They are linked to the issues 'Values and beliefs', 'Digital world' and 'Climate change, energy and resources'. It is hoped that the ideas in this book will help you structure your lessons in an active learning way with input from you as the teacher to help guide and support learners to become more effective at being able to analyse issues and suggest courses of action to help resolve these issues.

You will notice that some activities in this section focus on issues of sustainability. We hope these activities will help to develop beliefs in the importance of being responsible members of the global community in your learners.

Analysis skills overview

Learning objectives	78A.01 Identify ideas and evidence from different perspectives within different sources, on a given issue. 78A.02 Explain how graphical or numerical data supports an argument or a perspective. 78A.03 Explain causes of a local or global issue and consequences on others. 78A.04 Suggest and justify different actions to make a positive difference to a national or global issue.
Topic ideas	Migration and urbanisation; Change in culture and communities; Development, trade and aid; Climate change, energy and resources; Values and beliefs
Key points	• Understanding that a cause is responsible for a situation or issue, and a consequence is the result of a situation or issue. • Confusion between the terms 'issue' and 'perspectives'. An issue is often a problem that needs resolving or something that can be debated. A perspective is a way of looking at something (e.g. an issue). • Confusion between the terms 'perspective', 'opinion' and 'viewpoint'. A perspective is a way of looking at something, based on evidence. An opinion is what someone thinks and is often unsupported. A viewpoint is the same as an opinion and is someone's view about something. • Understanding the difference between a global, national, local and personal perspective.

Key points	• Evidence can be in the form of graphs, photos, video clips, audio recordings and written texts (newspaper/magazine articles, books, leaflets, newsletters, blogs etc.) • Closed questions (for example, those requiring 'Yes' or 'No' answers) are easy to analyse and findings can be presented as a graph. • Open questions often start with 'Why?' and 'How?' and are more difficult to analyse. Research findings from open questions are often presented as a summary. • A course of action is something that someone does to help resolve or make a positive difference to an issue • A course of action should relate to the issue. A local issue often needs a local course of action.
Language support	Pre-teach key vocabulary: cause; consequence; issue, perspective (local, national, global, personal, cultural); double bar graph (title, axis, labels, scale, bars); prediction; conclusion; identify; explain; resources; evaluate; course of action; solution; stakeholder; open question; closed question; bias; conclusion. Also include any issue-specific vocabulary for the topics – Migration and urbanisation; Digital world; Change in culture and communities; Development, trade and aid; Climate change, energy and resources; Values and beliefs. Handout of words/phrases signalling cause and consequence, and examples of their use: • Signalling cause – because, due to, since, as, so/as long as … , now that. • Signalling consequence – as a result, therefore, that's why, so, consequently, this means, this leads to, for this reason, due to this, if … then.
Cross-skills links	**Research** 78Rs.01 Construct relevant research questions. 78Rs.02 Identify and begin to reference a range of print and multimedia sources and use them to locate relevant information and answer research questions. 78Rs.03 Select an appropriate method and conduct research to test predictions and begin to answer a research question. 78Rs.04 Select, organise and record relevant information from a range of sources and findings from primary research, using appropriate methods. **Evaluation** 78E.01 Evaluate sources, considering the author and purpose, recognising that some sources may be more credible than others. 78E.02 Discuss the effectiveness of an argument, making explicit reference to its structure and use of evidence. **Reflection** 78Rf.03 Consider ways that personal perspective on an issue may have changed as a result of conducting research or exploring different perspectives. 78Rf.04 Identify skills learned or improved during an activity and relate to personal strengths and areas for improvement.

Cross-skills links	Collaboration 78Cl.01 Work positively within a team to achieve a shared outcome and improve team work, for example by contributing useful ideas, offering solutions to problems, encouraging other team members to participate and being open to others' ideas. 78Cl.02 The team assigns roles and divides tasks fairly, considering the skills of team members and the time available, resolves disagreements and works together to achieve a shared outcome. Communication 78Cm.01 Present information and arguments clearly with some reasoning, referencing sources where appropriate. 78Cm.02 Listen to ideas and information and offer relevant and well-judged contributions that demonstrate understanding of the issue.

Let's start thinking about analysis!

Good for: Enthusing your learners about the skill they are going to work on. The questions give learners ideas about the issues they might explore as they develop their analysis skills. The first idea suggested is the Challenge 'Beliefs about food' and the topic 'Values and beliefs'. The second idea is based on the topic 'Digital world', but it is not closely linked to a Challenge. However, the downloadables provide everything your learners need to complete the activities in Section 2 and become proficient at analysis.

Activity: Look at these pages with your learners. You could begin with a quick question and answer session.

Ask learners:

- What does 'analysis' mean?
- What kinds of questions could we ask?
- Where might we get our information?
- What issue shall we explore?

Ask learners to each write down one question they have about this section, e.g. on a sticky note. Collate and display their questions so that they are easy to refer to as you work through this section. In that way, learners can see their questions being answered.

Starting with analysis skills: Lesson 1

Lesson 1 focuses on being able to explain the term 'analysis' and how to analyse something and summarise relevant information gained from discussion.

CAMBRIDGE STAGE 8 ANALYSIS LEARNING OBJECTIVES

78A.01 Identify ideas and evidence from different perspectives within different sources, on a given issue

LEARNING GOALS

To start to:

- explain the term 'analysis'
- explain how to analyse something
- summarise relevant information.

How will I know if I reach my goals?

Good for: Learners to give examples of their learning from the lesson. They can complete the table at any point in the lesson but might do it at the end.

Resources needed

- Learner's Skills Book 8
- Downloadable 2.1

Prior learning (approx. 5 mins)

Good for: Building on previous knowledge, learning and understanding. This might be from Cambridge Primary Global Perspectives, from Cambridge Global Perspectives Stage 7, from other subject areas or from previous Cambridge Global Perspectives Stage 8 lessons. It asks learners to produce words/phrases related to the picture(s) and for use in the next activities.

Activity: Find out what words/phrases learners already know to be able to analyse the picture in the Starter activity and explain what analysis is. See Downloadable 2.1 and the Worked Example for picture ideas.

Differentiation: Learners work in pairs and then share with another pair to gain further ideas (they need to have the same picture).

Suggested ideas: Use four or more different pictures (see Downloadable 2.1 and the Worked Example for ideas) to do with the same issue as, in the Starter activity, learners will work in groups, each group with one of the pictures. Each picture can be copied twice and given to two different pairs to enable sharing for this activity.

Not issue specific but see the Worked Example.

Starter activity (approx. 10 mins)

Good for: Enabling learners to start thinking about how to analyse something (explaining what the picture shows).

Activity: Using words/phrases from their Prior learning, learners write an explanation about what their picture shows. (See Downloadable 2.1 and the Worked Example for picture ideas.)

Ways of working: Pair work to complete the written explanation about the picture.

Suggested answers: Any reasonable and relevant response, depending on the pictures/issue.

Main activity (approx. 20–25 mins)

Good for: Explaining an issue in more detail (including causes, consequences and perspectives).

Activity: Allow each small group to choose an issue (see the Worked Example). Each group works together to answer the questions in task 1. Give a specific time for discussion. Learners then produce a commentary summarising their discussion and record this commentary. Use some (e.g. three) of the recorded commentaries as a listening activity with learners making notes about the other issues.

Differentiation: Small group work for support. Choice of issues.

Ways of working: In small groups to discuss answers to the questions and write a transcript and commentary. Whole-class listening to commentaries and recording information about each of the issues.

Different opinions/perspectives: The activity encourages learners to look at their issue from different perspectives for example, their own and their teammates.

Learner response and feedback: Encourage learners to focus on their issue only and encourage each member of the group to keep the others focused on the tasks. Stress that they should listen to each other as they write their transcript and record their commentary for their issue.

Suggested answers/ideas: See the Worked Example below.

Worked Example for the Prior learning, Starter and Main activities

Topic: Values and beliefs

Issue: Beliefs about foods

See Downloadable 2.1.

Prior learning and Starter activity:

Suggested pictures and issues:

- Animal welfare for a better world
- Food allergies
- Eating out culturally
- Religious food festivals/celebrations
- Fast/junk food
- Vegetarian/vegan/plant-based.

These are used throughout the Prior learning, Starter and Main activities.

Main activity:

Suggested issues as for the Prior learning and Starter activities for small groups to choose from for discussion.

Questions for task 1 are in the Learner's Skills Book.

Suggested answers/ideas:

1 Picture: A range of food items that are all plant-based or vegetarian.

a Eating fruits and vegetables/a plant-based diet; not eating meat; not eating a diet of junk food but eating a healthy diet that consists mostly of fruits and vegetables.

b Because if we don't eat a diet rich in fruits and vegetables, we are more likely to suffer disease and need more medical attention, which could cost the country a lot of money. This money could be used for other causes, such as free education for all.

c People must eat a more plant-based diet to save the planet. Livestock farming uses approximately 77 per cent of global agricultural land. Livestock farming is responsible for destroying wildlife habitats and greenhouse gas emissions. If people ate less meat, there wouldn't need to be as much livestock farming.

d Answers might start with 'We think … '

e Answers might start with 'We chose this issue because … '

4 The type of information gained will be reasons for or causes of a healthy/plant-based diet and against a diet rich in animal products/junk food; consequences of eating meat, not eating more of a plant-based diet; perspectives/viewpoints of the teams.

5 Refer learners to the Tips.

Independent reflection activity (approx. 5–10 mins)

Good for: Learners to give examples of what they have found the most difficult in the lesson. This might be skill or content specific; for example, summarising information from discussion, gaining information from others or identifying the type of information gained. Encourage learners to reflect on all the skills (research, analysis, evaluation, reflection, communication, collaboration) they have used this lesson; for example, collaboration skills in discussion and deciding what to put in the commentary. This activity can be done in class, at home or in self-study time.

Starting with analysis skills: Lesson 2

Lesson 2 focuses on explaining what an issue and a perspective are and the difference between the them.

CAMBRIDGE STAGE 8 ANALYSIS LEARNING OBJECTIVES

78A.01 Identify ideas and evidence from different perspectives within different sources, on a given issue

LEARNING GOALS

To start to:

- explain what an issue is
- explain what a perspective is.

How will I know if I reach my goals?

Good for: Learners to give examples of their learning from the lesson. They can complete the table at any point in the lesson but might do it at the end.

Resources needed

- Learner's Skills Book 8
- Downloadable 2.2

Prior learning (approx. 5–10 mins)

Good for: Building on previous knowledge, learning and understanding. This might be from Cambridge Primary Global Perspectives, from Cambridge Global Perspectives Stage 7, from other subject areas or from previous Cambridge Global Perspectives Stage 8 lessons.

Activity: Learners review words/phrases that signal causes and consequences to look out for in texts when researching and to use in their own work. For example, 'because' is used to say why something has happened (cause) and 'as a result' is an example of a phrase signalling a consequence.

Differentiation: Learners work in pairs for support. Pairs can share with another pair to gain further ideas, but more time is needed for this.

Suggested answers:

1 Causes: because, due to, since, as, so long as … , as long as … , now, that.

2 Consequences: as a result, therefore, that's why, so, consequently, this means, this leads to, for this reason, due to this, if … then.

Not issue specific.

Starter activity (approx. 10–15 mins)

Good for: Reviewing the difference between issues and perspectives.

Activity: Give learners a sub-topic (e.g. Beliefs about foods).

1 Learners work together to come up with as many issues to do with the sub-topic as possible in a specific time (e.g. 5 mins). They put them on a mind map.

2 Sharing with another pair will extend their list/diagram of issues.

3 Learners explain what an issue is in their own words.

4 They explain how an issue differs from a perspective.

Ways of working: Individual, pairs and whole-class discussion to review understanding of the difference between issues and perspectives.

Suggested examples for the sub-topic 'Beliefs about foods':

- Issues: animal welfare, climate change, loss of culture/traditions, weight issues, health issues.
- Perspectives: global, national, local, personal, cultural.
- An issue is an important problem for debate or discussion. An issue often needs a course of action to help resolve it.
- A perspective is a way of looking at something.

Main activity (approx. 20–25 mins)

Good for: Exploring the difference between issues and perspectives in a text to help clarify understanding of the difference. For task 2, the three further issues and perspectives do not need to come from the text, but they should be related to the issue.

Activity: Learners identify and explain issues and perspectives from the text. The text can be written, or an audio or video clip (see the Downloadable 2.2 and the Worked Example).

Differentiation: Text lengths can vary, or a video clip might be suitable. Learners can refer to their definitions of the terms 'issue' and 'perspective'. They can read the text as a class and highlight issues and perspectives in two different colours. Then class discussion.

Ways of working: Individually, in pairs or whole class to share ideas and clarify own thinking/understanding.

Different opinions/perspectives: The lesson is about encouraging learners to see examples of different perspectives.

Learner response and feedback: Learners ask each other why they have underlined/noted what they have. Encourage learners to look at the definitions of the terms 'perspective' and 'issue' to give feedback.

Suggested answers:

1 These will vary according to the text (see the Worked Example).

2 Further issues – anything that might need a course of action. Further perspectives – ways of looking at issues; for example, from scientists, politicians, parents, teachers, doctors, environmentalists, nutritionists, individuals and so on.

Worked Example for the Main activity

Topic: Values and beliefs

Sub-topic: Beliefs about foods

See Downloadable 2.2.

WHY CHOOSE A PLANT-BASED DIET?

Plant-based diets are in the media a lot at the moment, but are they are as popular as health enthusiasts might like us to believe?

Most nutritionists agree that a plant-based diet is good for your health. People who follow plant-based diets generally eat a lot of vegetables, wholegrain bread and cereals, legumes like lentils and beans, and whole fruits. Unless they are vegan or vegetarian, they also include small amounts of lean meats, fish and some dairy products like milk or cheese in their diets.

Healthwise, a predominantly plant-based diet has been shown to reduce the risk of obesity and chronic diseases. This is because plants are rich sources of many nutrients, which are important for good health. Plants provide us with vitamins, minerals, protein, fibres and healthy fats.

According to the Farmers' Union in Australia (2019), however, meat can also be a rich source of nutrients, providing protein, iron, zinc and vitamin B. But they agree that highly processed meats such as burgers contain a lot of saturated fat and salt, and have been linked to a higher risk of heart disease and cancer. On the other hand, fish and white meat have been linked to a lower risk of these diseases.

Environmentalists call for a global reduction in the amount of meat people eat for many reasons, not least to help reduce problems such as a shortage of water for human consumption, biodiversity and ecosystem loss, and global warming.

According to the Global Water and Waste Foundation (2019), approximately 2500 gallons of water are needed to produce just one pound of beef. In contrast, it only takes about 25 gallons of water to produce one pound on wheat. The Foundation's concern is that the water saved by not producing meat can help to feed the ever-increasing global population by producing more wheat and plant-based foods. This concern is supported by the Sustainable Food Organisation (2019). It is trying to raise awareness that breeding a lot of livestock results in a huge amount of manure, which causes water and air pollution, and contributes to global warming due to the amount of gas produced. Unless there is more of a movement towards a vegan diet globally, the effects of climate will continue, including more frequent and extreme heat and droughts, rising sea levels and increased flooding, loss of biodiversity due to loss of habitat, longer and more damaging wildfires, and more destructive natural disasters like hurricanes.

Suggested answers:

1 a Issues: poor health, chronic diseases, environmental (shortage of water, water and air pollution), lack of food globally, biodiversity and ecosystem loss, global warming, more frequent and extreme heat and droughts, rising sea levels and increased flooding, habitat loss, longer and more damaging wildfires, and more destructive natural disasters like hurricanes.

b Perspectives: from nutritionists, doctors, vegans, vegetarians, scientists, environmentalists, global (Global Water and Waste Foundation; Sustainable Food Organisation), national (Farmers' Union in Australia).

c Other: causes (producing meat), consequences (see issues above), course of action (follow a more plant-based diet).

2 Responses will depend on the issue.

Independent reflection activity (approx. 5–10 mins)

Good for: Encouraging learners to consider what they found interesting during the lesson. Ask them to be as honest as they can. There is no correct response and they can choose more than one option. Encourage explanation but not all learners will be able to do this. Encourage learners to reflect on how they have used research skills this lesson; for example, by reading the text and identifying certain features. This activity can be done in class, at home or in self-study time.

Starting with analysis skills: Lesson 3

Lesson 3 focuses on further understanding of the difference between an issue, a perspective and a course of action. Learners will also analyse data and explain how data can support an argument.

CAMBRIDGE STAGE 8 ANALYSIS LEARNING OBJECTIVES

78A.01 Identify ideas and evidence from different perspectives within different sources, on a given issue

78A.02 Explain how graphical or numerical data supports an argument or a perspective

78A.04 Suggest and justify different actions to make a positive difference to a national or global issue

LEARNING GOALS

To start to:

- understand the difference between an issue, a perspective and a course of action
- explain how data from a graph can support an argument
- suggest courses of action to make a positive difference to an issue.

How will I know if I reach my goals?

Good for: Learners to give examples of their learning from the lesson. They can complete the table at any point in the lesson but might do it at the end.

Resources needed

- Learner's Skills Book 8
- Downloadable 2.3

Prior learning (approx. 5–10 mins)

Good for: Building on previous knowledge, learning and understanding. This might be from Cambridge Primary Global Perspectives, from Cambridge Global Perspectives Stage 7, from other subject areas or from previous Cambridge Global Perspectives Stage 8 lessons.

Activity: Learners reflect on their understanding and explain what they think an issue, a perspective and a course of action is to their partner. They evaluate whether their own understanding has deepened as a result of explaining to their partner. They give an example for each term.

Differentiation: Learners work in pairs.

Suggested answers/ideas: Any reasonable and relevant response.

1 **a** An issue is an important problem for debate or discussion.

b A perspective is a certain viewpoint or way of looking at an issue.

c A course of action is something you can do to help make a positive difference to an issue.

3 **a** A water shortage is an issue.

b Cultural perspective is a type of perspective.

c Giving a presentation to raise awareness is a course of action.

Not issue specific.

Starter activity (approx. 10–15 mins)

Good for: Analysing data and exploring bar graphs so that learners can create their own in the Main activity.

Activity: Show learners data in a graph format and hand out related questions (see Downloadable 2.3 and the Worked Example). Learners use the graph to answer the questions. They can work individually or in pairs. Class discussion to go through answers.

Differentiation: Learners work in pairs. You can give different questions to different groups. You can ask learners to come up with their own questions and answers.

Suggested answers/ideas: See the Worked Example.

Any issue can be used, but it's useful to use the issue decided on for the Main activity.

Worked Example for the Starter activity

Topic: Values and beliefs

Sub-topic: Beliefs about foods

See Downloadable 2.3.

1 Bar graph showing why people eat the foods they do.

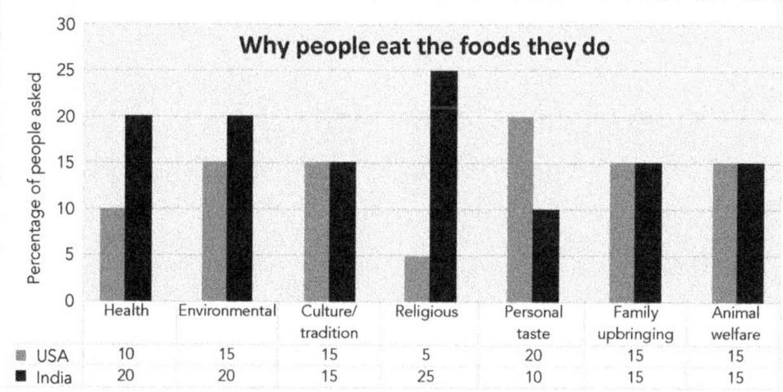

2 Questions to ask:

a What does the graph show?

b Which reason(s) did most people in the USA give as to why they eat the foods they do?

c What percentage of people asked in the USA said that they ate the foods they do due to animal welfare?

d Which is/are the most important reason(s) people in India give for the foods they eat?

e What percentage of people in India said that they ate the foods they do for their health?

f Which are the most significant differences in the reasons why people in the USA and India eat the foods they do?

Answers:

2 **a** The reasons why the people asked in the USA and India eat the foods they do.

b Personal taste

c 15%

d Religious reasons

e 20%

f People in India eat the foods they do mostly for religious reasons, but also for their health, and to protect the environment and animals, whereas people in the USA eat the foods they do mostly due to personal taste, although the environment, animal welfare and culture/traditions are also important reasons. The people from both countries think that family upbringing makes a difference to the foods they eat, but in the USA, they are less concerned about eating for religious reasons.

3 Perhaps the information might support the idea that people eat the foods they do for different reasons depending on where they are from and the upbringing they have had, and that education might be important in influencing the foods people eat, perhaps so that they eat more healthily.

Main activity (approx. 20–25 mins)

Good for: Reviewing predictions and creating supporting evidence for an argument.

Activity:

1 Give learners a set of data. You can create this in class and base it on the same issue as the Starter activity. For example, ask learners to put their hands up to tell you the reasons they eat the foods they do (use could you the same categories as in the graph in the Worked Example for the Starter activity). You can divide the data by gender or by culture/heritage.

Before creating a graph, learners write predictions based on the data; for example:

- I predict the most chosen reason will be …
- I predict the least chosen reason will be …
- I predict that boys/local people will eat the foods they do because of …
- I predict that girls/foreigners will eat the foods they do because of …
- I predict that most of my classmates will not have considered …

2 Model (or elicit from learners) how to create a double bar graph using key terms for the five parts of a graph (title, axis, labels, scale, bars). Explain that these parts each help to interpret the data/information.

Learners create a double bar graph as in Downloadable 2.3 and the Worked Example for the Starter activity but for the new set of data. For a double bar graph, they need to divide the data by gender/culture – boys/girls or local/foreign.

3 Learners check their predictions and answer the questions.

4 Learners suggest ways of influencing people to eat in a healthier and/or more mindful way, perhaps by talking with their parents or suggesting they go shopping with their parents to choose healthier options. They might also suggest that they help cook a different meal to usual, perhaps one that is from a different culture and might be healthier or not involve eating meat.

Differentiation: Learners can work individually and share in pairs once complete or work in pairs and share in fours. Model how to create a double bar graph for task 2. Some learners can write a conclusive statement that can be supported by their data; for example, 'Most people in the class eat the foods they do because of their family upbringing'.

Ways of working: In pairs for support and to clarify own thinking. Whole-class feedback on the presentation of the data and the importance of this data as supporting evidence for an argument.

Different opinions/perspectives: Stress that presenting data in a graph is a good way of presenting different viewpoints/opinions on an issue. Graphs are especially useful for presenting information gained from primary research.

Learner response and feedback: It doesn't matter that learners find creating graphs a challenge. A graph might not be a suitable way of presenting data, but learners should know that it is one of the ways of presenting evidence to support an argument or a perspective. They can also just summarise their findings as a paragraph. Peer feedback included so learners can clarify their own understanding and gain ideas from their peers.

Suggested answers: Answers will vary, as different learners will predict different outcomes from their graphs. Graphs should look similar if the same data is used. Learners can explore how and why any graphs look different.

Independent reflection activity; Self-assessment; Issue review (approx. 15–20 mins)

Good for: Encouraging learners to consider their learning in lessons. Encourage learners to reflect on the skills (research, analysis, evaluation, reflection, communication, collaboration) they have used this lesson; for example, research skills as they were testing predictions and communication skills as they created a graph to communicate research findings.

Learners also complete the self-assessment to set their own learning targets before they move on. They think about and shade where they think they are at this time in their learning. 'With help' refers to guidance given (pointing a learner in the right direction, although examples should still come from the learner); for example, from you, other learners, previous work done by the learner in their Learner's Skills Book.

For the Issue review, learners explore the issue used in this section to develop analysis skills.

These activities can be done in class, at home or in self-study time.

Suggested examples:

78A.01 *Identify ideas and evidence from different perspectives within different sources, on a given issue.* Learners give examples of perspectives (global, national, local, personal and cultural). Any reasonable response taken from Lessons 1–3 for their summary.

78A.02 *Explain how graphical or numerical data supports an argument or a perspective.* Graphical or numerical data can be used as evidence to test a prediction and to help support an argument. Learners can refer to their graph from Lesson 3.

78A.03 *Explain causes of a local or global issue and consequences on others.* Analysis is looking deeper at an issue: not just describing the issue, but also considering what might have caused it and what might happen as a result of it. Signal words can help learners recognise causes and consequences.

Signal words for causes: because, due to, since, as, so long as … , as long as … , now, that.

Signal words for consequences: as a result, therefore, that's why, so, consequently, this means, this leads to, for this reason, due to this, if … then.

78A.04 *Suggest and justify different actions to make a positive difference to a national or global issue.*

- An issue is an important problem for debate or discussion.
- A perspective is a certain viewpoint or way of looking at an issue.
- A course of action is something you can do to help make a positive difference to an issue.

Learners to give relevant examples for each from Lessons 1–3. Actions to make a positive difference to an issue can come from Lesson 3.

Developing analysis skills: Lesson 4

Lesson 4 focuses on the questions that might be asked before being able to resolve an issue and taking action to help resolve or make a positive difference to an issue.

CAMBRIDGE STAGE 8 ANALYSIS LEARNING OBJECTIVES

78A.04 Suggest and justify different actions to make a positive difference to a national or global issue

LEARNING GOALS

To develop knowledge and understanding about:

- questions to ask to decide on suitable courses of action to help resolve an issue
- taking action to help resolve or make a positive difference to an issue.

How will I know if I reach my goals?

Good for: Learners to give examples of their learning from the lesson. They can complete the table at any point in the lesson but might do it at the end.

Resources needed

- Learner's Skills Book 8
- Downloadable 2.2

Prior learning (approx. 5–10 mins)

Good for: Building on previous knowledge, learning and understanding. This might be from Primary Cambridge Global Perspectives, from Stage 7 Cambridge Global Perspectives, from other subject areas or from previous Stage 8 Cambridge Global Perspectives lessons.

Activity: Using the text from Lesson 2 (see Downloadable 2.2), learners review all the issues that might need resolving.

Differentiation: Allow learners to look back in their Learner's Skills Book. Some will not need to. Learners can work in pairs for support.

Suggested answers/ideas: Any reasonable and relevant response, but responses will be from the text used.

Not necessarily issue specific. You can ask learners to brainstorm a list of issues in their groups and share with the class.

Starter activity (approx. 10–15 mins)

Good for: Getting learners to think about questions to ask to approach solving issues.

Activity: Learners write questions to help decide on a course of action to help resolve an issue or make a positive difference to an issue. Elicit one or two examples from learners first. Refer learners to the Tips if necessary.

Ways of working: Individual, pair and whole-class discussion.

Suggested answers:

1 a What is the issue? It is important that learners understand that it is a problem/something that has a course of action to help resolve or make a positive difference to the issue.

b Why is it an issue? When explaining why it is an issue, different suggestions for actions might more readily come to mind.

c Who does the issue affect? This is an important question to decide on a realistic course of action to help make a positive difference to the issue.

d Which resources/information do I need? The answer to this will determine the answer to the next question.

e Where do I get this information? Primary and/or secondary research sources?

f How will I know if my course of action will work/make a positive difference/help to resolve the issue? It is useful to evaluate a course of action to determine whether it is realistic/will work to make a positive difference.

Not issue specific.

Main activity (approx. 20–25 mins)

Good for: Exploring a strategy to help resolve issues and getting learners to plan.

Activity:

1 Give learners a list of issues to choose from (issues could be based on a specific problems that learners are familiar with and are personal to them).

Learners choose an issue. Before they complete the table, first model with a basic example; for example:

Issue: When should I do my Cambridge Global Perspectives independent reflection activity?

Possible action 1: Straight after the Cambridge Global Perspectives lesson.

Reason against: I have another lesson to get to then.

Possible action 2: Straight after school on the day of the lesson.

Reason against: I have football straight after school.

Possible action 3: After dinner at home on the day of the lesson

Reason for: This is a good idea as I will have time and can do it in my room in the quiet and I will still remember what we did in the lesson as it's the same day.

Other factors: I also know I won't be disturbed if I tell my family what I'm doing so I will be able to do a better job of it.

2 You can elicit possible action 3 from learners and the reasons why this might be the best action.

See the Worked Example that follows for an issue-specific example.

Discuss how learners found this strategy. Did it help them understand problem solving a bit more?

Differentiation: Learners can work in pairs for support. They could use a graphic organiser/table to organise their thoughts.

Ways of working: Individually/in pairs to share ideas and clarify own thinking. Whole-class discussion about problem-solving strategies.

Different opinions/perspectives: Encourage learners to consider different levels of help/action: global, national, local and personal.

Learner response and feedback: Encourage learners to evaluate each other's courses of action. Are they realistic (do-able, don't cost much, not too large-scale)? Will they work? Do they relate to the issue?

Suggested answers: These depend on the issues given/chosen. See the Worked Example next.

Worked Example for the Main activity

Topic: Digital world

Issue: What can we do about the amount of time teenagers spend on their mobile phones?

Possible action 1: Poster persuading of the dangers of spending too much time on mobile phones.

Reasons for/against: Easy to do as an individual or in pairs; time to make the poster; resources for the poster.

Other factors: Where to put the poster? How many posters? How large? What to say on the poster? What visuals to put on the poster? Who does what when creating the poster?

Possible action 2: Persuade the headteacher to hold a digital technology awareness day after school, during the school day or at the weekend.

Reasons for/against: Can invite parents, local community, reach a wide audience; get the school interested; would take time for planning, a day of not having lessons, or a weekend day.

Other factors: Who to involve? Who does what? When to organise it for? Resources needed?

Possible action 3: A presentation promoting the dangers of spending too much time on mobile phones/on the internet.

Reasons for/against: Can be done individually or in small groups, in class. Date and time for the gathering needed.

Other factors: Need permissions (class and headteacher). Decide on who presents what, resources needed for the presentation, who the audience is.

Independent reflection activity (approx. 5–10 mins)

Good for: Encouraging learners to consider their learning from the lesson about whether they feel more able to come up with ideas to resolve issues. Encourage learners to reflect on other skills (research, evaluation, reflection, communication, collaboration) they have used this lesson as well as analysis skills; for example, evaluation skills to evaluate each course of action in the Main activity. This activity can be done in class, at home or in self-study time.

Developing analysis skills: Lesson 5

Lesson 5 focuses on understanding the difference between a local and a personal perspective, exploring how graphs can be evidence to support an argument and explaining the causes and consequences of issues.

CAMBRIDGE STAGE 8 ANALYSIS LEARNING OBJECTIVES

78A.01 Identify ideas and evidence from different perspectives within different sources, on a given issue

78A.02 Explain how graphical or numerical data supports an argument or a perspective

78A.03 Explain causes of a local or global issue and consequences on others

LEARNING GOALS

To develop knowledge and understanding about:

- the difference between a local and a personal perspective
- how graphs can be used as evidence to support an argument
- how to explain the causes and consequences of issues

How will I know if I reach my goals?

Good for: Learners to give examples of their learning from the lesson. They can complete the table at any point in the lesson but might do it at the end.

Resources needed

- Learner's Skills Book 8
- Downloadables 2.4 and 2.5

Prior learning (approx. 5–10 mins)

Good for: Building on previous knowledge, learning and understanding. This might be from Primary Cambridge Global Perspectives, from Stage 7 Cambridge Global Perspectives, from other subject areas or from previous Stage 8 Cambridge Global Perspectives lessons.

Activity: Review learning about the difference between a local and a personal perspective, and give examples for each. Learners write initial definitions of what they think a local and a personal perspective are. They can come back to this at the end of the lesson to make any amendments or add anything. After discussion, they give an example of a local and a personal perspective.

Differentiation: Refer learners to the Tips in their Learner's Skills Book if necessary. Learners work in pairs and then share ideas with the whole class.

Suggested answers: Any reasonable and relevant responses.

1 **a** A local perspective is a view that a particular community has on an issue. It is usually explained by local policies and speeches made by local politicians and might be supported by other groups within that community, such as religious groups.

b A personal perspective is what an individual thinks about something depending on their upbringing/education and what they have learned from various information sources throughout their life.

3 **a** School teachers in the community feel that teenagers spend too much time on their mobile phones and not enough time out in nature doing physical activity.

b I think that mobile phones are really useful as I can use mine for research and to connect with others, so improving my research and communication skills.

Starter activity (approx. 10 mins)

Good for: Discussion about how evidence in graphs can help support an argument.

Activity: Show learners a graph to do with the issue that allows them to answer the three questions in the Learner's Skills Book. For example, you could use a graph about the excessive use of mobile phones by teenagers to support the argument that teenagers waste too much time on their mobile phones/the internet rather than being outside in nature doing physical activity. See Downloadable 2.4.

Ideas for graphs:

https://www.forbes.com/sites/kevinanderton/2019/03/21/research-report-shows-how-much-time-we-spend-gaming-infographic/?sh=1e121fe73e07

https://www.statista.com/chart/11651/screen-time-dominates-kids-play/

Ways of working: Individual, pair and whole-class discussion.

Suggested answers: Depends on the graph given. Can be issue specific.

Main activity (approx. 20–25 mins)

Good for: Answering questions about the content of a text, in particular related to identifying issues and perspectives and explaining the causes and consequences of an issue.

Activity: Discussion about the ideas and evidence in the text. The Downloadable 2.5 and the Worked Example use written text on a local perspective from one particular community, but any perspective can be used, and the text can be in any form as long as the content enables learners to answer the questions in the Learner's Skills Book.

Differentiation: Learners can work in pairs for support. They can look back at their Prior learning or the lesson tips and the glossary to establish what is meant by the different terms – issue, cause, consequence, perspective, course of action.

Ways of working: Individually and in pairs to share ideas and clarify own thinking. Whole-class discussion about ideas in the text.

Different opinions/perspectives: Learners are exploring a local perspective.

Learner response and feedback: Encourage learners to discuss the ideas in the text in pairs/as a class.

Suggested answers: Answers depend on the text used (see the Worked Example below).

Worked Example for the Main activity

Topic: Digital world

See Downloadable 2.5.

SUMMER NEWSLETTER

It has come to our attention that parents and teachers are unhappy about the amount of time teenagers in our community are spending using their mobile phones. Many parents say that they are finding it difficult to communicate with their children because they always seem to have their phone to their ear and are not paying attention when parents want to talk with them. Parents also worry about the health of their children as they have noticed a lack of physical activity, and children in the area are increasingly becoming overweight. Reading the national media suggests that mobile phones can affect memory function and can result in more significant health issues in later life, which also worries parents and teachers alike.

Trying to limit mobile phone use doesn't seem to work as this simply leads to arguments in the family, and teenagers just hide themselves away in their bedrooms with their phones even more. If not using their phones, they use their laptops instead as it's just as easy to access social media on both. Even though mobile phones are not allowed in school, as soon as the youngsters leave school, they are once again hooked on their phones.

As a community, it's our responsibility to educate young people about the dangers of being addicted to mobile phones and, in particular, social media. Teenagers don't appear to have time for anything else apart from connecting with others via social media at every hour of the day that they can, even when they are supposed to be sleeping. This is resulting in many overweight teenagers, as they are not getting out and doing any physical activity. Even when out and about, they walk slowly so as to concentrate on what they're doing on their phones rather than on the world around them.

We are, therefore, going to hold a series of activities in the community to encourage teenagers to consider when and how they use their mobile phones. There will be a series of short talks, with entertainment and food provided to encourage attendance. Each talk will focus on an area of mobile phone use, from sleep deprivation to memory loss. We hope to invite some local celebrities who might also influence our teenagers to think more deeply about their mobile phone use.

Gabriel Hano
Community leader
June 2022

Suggested answers:

2 **a** Teenagers are addicted to their mobile phones, and parents, teachers and community leaders are unhappy about this, so the article is suggesting a way of reaching teenagers about the issues involved with mobile phone addiction and how to reduce usage.

b No correct response. Ideas include: mobile phones, laptops, access to social media, lack of physical activity, memory function, health issues, sleep deprivation etc.

c Addiction to/too much time spent on mobile phones/social media; lack of physical activity; loss of (teenagers') memory function; health issues in later life; lack of face-to-face communication (with parents); arguments (in the family).

d Too much time spent on social media; always on their phone; limited physical activity; overweight teenagers; arguments; using alternative means for social media (laptops). Encourage learners to look for the words/phrases that signal causes – because, due to, since, as, so long as … , as long as … , now that.

e Not paying attention to parents wanting to communicate (with them); can affect memory function; health issues in later life; overweight (teenagers); sleep deprivation; no time for anything else. Encourage learners to look for the words/phrases that signal consequences – as a result, therefore, that's why, so, consequently, this means, this leads to, for this reason, due to this, if … then.

f Perspectives from parents, teachers, community leaders, local perspective (community), teenagers (inferred).

g Educate young people about the dangers of being addicted to mobile phones; series of local activities; short talks with entertainment and food and inviting some celebrities.

Independent reflection activity (approx. 5–10 mins)

Good for: Encouraging learners to reflect on what helped them learn in this lesson and how they helped someone else learn. This activity can be done in class, at home or in self-study time.

Developing analysis skills: Lesson 6

Lesson 6 focuses on understanding the difference between a global, a national and a personal perspective, and being able to explain and give examples for each.

CAMBRIDGE STAGE 8 ANALYSIS LEARNING OBJECTIVES

78A.01 Identify ideas and evidence from different perspectives within different sources, on a given issue

LEARNING GOALS

To develop knowledge and understanding about:

- the difference between a global, a national and a personal perspective
- identifying and explaining different perspectives from an information source
- explaining my own personal perspective.

How will I know if I reach my goals?

Good for: Learners to give examples of their learning from the lesson. They can complete the table at any point in the lesson but might do it at the end.

Resources needed

- Learner's Skills Book 8
- Downloadables 2.6 and 2.7

Prior learning (approx. 5–10 mins)

Good for: Building on previous knowledge, learning and understanding. This might be from Cambridge Primary Global Perspectives, from Stage 7 Cambridge Global Perspectives, from other subject areas or from previous Stage 8 Cambridge Global Perspectives lessons.

Activity: Review learning to start to think about formulating a personal perspective about the issue in the Main activity of Lesson 5. Encourage learners to give reasons why their personal perspective might have changed/developed. Personal perspectives are covered further in Section 4 Reflection.

Differentiation: Learners can work in pairs for support. Allow learners to look in their Learner's Skills Book for the definitions of global, national and personal perspectives.

Suggested answers: Any reasonable and relevant response. For example, learners might say that they used to think mobile phones/technology was a good thing and now they don't because of the information they gained from different perspectives in the different sources such as the community newsletter in Lesson 5.

Starter activity (approx. 10–15 mins)

Good for: Stimulating thinking about different perspectives.

Activity: See Downloadable 2.6. Show learners a picture of mobile phones or that illustrates the chosen issue, for example:

- family members all using their mobile phones with the youngest child looking bored or a group of friends all focused on their own phones (global perspective: as many people around the world have a mobile phone and many are addicted to their mobile phone, it's becoming an increasingly global issue).
- a picture of a classroom and a mobile phone with a cross through it next to a map of France (national perspective: mobile phones banned in schools in France).

Learners decide what perspective they think the picture explores and give reasons why they think the way they do.

Ways of working: Individual, pair and whole-class discussion.

Suggested answers: Depends on the picture given. No correct answer but reasoning is important.

A global perspective may come from a specific country, organisation, institution or even an individual, but it will have influence that spreads beyond any one country.

A national perspective is based on the needs/wants/concerns of a whole country.

A personal perspective is the perspective of an individual based on research done about an issue and the different perspectives explored.

Main activity (approx. 20–25 mins)

Good for: Identifying and explaining different perspectives from an information source.

Activity:

1 Learners complete the table, giving the title of the text and making notes about the global, national and personal perspective (see Downloadable 2.7 and the Worked Example). Class discussion to explore the difference between a global, a national and a personal perspective.

3 Learners then choose one of the perspectives, or you can give them one. They write a short paragraph explaining the perspective and give reasons why they agree with it or not.

Differentiation: Learners can work in pairs for support. Refer learners to the Glossary at the back of the Learner's Skills Book and the Tips for definitions of different perspectives.

Ways of working: Pairs to share ideas, clarify own thinking and as support.

Different opinions/perspectives: The activity focuses on the understanding of information from different perspectives within different information sources.

Learner response and feedback: Encourage learners to give feedback to each other by asking questions: What is the main idea of the text? Where are the perspectives? How do you know the information is from a global/national/personal perspective? Do you agree with this perspective? Why/why not?

Suggested answers: Answers will vary. Remind learners how to determine a national, a global and a personal perspective:

- A global perspective may come from a specific country, organisation, institution or even an individual, but it will have influence that spreads beyond any one country; for example, 'Mobile technology has more benefits than disadvantages, globally.'
- A national perspective is based on the needs of a whole country; for example, 'Without mobile technology, we would not have the possibilities for learning that we do now.'
- A personal perspective is what an individual thinks about something according to their experience, research or reflecting on other perspectives.
  A personal perspective must be based on evidence. Otherwise it is just an opinion.

Worked Example for the Main activity

Topic: Digital world

See Downloadable 2.7.

Note that the sources referenced have been created for the purpose of this activity and are not real websites.

THE POTENTIAL OF MOBILE TECHNOLOGY FOR LEARNING

Brandon March, *Global Learning Magazine*, August 2019

Mobile phones are bringing learning and education to millions of people globally, said a spokesperson for the Global Learning Partnership (2019). With recent investment in tools that aid in the teaching and learning process, millions of young people around the world are benefitting from an education that they can't get face-to-face, either due to cost or availability in their local area. Everyone has a mobile phone, and with mobile technology, the potential for educating millions of young people is incredible. Not only do youngsters across the globe use their mobile phones for entertainment, a growing number are now realising the potential for reading and for learning.

'Personalising education and bringing it directly to homes around the world is extremely motivating,' stated a representative of the Worldwide Education Institution in a 2018 report on teaching and learning using digital technologies. They added that because of this motivation, participation is better, and youngsters are acquiring knowledge and skills at a quicker rate than they might do in a traditional classroom setting.

Here, in sub-Saharan Africa, the government feel that reading is an essential life skill. Statistics revealed that there were very few youngsters with access to expensive smart phones with 4G or 5G, but they do all have basic mobile phones. Even a basic mobile phone, with a 2G network provided by our government, can access electronic books and, for this reason, Worldreader is widely used to enable young people to learn to read and enjoy a world of books. There are over 4000 books to choose from, and these are divided into different age groups so everyone can enjoy books whilst also improving their English as, although some of the books are in local languages, the majority are in English.

As well as improving English vocabulary and grammar, the Worldreader programme has been shown locally to improve memory and focus, imagination and empathy, strengthen writing abilities, and lower stress and enable better sleep, other reasons why it's so popular.

Personally, having had experience of education both in a traditional classroom setting and as a home-schooled student using mobile technology for language learning and acquisition, I can say that there are advantages and disadvantages of both – not least, perhaps, the isolation of learning on your own. However, if virtual schools could provide areas for social networking and collaboration then maybe a school setting might not be the best way of learning, and if governments can provide better bandwidths around the world, then more and more youngsters will be able to receive an education.

References

Global Learning Partnership (2019). 'How mobile technology can transform global education'. [Online], https://www.glpartnership.org/tech/073493848bn4 (Accessed 08/08/2023).

Worldwide Education Institution (2019). 'The potential of mobile technology for learning'. [Online], https://www.wei.org/mobile-technology-for-learning (Accessed 09/09/2023).

Suggested answers:

Title of the text	The potential of mobile technology for learning
Global perspective	Global Learning Partnership – mobile phones mean more and more young people around the globe have access to education through technology; Worldwide Education Institution – young people are motivated to use mobile phones for learning so participation is high, and skills and knowledge better than gained from a normal classroom/lesson.
National perspective	Sub-Saharan Africa – Worldreader (2G network provided by the government) has more than 4000 books for different age groups – reading helps with vocabulary and grammar, learning English, memory, focusing, lowering stress, giving better sleep.
Personal perspective	Writer of article (Brandon March) has experience of both school and learning on own. He thinks there are advantages and disadvantages to both. He missed social interaction by not being in a school environment. He thinks technology will improve so that learning via mobile phone is not so solitary.
Reference	March, B. (2019). 'The potential of mobile technology for learning'. *Global Learning Magazine*.

3 a The national perspective of sub-Saharan Africa is that young people learn from reading, so the government has provided access to Worldreader for youngsters not only to learn English vocabulary and grammar but also to aid in writing, to improve memory and focus, and to reduce stress.

b For example, I think that the national perspective of sub-Saharan Africa shows that there are a lot of benefits of using mobile phones for learning. I think that other governments also need to provide free 2G network coverage and basic mobile phones so that more youngsters around the world can access Worldreader and other applications for learning.

Independent reflection activity; Self-assessment; Issue review (approx. 15–20 mins)

Good for: Encouraging learners to consider their learning and progression in learning in lessons. Ask them to be as honest as they can. Encourage learners to give examples and think about how they can further develop their understanding of the differences between global, national and personal perspectives; for example, by asking you or their peers or by coming up with examples of their own.

Learners also complete the self-assessment to set their own learning targets before they move on. They think about and shade where they think they are at this time in their learning. 'With help' refers to guidance given (pointing a learner in the right direction, although examples should still come from the learner); for example, from you, other learners, previous work done by the learner in their Learner's Skills Book.

For the Issue review, learners explore the issue used in this section to develop analysis skills.

These activities can be done in class, at home or in self-study time.

Suggested examples:

78A.01 *Identify ideas and evidence from different perspectives within different sources, on a given issue.* Ideas from global, national, personal perspectives. Example of a national perspective: 'Reading is an important skill and we want to encourage all young people to read to improve their vocabulary and grammar.'

78A.02 *Explain how graphical or numerical data supports an argument or a perspective.* Graphical or numerical data can be used as evidence to test a prediction and to help support an argument. Learners can refer to the work done in Lesson 5.

78A.03 *Explain causes of a local or global issue and consequences on others.* Analysis is to break something down; for example, into causes and consequences. Analysis is more than describing, it is explaining something. For example, 'Mobile technology means that more young people around the world have access to materials to enable learning' (consequence); 'More opportunities for education for all have been created by technology' (cause: technology; consequence: more education for all opportunities).

78A.04 *Suggest and justify different actions to make a positive difference to a national or global issue.* Suitable questions include:

- What is the issue?
- Why is it an issue?
- Who is affected by the issue?
- What resources do I need to help resolve the issue?
- Where do I get these resources? Primary and/or secondary research sources?
- How will I know if my course of action is realistic/ will work to help resolve the issue/make a positive difference to the issue?

Learners can refer to examples from Lesson 4.

Getting better at analysis skills: Lesson 7

Lesson 7 focuses on understanding Cambridge Global Perspectives key terms, identifying different groups of stakeholders and explaining the perspective of a specific group of stakeholders.

CAMBRIDGE STAGE 8 ANALYSIS LEARNING OBJECTIVES

78A.01 Identify ideas and evidence from different perspectives within different sources, on a given issue

LEARNING GOALS

To get better at:

- understanding Cambridge Global Perspectives key terms
- identifying different groups of stakeholders
- explaining the perspective of a group of stakeholders.

How will I know if I reach my goals?

Good for: Learners to give examples of their learning from the lesson. They can complete the table at any point in the lesson but might do it at the end.

Resources needed

- Learner's Skills Book 8
- Downloadables 2.8 and 2.9

Prior learning (approx. 5 mins)

Good for: Building on previous knowledge, learning and understanding. This might be from Cambridge Primary Global Perspectives, from Cambridge Global Perspectives Stage 7, from other subject areas or from previous Cambridge Global Perspectives Stage 8 lessons.

Activity: Review learning from Section 2 Analysis, Lessons 1–6. Read out or hand out the quick quiz questions (see Downloadable 2.8 and below). Learners write down questions and answers.

Differentiation: Allow learners to look back in their Learner's Skills Book. Some will not need to. Learners to work individually and then share ideas with a partner/whole class in the Starter activity.

Quick quiz questions and Suggested answers: Answers to be discussed in the Starter activity.

1 What is an issue?	A problem, something that needs resolving.
2 What is a perspective?	A view of the world made up of opinions and viewpoints, and supported by evidence.
3 What is an opinion/viewpoint?	What someone thinks about something, which may/may not be supported by evidence.
4 What's the difference between a global and a national perspective?	A global perspective may come from a specific country, organisation, institution or even an individual, but it will have influence that spreads beyond any one country, e.g. 'Globalisation has more benefits than disadvantages globally.' A national perspective is based on the needs of a whole country, e.g. 'Without globalisation, we would not be as economically developed as we now are, and more people would be living in poverty.'
5 Why might a graph be useful when researching and analysing an issue?	To gain evidence for a perspective; to present findings from primary research.

Starter activity (approx. 10–15 mins)

Good for: Reviewing quiz answers, learning from Cambridge Global Perspectives Stage 8 and writing questions about Cambridge Global Perspectives terms.

Activity:

1 Elicit and discuss answers to the questions in the Prior learning activity. Whole-class discussion to clarify thinking and gain new learning. Check that all learners know the answers to all outstanding questions. You might ask learners to write down the questions and answers for future reference.

Learners also write five further questions; they can ask another pair to answer these.

Suggested answers/ideas: See Prior learning activity.

2 Further suggestions for questions:
- What's the difference between a local and a national perspective?
- What does the term 'analysis' mean?
- What is a personal perspective?
- What is a course of action?
- What is evidence?
- Give an example of …

3 Learners may have got an answer wrong because the question wasn't clear, it wasn't clear what the question was asking, or they didn't know/had forgotten the answer.

Not issue specific.

Main activity (approx. 20–25 mins)

Good for: Identifying the stakeholders interested in an issue and exploring different perspectives on the issue.

Activity:

1 Give learners a choice of issue (see the Worked Example for ideas). Learners complete the diagram for their issue.

2 Learners choose one of the groups of people from their diagram in task 1. They discuss it with a partner and summarise the issue from the perspective of this group of people (see the Worked Example for the Main activity).

3 Learners share their ideas with another pair and change/add to their summaries.

Differentiation: Give learners a copy of Downloadable 2.9. Talk through the Worked Example, eliciting/explaining why it might be important to consider different perspectives. When completing their own diagrams, learners can work in small groups on an issue of their choice for support and feedback.

Ways of working: Whole class and small groups. Whole-class discussion about stakeholder groups.

Different opinions/perspectives: This lesson focuses on different stakeholder groups and their different perspectives on an issue.

Learner response and feedback: Encourage learners to ask each other questions such as:

- Who would be interested in this issue?
- Why would they be interested?
- What might their perspective be and why?

Suggested ideas: (See the Worked Example).

Worked Example for the Main activity

Topic: Climate change, energy and resources

See Downloadable 2.9.

1 **Issue:** Is it possible for humans to lead more sustainable lives?

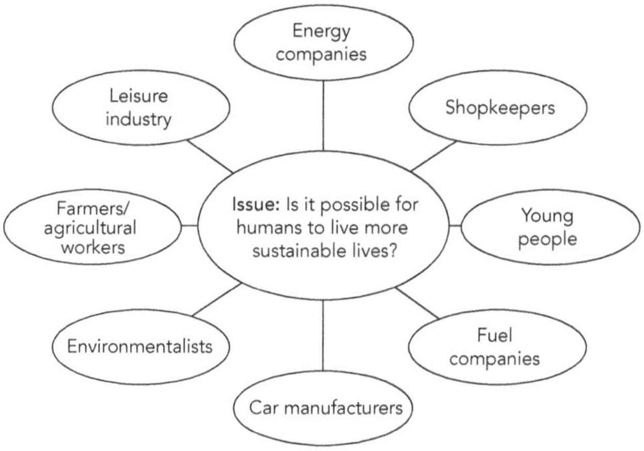

Stress that each circle contains a stakeholder group (and therefore a relevant perspective) that could inform learners' understanding of a particular issue. You can also suggest that there are sub-groups within these groups that might have differing perspectives. For example, within energy companies, different types of energy (e.g. renewable versus coal) might have different perspectives; within farmers/agricultural workers, organic farmers might have a different perspective to other farmers etc.

Suggested issues on climate change, energy and resources:

- Should single-use plastic be banned nationally?
- Should animal products be banned from the school canteen?
- Should there be a week of activities in school to raise awareness about sustainable living?
- Should one lesson per week be about how to live more sustainable lives?
- Should people in restaurants be charged more if they leave food?
- Should everyone be charged according to the quantity of water they use rather than the same rate per household?

2 Example summary for energy companies: Energy companies that promote the use of renewable energy sources such as solar and wind power will agree that it is possible for humans to live more sustainably if they switch from using traditional sources of fuel such as gas and electricity to solar and wind power. However, energy companies selling gas and electricity will argue that it is cheaper for people to use gas and electricity and that renewable sources of energy are not accessible or cost-effective in many areas.

Independent reflection activity (approx. 5–10 mins)

Good for: Encouraging learners to consider their learning from the lesson, what they think they have done well in terms of working on their own, joining in discussions, asking for help/support, helping their partner etc. Encourage learners to reflect on the skills (research, analysis, evaluation, reflection, communication, collaboration) they have used this lesson; for example, analysis skills to explain the perspective of energy companies about the issue of living more sustainably. This activity can be done in class, at home or in self-study time.

Getting better at analysis skills: Lesson 8

Lesson 8 continues the sequence from Lesson 7 and focuses on gaining information from different perspectives by analysing a text and asking questions.

CAMBRIDGE STAGE 8 ANALYSIS LEARNING OBJECTIVES

78A.01 Identify ideas and evidence from different perspectives within different sources, on a given issue

78A.02 Explain how graphical or numerical data supports an argument or a perspective

LEARNING GOALS

To get better at:

- giving examples of different groups of stakeholders
- finding ideas and evidence from different perspectives
- asking questions to gain information from a specific group of people.

How will I know if I reach my goals?

Good for: Learners to give examples of their learning from the lesson. They can complete the table at any point in the lesson but might do it at the end.

Resources needed

- Learner's Skills Book 8
- Downloadables 2.10 and 2.11

Prior learning (approx. 5–10 mins)

Good for: Building on previous knowledge, learning and understanding. This might be from Cambridge Primary Global Perspectives, from Cambridge Global Perspectives Stage 7, from other subject areas or from previous Cambridge Global Perspectives Stage 8 lessons.

Activity: Review learning about stakeholders from Lesson 7. Use the issue from the Main activity in Lesson 7.

Differentiation: Learners can work together. Some learners will need to refer back to Lesson 7.

Suggested answers:

1 A stakeholder is a person, group or organisation that has a direct or indirect concern or interest in an issue.

2 For example, for the issue of sustainability: families, communities, governments, car manufacturers etc.

3 No. Families might like the idea of leading a more sustainable life, but traditional car manufacturers might feel differently as their livelihood is threatened if people buy fewer cars or hybrid cars (that don't run on fossil fuels but run on hydrogen, for example).

Not issue specific.

Starter activity (approx. 10–15 mins)

Good for: Finding different perspectives on an issue.

Activity: Give learners a short text (see Downloadable 2.10 and the Worked Example). Learners read the text and identify and consider the perspectives put forward in it.

Ways of working: Individual, pair and whole-class discussion to clarify thinking and gain new learning.

Suggested answers: See the Worked Example.

Worked Example for the Starter activity

Topic: Climate change, energy and resources

See Downloadable 2.10.

SHOULD WE CHANGE TO A PLANT-BASED DIET TO CREATE A MORE SUSTAINABLE PLANET?

A predominantly plant-based diet is being recommended globally by the World Health Fund (2019) for a number of reasons. Firstly, many lives will be lengthened as, according to scientists, approximately 11 million people a year die from diseases related to unhealthy eating. Also, if people continue to eat an unsustainable diet, which includes most animal products, the natural world as we know it will not survive due to climate change and global warming.

Suggested answers:

1 A global perspective – the World Health Fund is a global organisation with global influence. A scientific perspective is also mentioned.

2 Families; food companies; restaurants; people working in the food and drink industry; livestock farmers; organic fruit and vegetable farmers; health agencies.

3 For example, livestock farmers are likely to have a different perspective to families as their livelihood depends on people eating meat, whereas families might want their children to eat more healthily to have longer lives with less illness.

4 Do further research.

Main activity (approx. 20–25 mins)

Good for: Finding out information from a specific stakeholder group by designing a questionnaire with some simple 'YES/NO' questions and some more open-ended questions (see Downloadable 2.11 and the Worked Example). For this activity, the stakeholder group is other Stage 8 learners.

Activity: Learners design ten questions to find out information from a learner perspective about an issue of their choice, or you could give each team/small group a different issue (see the Worked Example). It's a good idea if learners work in teams for this activity and produce one questionnaire per team as they will be working in these teams in Lesson 9.

Differentiation: Learners work in teams/small groups to share ideas, and give and gain feedback.

Ways of working: In teams/small groups.

Different opinions/perspectives: The lesson focuses on gaining a different perspective.

Learner response and feedback: Encourage learners to work in teams/small groups to give feedback to each other on the questions and choose the best ten questions, keeping their issue in mind. Questions to ask when compiling the questionnaire:

- Is it clear what the question is asking?
- Is the question short and to the point?
- Is the question direct (does it use 'you')?
- Can the question be answered with 'YES/NO'?
- Does the question give further information to help answer the issue question?

Learners should also ask you for feedback on their final questionnaire and then make any changes to the questions before they hand it out for completion by the stakeholder group.

Suggested answers/ideas: See the Worked Example below.

Worked Example for the Main activity

Topic: Climate change, energy and resources

See Downloadable 2.11.

Issue: Living a more sustainable life

Suggested questions:

- Can humans live more sustainably?
- Should there be restrictions on vehicles in city centres?
- Should there be a law to ban single-use plastics?
- Is recycling important for sustainable living?
- Is saving water important for sustainable living?
- Is it important to eat local foods?
- Is it important to have access to clean air?

Suggested questionnaire:

Student Questionnaire – Stage 8			
Team:			
Closed questions (Yes/No answer)		Yes	No
1	Do you think having access to clean air is important?		
2	Do you think it is important to eat local foods?		
3	Do you think saving water is important?		
4	Do you think recycling is important?		
5	Do you think there should be a law forbidding single-use plastics?		
6	Do you think there should be restrictions on vehicles in city centres?		
7	Do you think you and your family might be able to live a more sustainable life?		
	More open-ended questions		
8	Why do you think recycling is important?		
9	How might you and your family live a more sustainable life?		
10	What suggestions do you have for raising awareness within the community about living a more sustainable life?		

Independent reflection activity (approx. 5 mins)

Good for: Encouraging learners to consider their learning from the lesson, what they found easy and what they needed help with; for example, they might have found it easy to design 'YES/NO' questions but more challenging to write more open-ended questions. This activity can be done in class, at home or in self-study time.

Getting better at analysis skills: Lesson 9

Lesson 9 focuses on using research conducted in Lesson 8 to suggest a course of action and produce an outcome to help resolve or make a positive difference to an issue.

CAMBRIDGE STAGE 8 ANALYSIS LEARNING OBJECTIVES

78A.02 Explain how graphical or numerical data supports an argument or a perspective

78A.03 Explain causes of a local or global issue and consequences on others

78A.04 Suggest and justify different actions to make a positive difference to a national or global issue

LEARNING GOALS

To get better at:

- using data from research into different perspectives on an issue to help support an argument
- explaining consequences of a local or national issue
- suggesting an action to make a positive difference to a local or national issue.

How will I know if I reach my goals?

Good for: Learners to give examples of their learning from the lesson. They can complete the table at any point in the lesson but might do it at the end.

Resources needed

Learner's Skills Book 8

Prior learning (approx. 5–10 mins)

Good for: Building on previous knowledge, learning and understanding. This might be from Cambridge Primary Global Perspectives, from Cambridge Global Perspectives Stage 7, from other subject areas or from previous Cambridge Global Perspectives Stage 8 lessons. This lesson consolidates learning from the whole of Section 2 Analysis.

Activity: Discuss findings from the Lesson 8 questionnaire.

Differentiation: Learners work in teams for this activity. They share their findings from the questionnaire and ask each other the questions in the Learner's Skills Book.

Suggested ideas: Not issue specific but should be linked to the issue of the questionnaire in Lesson 8.

Starter activity (approx. 10 mins)

Good for: Discussing an issue from their questionnaire in Lesson 8.

Activity: Teams work together to review an issue from their questionnaire in Lesson 8. They:

- identify the issue
- review the information gained from the responses to their questionnaire
- decide whether they need to do further research
- decide on a course of action to help resolve or make a positive difference to their issue.

As a result of this action, they can produce an outcome in the Main activity, such as a letter/email, presentation, event, video clip, podcast, leaflet etc.

Suggested answers: Should be specific to the responses gained from the questionnaire in Lesson 8 (see the Worked Example).

Worked Example for the Starter activity

Topic: Climate change, energy and resources

Suggested questions from Lesson 8:

- Can humans live more sustainably?
- Should there be restrictions on vehicles in city centres?
- Should there be a law to ban single-use plastics?
- Is recycling important for sustainable living?
- Is saving water important for sustainable living?
- Is it important to eat local foods?
- Is it important to have access to clean air?

Suggested answers for the issue 'Is recycling important for sustainable living?'

a Recycling

b The majority of classmates asked think it's important to recycle paper, cardboard and wood because it saves trees and forests, which are wildlife habitats, and helps prevent flooding, which is a problem locally as well as nationally.

c Yes.

d To gain a national perspective, we could create a presentation for the community to explain the consequences of not recycling paper, cardboard and wood, and why we should all recycle these items.

Main activity (approx. 20–25 mins)

Good for: Suggesting a course of action and producing an outcome such as a presentation, leaflet, series of posters to help resolve or make a positive difference to a local or national issue.

Activity: Learners work in teams. They do further research if necessary and decide who finds out what. They discuss their course of action and what they are going to produce as their outcome to help resolve or make a positive difference to their issue.

Differentiation: Learners work in groups of four for feedback, support and guidance. Give some website addresses or enable learners to look for their own depending on their issue.

Ways of working: Small groups to develop team-working skills.

Different opinions/perspectives: Stress that the aim is to suggest a course of action that takes different perspectives (global, national, local) into consideration and to produce an outcome to help resolve or make a positive difference to their issue at a local or national level.

Learner response and feedback: Encourage learners to give feedback to each other on the information gained. Ask questions: What else did you learn? How can we use what you've learned? Do your findings make a case for this course of action and outcome? Refer learners to Lesson 4 for more about how to come up with a course of action and outcome.

Independent reflection activity; Self-assessment; Issue review (approx. 15–20 mins)

Good for: Encouraging learners to consider their learning and progression in learning in lessons. Ask them to be as honest as they can. Encourage learners to reflect on the skills they have used today and how they can develop them further; for example, research skills to find further information to include in their outcome. To develop research skills further, they might use fewer, more specific words in their search engine.

Learners also complete the self-assessment to set their own learning targets. They think about and shade where they think they are at this time in their learning. 'With help' refers to guidance given (pointing a learner in the right direction, although examples should still come from the learner); for example, from you, other learners, previous work done by the learner in their Learner's Skills Book.

For the Issue review, learners explore the issue used in this section to develop analysis skills.

These activities can be done in class, at home or in self-study time.

Suggested examples:

78A.01 *Identify ideas and evidence from different perspectives within different sources, on a given issue.* Ideas should include the issue; global, national, local and personal perspectives; course(s) of action; outcomes. Groups of stakeholders include parents, teachers, medical professionals, health agencies – it depends on the issue. For example, the perspective of a group of livestock farmers will be different from that of a group of organic fruit and vegetable farmers regarding the issue of sustainable living.

78A.02 *Explain how graphical or numerical data supports an argument or a perspective.* Relevant information to help develop a perspective and support an argument might come from graphs as well as articles on the internet. Example questions to gain information can come from work done in Lessons 7–9.

78A.03 *Explain causes of a local or global issue and consequences on others.* For example, one cause of climate change might be the carbon dioxide from vehicles. A consequence of not recycling paper, cardboard or wood is that more trees will be cut down to provide more paper, cardboard and wood, resulting in the loss of wildlife habitats and more flooding.

- Words/phrases that signal causes: because, due to, since, as, so long as … , as long as … , now that.
- Words/phrases that signal consequences: as a result, therefore, that's why, so, consequently, this means, this leads to, for this reason, due to this, if … then.

78A.04 *Suggest and justify different actions to make a positive difference to a national or global issue.* Relevant courses of action for a specific local issue might include giving a talk or presentation to raise awareness that the issue needs everyone to participate for it to be resolved; posters or leaflets to promote the importance of something to help resolve a local issue or make a positive difference to an issue; an event where people actively do something to help resolve an issue. Learners might give examples from work done in Lessons 7–9.

[redacted]

Showcasing your skills: Analysis

Good for: Showing learners how others felt at the end of this section after practising and developing their analysis skills. Your learners have learned a lot about how to identify issues, what causes and consequences are, how to identify and explain perspectives and come up with one solution. Teachers are part of the journey but are also on their own journey, so you will see the response of a teacher here too.

This section includes a lot of new skills practice so don't worry if your learners haven't mastered all of them. So long as they have made some progress and learned some of the skills, they have made a successful start. We are all developing and learning all the time.

Activity: This is an opportunity for your learners to reflect on elements of their work in this section that they are particularly pleased with. Read through and discuss the reflections with your class. Then try one of these reflection tasks with your learners:

- 'Reflect and sketch': Learners could use pictures, numbers and symbols (but no words) to illustrate what they have done well in this section.
- 'Two stars and a wish' means 'Two things I am pleased with and one thing I want to improve on'. Ask your learners to write their own 'two stars and a wish' on a sticky note and stick it on the board.

Projects: If learners have had ample opportunities to practise the other skills required, they could also showcase their analysis skills by attempting any of the three projects available at cambridge.org/go, all three of which have analysis learning objectives.

Section 3 Evaluation

Introduction

The learning objectives for evaluation skills for Stage 8 are the same as those for Stage 7 and focus on the following:

- evaluating sources
- evaluating arguments.

However, you might also find opportunities within these lessons to develop some of the other Cambridge Global Perspectives skills. For example, when selecting, organising and recording relevant information from a range of sources and findings from research using appropriate methods, not only will learners be developing evaluation skills, they will also be developing their research skills.

The ideas given in this Teacher's Resource are suggestions only, and the activities can be used with any of the Cambridge Global Perspectives Challenges or topics for Stages 7 to 9. Downloadables and Worked Examples are provided for many learning activities. They are linked to the the topics 'Migration and urbanisation' and 'Digital world'. Issues relating to sustaining the planet and its resources are explored through some of the activities in this section. It is hoped that the ideas in this book will help you structure your lessons in an active learning way with input from you as the teacher to help guide and support learners to become more effective at being able to evaluate sources and arguments when exploring information to answer research questions.

Evaluation skills overview

Learning objectives	78E.01 Evaluate sources, considering the author and purpose, recognising that some sources may be more credible than others. 78E.02 Discuss the effectiveness of an argument, making explicit reference to its structure and use of evidence.
Topic ideas	Migration and urbanisation; Digital world; Change in culture and communities; Development, trade and aid; Climate change, energy and resources; Values and beliefs
Key points	• Understanding the difference between analysis and evaluation: analysis is to break something down to make it clearer/more understandable; evaluation is to judge the qualities of something – its strengths and limitations. • Recognising what 'fake news' is and why it is created: news that is not true, is exaggerated or made up, and often created to persuade people to buy something or vote for something. • There are different ways that a source can be unreliable; for example, it is out of date, lacks expert evidence or contains bias. • There are two definitions for an argument. The first is an exchange of differing views, often in an angry way. The second, used for Cambridge Global Perspectives, is a set of reasons and evidence in support of an idea, perspective or action. • There is a difference between fact and opinion: facts are supported with evidence; opinion is unsupported. • Understanding what bias is and why sources of information might contain bias. • Most sources of information contain some form of bias, often political or commercial.

Language support	Pre-teach key vocabulary: evaluation; strengths; weaknesses; limitations; reliable, unreliable; fake news; news links; audience; author; purpose; evidence; claim; conclusion; logical; argument; reason; believable; convincing; debate; fact; opinion; bias; jokes; gender; entertain; inform; persuade; describe; instruct; advise; argue. Also include any issue-specific vocabulary for the topics – Migration and urbanisation; Digital world; Change in culture and communities; Development, trade and aid; Climate change, energy and resources; Values and beliefs.
Cross-skills links	**Research** 78Rs.02 Identify and begin to reference a range of print and multimedia sources and use them to locate relevant information and answer research questions. 78Rs.03 Select an appropriate method and conduct research to test predictions and begin to answer a research question. 78Rs.04 Select, organise and record relevant information from a range of sources and findings from primary research, using appropriate methods. **Analysis** 78A.01 Identify ideas and evidence from different perspectives within different sources, on a given issue. 78A.02 Explain how graphical or numerical data supports an argument or a perspective. **Reflection** 78Rf.03 Consider ways that personal perspective on an issue may have changed as a result of conducting research or exploring different perspectives. 78Rf.04 Identify skills learned or improved during an activity and relate to personal strengths and areas for improvement. **Collaboration** 78Cl.01 Work positively within a team to achieve a shared outcome and improve team work, for example by contributing useful ideas, offering solutions to problems, encouraging other team members to participate and being open to others' ideas. 78Cl.02 The team assigns roles and divides tasks fairly, considering the skills of team members and the time available, resolves disagreements and works together to achieve a shared outcome. **Communication** 78Cm.01 Present information and arguments clearly with some reasoning, referencing sources where appropriate. 78Cm.02 Listen to ideas and information and offer relevant and well-judged contributions that demonstrate understanding of the issue.

Let's start thinking about evaluation!

Good for: Enthusing your learners about the skill they are going to work on. Evaluation is a complex skill and it can take time to master. Learners need to learn how to place their own value on sources of information as well as on arguments and claims.

The questions give learners ideas about the issues they might explore as they develop their evaluation skills. The first idea suggested is the Challenge 'What are the challenges and opportunities of migration?' and the topic 'Migration and urbanisation'. Although they are not closely linked to a Challenge, the downloadables provide everything your learners need to complete the activities in section 3 and become proficient at evaluation. The downloadables are based on the topics 'Migration and urbanisation' and 'Digital world'.

Activity: Look at these pages with your learners. You could begin with a quick question and answer session. Ask learners:

- What does 'evaluation' mean?
- What kinds of questions could we ask?
- Where might we get our information?
- What issue shall we explore?

Ask learners to each write down one question they have about this section, e.g. on a sticky note. Collate and display their questions so that they are easy to refer to as you work through this section. In that way, learners can see their questions being answered.

Starting with evaluation skills: Lesson 1

Lesson 1 focuses on explaining the term 'evaluation', understanding the difference between evaluation and analysis, and being able to recognise a fake news item.

CAMBRIDGE STAGE 8 EVALUATION LEARNING OBJECTIVES

78E.01 Evaluate sources, considering the author and purpose, recognising that some sources may be more credible than others

LEARNING GOALS

To start to:

- explain the term 'evaluation'
- understand the difference between evaluation and analysis
- understand what 'fake news' is, why it is created and how to recognise it.

How will I know if I reach my goals?

Good for: Learners to give examples of their learning from the lesson. They can complete the table at any point in the lesson but might do it at the end.

Resources needed

- Learner's Skills Book 8
- Downloadable 3.1

Prior learning (approx. 5–10 mins)

Good for: Building on previous knowledge, learning and understanding. This might be from Cambridge Primary Global Perspectives, from Cambridge Global Perspectives Stage 7, from other subject areas or from previous Cambridge Global Perspectives Stage 8 lessons.

Activity: Learners answer the questions and then identify which questions focus on analysis and which focus on evaluation to help them understand the difference between analysis and evaluation. They then write a definition for each term.

Differentiation: Learners work in pairs to discuss and then write their own ideas. Class discussion about answers to questions, but more importantly, leading into discussion about what the terms 'analysis' and 'evaluation' mean.

Suggested answers:

1 **a** We discuss issues that are in the news that are relevant to me and my family/friends; it allows us to share our opinions; we are not just learning about specific issues but developing skills for all subjects, and that will be useful in life.

- **b** I work with my friends.
- **c** Once a week on Mondays.
- **d** Yes, because I'm able to work with my friends and we discuss interesting issues. We don't just talk about the content of texts, we talk about how different issues affect different people. OR: No, because I'm unable to work on my own enough as there is a lot of pair and group work; I'm not confident enough to share my opinions.
- **e** Not really, although we could do more writing as we have a lot of discussions and I will only remember things if I write them down, although I don't want to do too much writing.

2 Questions a, b, c focus on analysis; questions d and e focus on evaluation.

4 Analysis is giving more details, explaining something in more detail. Analysis questions often start with 'What?', 'When?', 'Who?', 'Where?'

Evaluation is giving the strengths/weaknesses of something with reasons in order to make a judgement about something (quality, importance, value etc.). Evaluation questions often start with 'Why?', 'How?'

Not issue specific.

Starter activity (approx. 10 mins)

Good for: Identifying statements that focus on evaluation and exploring the difference between evaluation and analysis.

Activity: Learners decide which one of the statements is not an evaluative statement.

Ways of working: Individual, pair and whole-class discussion.

Suggested answers:

1 Evaluation is a judgement about something. All the statements are evaluation apart from E, which is analysis (cause).

3 Learners identify how they might become more confident in understanding the difference between evaluation and analysis; for example, by asking their partner or you, or by explaining the difference to someone else.

Not issue specific.

Main activity (approx. 20–25 mins)

Good for: Enabling learners to consider what fake news is and why it is created.

Activity:

1 Learners discuss what fake news is, why it is created and why it matters.

2 Learners look at a news item you give them (see Downloadable 3.1 and the Worked Example) and decide if it is real or fake, and why. Learners answer the questions in pairs and then take part in class discussion about the answers and what to look out for to tell if a news item is fake.

Differentiation: Pair work and class discussion. You can give different fake news items according to the issue and ability of learners.

Ways of working: Individual, pairs and whole class.

Different opinions/perspectives: Encourage learners to look at the fake news stories from different perspectives – who might think these stories are true and why?

Learner response and feedback: Encourage learners to discuss with each other for task 2 in particular. Questions to ask:

- What is the news item about?
- Does it make sense to you?
- Why do you think it was created?
- Does it seem like a joke to you?
- Do you think this is possible? Why?/Why not?

Suggested answers/ideas:

1
- **a** Fake news is news that is presented as fact but is actually made up for a specific reason; for example, to gain political favour or to persuade people to visit a website, perhaps to buy something.
- **b** It is often created to deliberately misinform or deceive readers into buying something or doing something; for example, voting for a political party.
- **c** Because we cannot be certain that what we are reading/listening to is true and, if we share it, we could make someone else believe something that isn't true.
- **d** No, because they do not want me to believe things that are not true; they want me to do well. The only reason they might give me fake news is if the lesson is about fake news and evaluating whether news is real or fake.

2 Answers will depend on the news item given (see the Worked Example below).

Worked Example for the Main activity

Topic: Digital world

See Downloadable 3.1.

PRESS RELEASE – JUNE 2020

Goverment agrees to £10 million buget for all youngsters between the ages of 11 and 18 to have a smart phone that can access 5G.

A goverment agency has just declared that in 2020, it will be providing all youngsters in India and Mumbai with a smart phone capable of accessing 5G. Ananya Gupta, a spokesperson for the agency, stated that in this age of digital technologies, we cannot ignore the fact that so many young people are unable to access 5G as they don't have the right type of phone. This comes at a time when schools are just starting to allow mobile phones to be used in school. Ananya said, 'Its a brilliant idea and I'm thrilled that we can do this'. Parents globally agree with Ananya and are overjoyed that they will no longer have to spend their hard-earned money buying the newest mobile phones for their children.

Suggested answers:

2 a The news item is fake.

b Reasons include that there are spelling errors, and you wouldn't use a spokesperson's first name in a press release. It is not likely that a government spokesperson would say this. It is too good to be true as it is unrealistic that the government will spend this amount of money for this purpose. It's also unlikely that mobile phones are allowed in school. Mumbai is in India, so facts are incorrect, and it's unlikely that parents globally will have been asked about this issue.

4 Responses will vary. Example: You need to check for any bias; check the date published; check the source of the information – that you can find the source somewhere else, or that you already know the source is reliable/credible; check the author – that they have written other things; check the website address is real; use a fact checker. You can encourage learners to use the acronym REAL:

R – ask, 'Is this **R**eal?'

E – ask 'What **E**vidence is presented?' (source, author, publication, website address, date and time, and any pictures)

A – ask 'Does it all **A**dd up?' (use own knowledge, ask others, check the details with a little further research)

L – **L**ook around. (Do any other sources have the same story/news item; e.g. TV, radio, magazine, newspaper etc.?)

Independent reflection activity (approx. 5–10 mins)

Good for: Learners to give examples of what they have found the most difficult in the lesson. This might be skill or content specific; for example, identifying how to tell if news items are real or fake. Encourage learners to reflect on the skills (research, analysis, evaluation, reflection, communication, collaboration) they have used this lesson; for example, collaboration skills to work with a partner. This activity can be done in class, at home or in self-study time.

Starting with evaluation skills: Lesson 2

Lesson 2 focuses on recognising that some facts are real and some are made up, and how to judge if a fact is real or fake.

CAMBRIDGE STAGE 8 EVALUATION LEARNING OBJECTIVES

78E.01 Evaluate sources, considering the author and purpose, recognising that some sources may be more credible than others

LEARNING GOALS

To start to:

- recognise that facts from news stories can be real or fake
- understand how to judge if a fact is real or fake.

How will I know if I reach my goals?

Good for: Learners to give examples of their learning from the lesson. They can complete the table at any point in the lesson but might do it at the end.

Resources needed

- Learner's Skills Book 8
- Downloadable 3.2
- Selection of newspapers from the same day reporting the same stories or access to computers and the internet

Prior learning (approx. 5 mins)

Good for: Building on previous knowledge, learning and understanding. This might be from Cambridge Primary Global Perspectives, from Cambridge Global Perspectives Stage 7, from other subject areas or from previous Cambridge Global Perspectives Stage 8 lessons.

Activity: Ask learners to answer the questions in task 1, then discuss them as a class.

Differentiation: Learners work individually or in pairs. They can look back at Lesson 1 if necessary.

Suggested answers:

1 **a** A printed, broadcast or digital report of factual information about important events in the world, country or local area.

b News or stories that are not true/made up.

c Often for political reasons to get people to vote for them, to discredit someone, to mislead people and for commercial/business reasons (to persuade or influence people to buy something).

Not issue specific.

Starter activity (approx. 5–10 mins)

Good for: Looking at news headlines to consider whether they might be true or made up.

Activity: Show learners some news headlines (from any issue). Learners discuss the news headlines to decide whether they are true or made up. See Downloadable 3.2.

Ways of working: Individual, pairs and whole class.

Suggested ideas for news headlines (see Downloadable 3.2):

1 **a** Joe Biden to adopt baby from South Africa'. This headline is made up. Learners will not be able to find any information about this in any sources. They should consider that Joe Biden is probably too old to adopt and what reasons might he have for adopting from South Africa?

b 'Actor Adam Sandler attacked by cheetah.' This is true, but learners might reasonably conclude that it seems unlikely: Adam Sandler is American and is unlikely to be near cheetahs very often.

c 'Scientists create water-activated self-folding straws'. This is true. If you search for this headline, you will find it in different information sources, and there are images showing scientists creating the straws.

Further ideas can be found by searching for 'fake news headlines' on the internet.

2 You could check to see if they have been reported in more than one information source.

Main activity (approx. 20–25 mins)

Good for: Further exploration of whether pieces of information that look like facts in information sources are real or fake, and how to find out.

Activity: Learners work with a partner to work through the tasks in their Learner's Skills Book. You can give learners a selection of newspapers from the same day reporting the same stories or you can let them have access to computers and the internet. Stress that supposed facts do not need to be statistical, but it might be easier to work with a statistical fact to start with. See the Worked Example for the Main activity.

Differentiation: Learners work in pairs for support and clarification, and share with another pair for feedback.

Ways of working: In pairs, whole class to share ideas, clarify own thinking/understanding.

Different opinions/perspectives: Encourage learners to see why some might believe the facts they find.

Learner response and feedback: Encourage learners to explore the information sources together. Learners give feedback to another pair in task 2, using the checklist in the Learner's Skills Book.

Suggested answers: These will vary according to the chosen news stories and supposed facts (see the Worked Example below).

[redacted]

Worked Example for the Main activity

Topic: Digital world

Suggested answers:

1 a For example: 'Automation could destroy millions of jobs in Australia'.

b 6.5 million jobs will be lost due to robots, as reported in *The News Daily*.

c *The Sydney Morning Herald*; *The West Australian*; *Australian Financial Review*

d It informs people about the risks to their livelihood from computer technology.

e Because it has been reported in different information sources. These information sources are well-known, trusted sources in Australia.

f The original source for the fact: a report by McKinsey, Australia. You might find out by reading the articles with the fact in them to see where it came from.

g 'The motoring industry would be most disrupted by autonomy'. The motoring industry is reported elsewhere as one of the industries that will be affected by automation, but the exaggeration 'most disrupted' in the source in task a is not reported elsewhere.

h By reading different sources to check what is actually written about this supposed fact.

2 Will depend on the supposed fact.

Independent reflection activity (approx. 5–10 mins)

Good for: Encouraging learners to consider what they found difficult during the lesson and why. Ask them to be as honest as they can. For example, they might have found identifying real and fake news headlines difficult because they all sounded believable. Encourage explanation, but not all learners will be able to do this. Encourage learners to reflect on how they used research skills this lesson; for example, by searching for the same fact in different information sources. This activity can be done in class, at home or in self-study time.

Starting with evaluation skills: Lesson 3

Lesson 3 focuses on further understanding of judging whether a source is reliable to use or not, and follows on from Lessons 1 and 2.

CAMBRIDGE STAGE 8 EVALUATION LEARNING OBJECTIVES

78E.01 Evaluate sources, considering the author and purpose, recognising that some sources may be more credible than others

78E.02 Discuss the effectiveness of an argument, making explicit reference to its structure and use of evidence

LEARNING GOALS

To start to:

- recognise that some facts in a news story might not be true
- identify bias in a source
- realise that news stories may contain bias or may not be credible
- realise that the argument in a source should make sense if it is to be trusted.

How will I know if I reach my goals?

Good for: Learners to give examples of their learning from the lesson. They can complete the table at any point in the lesson but might do it at the end.

Resources needed

- Learner's Skills Book 8
- Downloadable 3.3
- Selection of newspapers from the Main activity in Lesson 2 or access to computers and the internet

Prior learning (approx. 5 mins)

Good for: Building on previous knowledge, learning and understanding. This might be from Cambridge Primary Global Perspectives, from Cambridge Global Perspectives Stage 7, from other subject areas or from previous Cambridge Global Perspectives Stage 8 lessons.

Activity: Learners work in pairs to discuss and write down how to check if a fact in an information source is real or fake. They share with another pair to gain further ideas and clarify own thinking.

Differentiation: Learners work in pairs. They can look back at work done in Lesson 2. Discuss responses in class.

Suggested answers: Any reasonable and relevant response. For example: check the author; ask/check if the fact is believable/a joke; check other sources to see if they contain the same fact; check the source is real etc.

Not issue specific.

Starter activity (approx. 10–15 mins)

Good for: Reviewing a news story from the Main activity in Lesson 2 to write the story using only correct facts in own words.

Activity: Learners review their work from the Main activity in Lesson 2 and write the story in their own words. Stress that they should write no more than four lines. Once written, they swap their stories with another pair, who try to find the sources used to write the story. This can be done using the newspapers from the Main activity in Lesson 2 or computers with internet access.

Differentiation: Learners work in pairs. Some might only write a couple of sentences for their story.

Suggested answers/ideas: Depends on the news story in the Main activity in Lesson 2.

Main activity (approx. 20–25 mins)

Good for: Evaluating an information source.

Activity: Learners review the information source (it can be text or a video clip; see Downloadable 3.3 and the Worked Example) and complete the table.

1 Whilst reading/watching, learners make notes about the main idea and the facts to help them answer some of the questions in task 2.

2 Learners use the internet to answer all the questions in the table to judge whether the information source is reliable or not. (If using a video clip, learners won't be able to complete point 6 in the table.)

3 With new knowledge from their completed table, learners decide whether or not the information source is real or fake, giving reasons.

5 Learners individually consider if they feel more confident about judging whether an information source is real or fake, and why. They give ideas for what might help them gain more confidence in this skill.

Differentiation: For tasks 2 and 3, learners can work individually and share in pairs once complete or work in pairs and share in fours.

Ways of working: Individually/in pairs for support and to clarify own thinking and understanding.

Different opinions/perspectives: Learners should keep in mind that the ideas/evidence in the source might come from different perspectives, which is fine as long as the source can be judged as reliable.

Learner response and feedback: Learners can help each other using the checklist, asking questions such as:

- Have you considered the whole story and not just the headline?
- Have you checked the author exists?
- Have you checked the date of the story?
- Does the story seem believable or a joke?
- Does the source refer to any other evidence – real people, other sources of information?

Suggested answers: Answers will vary depending on the source given (see the Worked Example).

Worked Example for the Main activity

Topic: Digital world

See Downloadable 3.3.

Information source: For example, BBC News video clip 'Will robots take our jobs and if so which ones?' (https://www.youtube.com/watch?v=skG3okhx2TU). This reliable/real source of information is a bit out of date (2014), it cites real people and studies, and is from the BBC, known to be a reputable source of information.

1 The main idea is that automation will replace people in some areas of the workforce.

Example facts: 47 per cent of jobs in the USA will become computerised. Research was conducted by the Pew Research Centre: 1900 experts responded, and 48 per cent of respondents are not optimistic about automation – they think manual and office workers will be affected; 52 per cent say robots will do lots of work, but humans will find different types of work.

2

	Checklist	Source	Notes
1	Has the story been reported anywhere else?	Yes	A few different websites report on this issue, including *The Guardian*.
2	Is the purpose of the story clear?	Yes	To inform youngsters and parents about the risk to future jobs from automation in a basic way
3	Have you heard of the organisation that published the story?	Yes	The BBC is known as a reputable organisation for news.
4	Does the story sound believable?	Yes	
5	Is the argument in the story logical	Yes	All the points follow on from each other and you can easily follow it. It gives examples for each point made, although it talks about half when in fact the percentages are 48% and 52%. It draws a conclusion.
6	Are there any errors in spelling or grammar (in text only)?	N/A	
7	Is the author of the story a real person?	Yes	He has reported about this issue elsewhere.
8	Is there anything odd about the dates?	Yes	2014 is a bit old.
9	Does the story contain bias?	Yes	It chooses which jobs to highlight – jobs already in decline; gives own opinion at the end based on the list of jobs highlighted that won't be automated. Some of the language hints at bias: 'masses of people'; 'effectively unemployed'.
10	Is there any other evidence to support the story?	Yes	Some evidence: a study; Pew Research Centre experts; two economists.

3 This is a real source as the facts can be found in other information sources; the evidence is from real sources that are well-known and can be trusted. The author is real and has reported on this issue elsewhere etc. (Encourage learners to summarise findings from their checklist in task 2.)

5 Answers will vary, depending on the learners. To help them further, they might state seeing more examples of real and fake news stories.

Independent reflection activity; Self-assessment; Issue review (approx. 15–20 mins)

Good for: Encouraging learners to consider their learning in lessons. Encourage learners to reflect on the skills they have used in the lesson, such as research skills to make notes and evaluation skills to complete their checklist. Working in pairs or individually might have helped them learn better, for example.

Learners also complete the self-assessment to set their own learning targets before they move on. They think about and shade where they think they are at this time in their learning. 'With help' refers to guidance given (pointing a learner in the right direction, although examples should still come from the learner); for example, from you, other learners, previous work done by the learner in their Learner's Skills Book.

For the Issue review, learners explore the issue used in this section to develop evaluation skills.

These activities can be done in class, at home or in self-study time.

Suggested examples:

78E.01 *Evaluate sources, considering the author and purpose, recognising that some sources may be more credible than others.* Evaluation is judging something to be good/bad, fair or not etc. Analysis is explaining something in more detail. Fake news is news that is not true, has been made up or has been exaggerated so as to be untrue. To check if facts are true, look for them in different information sources.

78E.02 *Discuss the effectiveness of an argument, making explicit reference to its structure and use of evidence.* If a source contains bias, it might affect the effectiveness of the argument in that it could be one-sided. Bias is usually for political or for business reasons as authors of information sources might be trying to influence an outcome or persuade someone to buy something/invest in something. An argument that does not make sense will generally be fake news as the facts will not add up. Learners can use any examples from Lessons 1–3.

Developing evaluation skills: Lesson 4

Lesson 4 focuses on understanding what an argument is in Cambridge Global Perspectives and how to write an effective argument.

CAMBRIDGE STAGE 8 EVALUATION LEARNING OBJECTIVES

78E.02 Discuss the effectiveness of an argument, making explicit reference to its structure and use of evidence

LEARNING GOALS

To develop knowledge and understanding about:

- the characteristics of an argument in Cambridge Global Perspectives
- the features of an effective argument
- writing an effective argument.

How will I know if I reach my goals?

Good for: Learners to give examples of their learning from the lesson. They can complete the table at any point in the lesson but might do it at the end.

Resources needed

- Learner's Skills Book 8
- Downloadables 3.4, 3.5 and 3.6

Prior learning (approx. 5–10 mins)

Good for: Building on previous knowledge, learning and understanding. This might be from Cambridge Primary Global Perspectives, from Cambridge Global Perspectives Stage 7, from other subject areas or from previous Cambridge Global Perspectives Stage 8 lessons.

Activity: Learners work with a partner to discuss and write down what they think an argument in Cambridge Global Perspectives is.

Differentiation: Allow learners to work in pairs for support. They can look at the Tip defining what an argument is the Learner's Skills Book if needed.

Suggested answers/ideas: There are two meanings of the word 'argument'. For Cambridge Global Perspectives lessons, an argument is logical reasoning to justify an idea, claim or perspective that is supported by evidence.

A useful video clip to explore what an argument is 'Analyzing the argument' on YouTube (https://www.youtube.com/watch?v=pP8dWURrEF0). See Downloadable 3.4.

Not issue specific.

Starter activity (approx. 10–15 mins)

Good for: Getting learners to think about deconstructing arguments and identifying what makes an effective argument, starting with a claim.

Activity: Discuss/elicit from learners what a claim is before they do the activity. Learners look at a picture, for example, the *Huffington Post* infographic 'The most common reasons we move in America' (https://www.huffpost.com/entry/the-most-common-moving_b_4738585)

(see Downloadable 3.5). Learners then write claims related to the issue.

Ways of working: Individual, pair and whole-class discussion.

Suggested answers (based on the suggested image):

1 People move in the USA… for family reasons, to go to university or college, for work-related reasons, due to natural disasters, because of changes in their marital status, for a better neighbourhood, for an easier commute, and so on.

3 A claim is a statement or assertion that something is true, often without providing supporting evidence or proof.

Main activity (approx. 20–25 mins)

Good for: Exploring what makes up an argument.

Activity: Give learners a text (see Downloadable 3.6 and the Worked Example). Learners identify the claim, reasons and evidence for this claim, determine whether the argument is convincing and say why/why not.

Differentiation: Learners can work in pairs for support. Consider the length of text (shorter or longer depending on learners) and the complexity of language (adaptations might be needed, pre-teach vocabulary or provide your own Language Support handout).

Ways of working: Individually/in pairs to share ideas and clarify own thinking. Whole-class discussion once argument has been evaluated.

Different opinions/perspectives: Encourage learners to consider what perspective the ideas in the text are from. For example, for the Worked Example, in favour of moving to a different country for different opportunities, perspectives are from a social perspective, from a cultural perspective, from a global perspective (evidence from two sources).

Learner response and feedback: Encourage learners to ask questions of each other:

- What do you think the author thinks?
- Why do you think the author thinks this?
- How do you know this?

Suggested answers: Depends on the text given (see the Worked Example below).

Worked Example for the Main activity

Topic: Migration and urbanisation

See Downloadable 3.6.

MOVING TO LIVE IN A NEW COUNTRY

There is no greater life experience than moving to a new country. The opportunities a new country brings are enormous. There are new discoveries such as culture and traditions, foods, places and, of course, the people. Since moving to Canada three years ago, I have not looked back. For young people nowadays, moving to live in a new country is easy to do and it doesn't have to be a permanent decision; you can try it for three or six months first and see how it goes.

Living in a new country can be hard work at first, perhaps due to language barriers or feeling lonely. If you choose somewhere you speak the language, then language is no problem, and you can easily make friends by enrolling on college courses, joining a sports club or finding a new hobby such as cooking local dishes or yoga. Of course, you will probably miss your friends and family, but you don't need to go halfway across the world, and they can visit. In fact, they will probably be really pleased to visit you in a different location and you might even see more of them. And don't forget, there's social media where you can keep up to date with all that's happening in your hometown, and all your friends and family can follow you as you explore new sights, sounds and tastes.

According to Gregorio, who has now lived in Mexico for four years, having moved from Spain, 'The language is almost the same. There is such a variety of food and I love Mexican burritos and tortillas. It was a great decision to move here and my friends come to stay a lot as they love the Mexican way of life too.'

Katrina moved from her hometown of Hamburg in Germany to Rome and, even though the language is different, she easily picked it up, and is thoroughly enjoying living and working in the Italian capital. 'I love the warm summers and the history of Rome. I often sit outside a little café and watch the world go about its daily business thinking how fortunate I am. I do miss my friends and family, so I chat with my mum at least once a week and friends message me often to find out what I'm doing. I go back to Germany for Christmas because Christmas in Germany is so special to me,' she said with a peaceful smile on her face.

There are just so many good reasons for moving to a new country – so don't be afraid to make that move.

Suggested answers:

1 **a** There is no greater life experience than moving to a new country.

b Reasons: lots of opportunities to explore a different culture and traditions, enjoy new foods, see new places, meet new people.

Evidence: Gregorio's statement; Katrina's statement.

c and **d** Answers will vary. The argument is convincing in some ways as it has reasons for moving and living in a new country and it has evidence (Gregorio's and Katrina's statements) to support these reasons (local foods, culture/history, language and weather). The evidence is anecdotal from people living there rather than any statistical evidence (e.g. number of people that have moved to live in a new country or enjoy living in a new country). The argument does mention some disadvantages (different language and missing family and friends) but it gives ways of making these a benefit rather than a disadvantage.

Independent reflection activity (approx. 5–10 mins)

Good for: Encouraging learners to consider their learning from the lesson about the skills they have used in the lesson (e.g. research skills to identify claims for a photo/image) and if they are starting to get a better understanding of what an argument is. Encourage learners not only to write what an argument is made up of but also to give basic examples if they can (some will struggle). For example: An argument is made up of a claim (living in a new country is a good idea), reasons (you can enjoy a different culture/traditions) and evidence (testimony from someone that moved to live in a new country and is enjoying it).

This activity can be done in class, at home or in self-study time.

Developing evaluation skills: Lesson 5

Lesson 5 focuses on the features of an effective argument: identifying claims, reasoning for claims and evidence in support of claims.

CAMBRIDGE STAGE 8 EVALUATION LEARNING OBJECTIVES

78E.02 Discuss the effectiveness of an argument, making explicit reference to its structure and use of evidence

LEARNING GOALS

To develop knowledge and understanding about:

- identifying claims
- identifying reasoning to justify a claim
- identifying evidence in support of a claim.

How will I know if I reach my goals?

Good for: Learners to give examples of their learning from the lesson. They can complete the table at any point in the lesson but might do it at the end.

Resources needed

- Learner's Skills Book 8
- Downloadables 3.7 and 3.8
- Newspaper/magazine articles or access to computers and the internet

Prior learning (approx. 5–10 mins)

Good for: Building on previous knowledge, learning and understanding. This might be from Cambridge Primary Global Perspectives, from Cambridge Global Perspectives Stage 7, from other subject areas or from previous Cambridge Global Perspectives Stage 8 lessons.

Activity: Review learning from Lesson 4 and learners choose the correct response.

Differentiation: Allow learners to look back in their Learner's Skills Book. Some will not need to. Learners to work individually and then share ideas with a partner/whole class. Some learners will struggle with task 3. Class discussion to gain ideas.

Suggested answers:

1 C

2 Question A might identify reasons; question B might identify evidence.

3 Claim: Moving abroad has more benefits than disadvantages; living in a new country brings new opportunities.

Reasons: You can meet new people, try new foods, see new places, experience a new culture/local tradition.

Evidence: A report from …/A questionnaire about …/… said …

Starter activity (approx. 10–15 mins)

Good for: Exploring the type of claims people can make.

Activity: Show learners a video clip (see Downloadable 3.7 and the Worked Example; it should be on the same issue as the issue for the Main activity). Learners write down one claim made in the video, reason(s) to justify the claim and evidence in support of the claim.

Ways of working: Individual, pair and whole-class discussion.

Suggested answers: Depends on the video clip given.

Worked Example for the Starter activity

Topic: Migration and urbanisation

See Downloadable 3.7.

Video clip idea: '5 Things that will change after you have lived abroad' on YouTube https://www.youtube.com/watch?v=h6mHboMySaI (Please check that this video is suitable for your learners.)

Suggested answers/ideas:

a **Claim:** Your outlook on life will change drastically. You cannot live like a tourist anymore. You cannot fit into your clothes anymore/you will put on weight. You will never have to pay for a hotel room again. You can make changes in your own country.

b **Reason(s):** You cannot live like a tourist anymore (when you visit a new country) as all you want to do is immerse yourself in culture. You want to find the best local hideouts, enjoy the local cuisine and learn how to cook it. You will have made new friends around the world. You will have done new things and learned new skills that you can bring back to your own country to make a difference.

c **Evidence:** Author of the clip; every seasoned traveller; the Club of the Restless.

Main activity (approx. 20–25 mins)

Good for: Researching to find interesting texts about the issue to practise identifying claims, reasoning and evidence.

Activity: Learners find an interesting text about the issue. This can be online or from a newspaper or magazine. They give the text reference and identify a claim, reason(s) for the claim and evidence in support of the claim (see Downloadable 3.8 and the Worked Example). You could also use the text from Lesson 4 for this activity.

Differentiation: Learners can work in pairs for support. You can give learners different newspaper articles. Learners can refer to Section 1 Research about referencing.

Ways of working: Individually/in pairs to share ideas and clarify own thinking. Whole-class discussion about claims, reasoning and evidence before learners start work.

Different opinions/perspectives: Encourage learners to think about the perspectives included in their article also (e.g. the perspective from which the reasoning and evidence come).

Learner response and feedback: Encourage learners to discuss in pairs/as a class the differences between a claim, reasoning and evidence. They can ask each other questions such as:

- What does the author think?
- Why does the author think this?
- How does the author know this?
- Have we included everything in the reference (author, date, title, publication or website if online, date accessed)?

Suggested answers: See the Worked Example below.

Resource for the Main activity

Topic: Migration and urbanisation

See Downloadable 3.8.

Living abroad is not always a positive thing

Many people talk about how they would love to live abroad and all the great things that they will be able to do and the adventures they will have. In my experience, living abroad is not all positive and here's why.

Firstly, you miss your friends and family too much and you feel like you are missing out on all they are doing. For example, my sister had her sixteenth birthday and I couldn't be there as I was on the other side of the world in Australia and it is too expensive for me to fly back more than once a year.

This happened to a friend of mine as well who missed his brother's wedding because he couldn't afford the trip back home for it. Next, you think you will have many adventures but you have the same ones you would have if you stayed at home.

In fact, you would have more as you would do things with your friends who you have known all your life. It's very difficult to make friends when you move to a different country. I was reading in a magazine that it takes someone on average a year to meet and make a new friend and this only happens if you make the first move by joining a club or taking up a hobby and approaching people – which many of us feel shy about doing. Often the friends we have back home are people we have known since primary school as, according to 'Friends' magazine (2023), it's easier to make friends then than when you older.

Amy Dexter https://www.amysblog.com
June 2023

Suggested answers:

1 a Text reference: Dexter, A. (2023). 'Living abroad is not always a positive thing'. [Online], https://www.amysblog.com (Accessed 24/08/2023).

b Claim: Living abroad is not always a positive thing.

c Reason(s): Miss friends and family too much; think you're going to have more adventures, but you don't; getting home for events is expensive.

d Evidence: experience of the author, experience of author's friend, *Friends* magazine.

Independent reflection activity (approx. 5–10 mins)

Good for: Encouraging learners to reflect on their own learning from the lesson and what helped them to learn, how they might have helped others. Encourage learners to reflect on the skills (research, analysis, evaluation, reflection, communication, collaboration) they have used this lesson; for example, research skills to find a suitable text for the Main activity. This activity can be done in class, at home or in self-study time.

Developing evaluation skills: Lesson 6

Lesson 6 focuses on developing learners' knowledge and understanding about bias, and the purposes and aims of different text types.

CAMBRIDGE STAGE 8 EVALUATION LEARNING OBJECTIVES

78E.01 Evaluate sources, considering the author and purpose, recognising that some sources may be more credible than others

LEARNING GOALS

To develop knowledge and understanding about:

- the meaning of the term 'bias' and judging if a text contains any bias
- the purpose of different texts
- the audience for different texts.

How will I know if I reach my goals?

Good for: Learners to give examples of their learning from the lesson. They can complete the table at any point in the lesson but might do it at the end.

Resources needed

- Learner's Skills Book 8
- Downloadables 3.9 and 3.10
- As an alternative to using Downloadable 3.10 newspapers or magazines, or access to the internet

Prior learning (approx. 5–10 mins)

Good for: Building on previous knowledge, learning and understanding. This might be from Cambridge Primary Global Perspectives, from Cambridge Global Perspectives Stage 7, from other subject areas or from previous Cambridge Global Perspectives Stage 8 lessons.

Activity: Discussing the meaning of the term 'bias'.

Differentiation: Allow learners to look at the Tips in their Learner's Skills Book. Some will not need to. Learners can work in pairs for support. In tasks 2 and 3, learners can revisit what they've written in task 1 after discussion to deepen their understanding. Examples might come from any of the texts explored in Lessons 1–5.

Suggested answers: Any reasonable and relevant response. For example:

- Bias is favour or prejudice for or against one person or group of people according to different opinions/perspectives/beliefs, often in a way that is thought to be unfair. A biased person favours one side or issue over another or is in favour of one action/reason over another for reasons that might be beneficial to them (also known as having a vested interest).
- Examples of bias: Political bias – 'Vote for us because we will make sure that we limit the number of immigrants coming into our country'; '90 per cent of Americans think that migration is beneficial to the country in a lot of ways'; 'Half the population (47 per cent) agree that further spending on a high speed rail network is unnecessary'. Commercial bias: 'The best steak in the whole of Texas!'; 'The best airline for flights to Canada'. For examples of commercials to illustrate gender bias, search YouTube for 'bias women commercials' and 'gender stereotype ads'.

Starter activity (approx. 10–15 mins)

Good for: Identifying the purpose of different texts and judging if they contain bias.

Activity: Reviewing the purpose of different text types and whether they contain bias. Learners look at three different video clips on the same issue; they discuss the videos with a partner and answer the questions about purpose and bias (see Downloadable 3.9 and the Worked Example).

Ways of working: Pair and whole-class discussion. This can be the same or a different issue to the issue for the Main activity. Stress to learners that the majority of texts contain some form of bias.

Suggested answers/ideas: Responses will vary depending on the video clips.

Worked Example for the Starter activity

Topic: Migration and urbanisation

See Downloadable 3.9.

Suggested video clips and answers:

1 a A YouTube video 'Studying abroad – why you should do it' aiming at students to persuade them to study abroad (https://www.youtube.com/watch?v=0PwNW7PAUzQ)

b A news item 'Syria to UK – an 11–year-old's story' aiming to inform of the situation in Syria and why a family moved from Syria to the United Kingdom (https://www.bbc.co.uk/newsround/34262108)

c An online video 'Culture Shock in America Part 1' from 'Study Abroad with Anne' aiming to entertain (https://www.youtube.com/watch?v=qTwntbHcwWA)

2 a Yes, it contains bias as it only considers the advantages (not the disadvantages) of studying abroad.

b Yes, it contains bias as it focuses on one family only and is mostly from the perspective and experiences of an 11-year-old girl.

c Yes, it contains bias as its intention is to make people laugh, even though it might not succeed. Therefore, it only shows the negatives of studying abroad.

Main activity (approx. 20–25 mins)

Good for: Evaluating text titles to predict who they might be aimed at, the purpose of each text and whether the text might contain bias.

Activity: Learners look at the text titles you give them (see Downloadable 3.10 and the Worked Example); they could also find their own text titles (from newspapers or magazines, or from the internet). They could do this activity in small groups of four, with pairs working together and exchanging text titles to complete the activity in their Learner's Skills Book.

Differentiation: Learners work in pairs for support. Refer learners to the Tips in their Learner's Skills Book for definitions of the words 'audience', 'purpose' and 'bias'.

Ways of working: Pairs to share ideas, clarify own thinking and as support.

Different opinions/perspectives: Encourage learners to think about the perspective that might be within each text from its title.

Learner response and feedback: Encourage learners to give feedback to each other by discussing each text title to answer the questions in their Learner's Skills Book.

Suggested answers: Answers will vary according to the text titles (see the Worked Example). Can be the same issue as for the Starter activity or can be a different issue.

Worked Example for the Main activity

Topic: Migration and urbanisation

See Downloadable 3.10.

Suggested text titles:

1 A 'Many countries in the north would be unable to function without a large population of foreign workers'

B My wonderful student life in Copenhagen'

C 'Ten best jokes about moving abroad'

2 a A The audience is most likely the general population who read the news to inform themselves about what's happening in the world; employers; workers.

B The audience is most likely groups of students and people who read blogs about places in the world; tourists; people who like travelling.

C The audience is most likely people who want a laugh or want entertaining; might be young people or comedians.

b A To inform; to educate; analyse the issue of migration; to argue/make the case for foreign workers/migration.

B Perhaps to entertain; to persuade others to go to Copenhagen; to inform about Copenhagen.

C To entertain or make people laugh.

c A Yes, as it might only give the positives of having foreign workers in the north.

B Yes, as judging from the text title, it only says what's good about living in Copenhagen.

C Yes, as it depends what the author/comedian thinks about moving abroad – if it's a good or bad thing or both.

4 Text titles give us a clue about the content of a text, might indicate the audience and purpose of the text, and might tell us if a text might contain bias. By looking at a text title, we can start to evaluate the reliability of the text. For example, text title B is a blog. It is one person's view of living in Copenhagen, so this is not necessarily a reliable source of information about what Copenhagen has to offer.

Independent reflection activity; Self-assessment; Issue review (approx. 15–20 mins)

Good for: Encouraging learners to consider their learning and progression in learning in lessons. Ask them to be as honest as they can.

Learners also complete the self-assessment to set their own learning targets before they move on. They think about and shade where they think they are at this time in their learning. 'With help' refers to guidance given (pointing a learner in the right direction, although examples should still come from the learner); for example, from you, other learners, previous work done by the learner in their Learner's Skills Book.

For the Issue review, learners explore the issue used in this section to develop evaluation skills.

These activities can be done in class, at home or in self-study time.

Suggested examples:

78E.01 *Evaluate sources, considering the author and purpose, recognising that some sources may be more credible than others.* Evaluation is judging if a source/argument is reliable/effective or not; checking the author exists and looking at the purpose of the information source (to inform, entertain, persuade etc.); judging if a source contains bias and why.

78E.02 *Discuss the effectiveness of an argument, making explicit reference to its structure and use of evidence.* An argument in Cambridge Global Perspectives is made up of a claim, reasoning and evidence. Being able to identify the features of an effective argument includes: claim (what the author believes), reason(s) (why the author believes this) and evidence (how the author knows this). Answers will vary for being able to write an effective argument. Examples can come from Lessons 1–6.

Getting better at evaluation skills: Lesson 7

Lesson 7 focuses on understanding the difference between the author of a text and the purpose for a text, and recognising different types of evidence to support claims.

CAMBRIDGE STAGE 8 EVALUATION LEARNING OBJECTIVES

78E.01 Evaluate sources, considering the author and purpose, recognising that some sources may be more credible than others

78E.02 Discuss the effectiveness of an argument, making explicit reference to its structure and use of evidence

LEARNING GOALS

To get better at:

- understanding the difference between audience and purpose
- recognising fact and opinion
- recognising bias.

How will I know if I reach my goals?

Good for: Learners to give examples of their learning from the lesson. They can complete the table at any point in the lesson but might do it at the end.

Resources needed

- Learner's Skills Book 8
- Downloadable 3.10

Prior learning (approx. 5–10 mins)

Good for: Building on previous knowledge, learning and understanding. This might be from Cambridge Primary Global Perspectives, from Cambridge Global Perspectives Stage 7, from other subject areas or from previous Cambridge Global Perspectives Stage 8 lessons.

Activity: Review learning of Cambridge Global Perspectives terms 'audience' and 'purpose'. Discussion about the difference between the audience for a text and what the purpose of a text is, and giving examples for both.

Differentiation: Allow learners to look at the Tips in their Learner's Skills Book. Some will not need to. Learners work with a partner.

Suggested answers:

Audience: Who the text is aimed at (examples: students, parents, teachers, governments, buyers, sports fans, community leaders, women etc.)

Purpose: What the text hopes to achieve (examples: to inform, persuade, entertain, argue, describe, analyse, instruct etc.)

Starter activity (approx. 10 mins)

Good for: Building understanding about the features of an effective argument: claim, reasoning and evidence (different types such as facts and opinions).

Activity: Learners discuss with a partner and share with the rest of the class.

Suggested answers:

1 **a** A claim is a statement or assertion that something is true.

b Types of evidence include facts, evidence from experts and organisations, from surveys/questionnaires, reports etc.

3 **a** Fact: a type of evidence, something that can be proven to be true.

b Opinion: what someone thinks; it isn't proven so, although it can be a type of evidence, it is weaker evidence than a fact.

Not issue specific.

Main activity (approx. 20–25 mins)

Good for: Finding relevant information from a text.

Activity: Give learners a text (see Downloadable 3.11 and the Worked Example). Learners work in pairs to complete the tasks in their Learner's Skills Book.

Differentiation: Learners work in pairs/small groups. Each partner/member of a small group can complete different tasks if divided and then share all responses at the end. For example, if working in pairs, one learner might complete tasks 1 a–c and another might do tasks 1 d–e. They share their answers, then discuss and answer task 2.

Ways of working: In pairs/small groups.

Different opinions/perspectives: Learners will be considering the perspective(s) of the ideas and evidence in the text and giving reasons for their chosen perspective.

Learner response and feedback: Encourage learners to ask each other questions such as:

- Why do you think that's a claim?
- Does the reasoning justify the claim?
- Why do you think that's evidence?
- Why do you think that's an example of bias?

Suggested answers/ideas: Any relevant response, depending on the text (see the Worked Example for the Main activity). Encourage learners to discuss how effective the text is for task 2 and how it might be more effective; for example, by including more factual (statistical) evidence and less opinion or by including more global examples. For task 3, encourage learners to give feedback to another pair to establish understanding of the features of an effective source and any action that needs to be taken if they are not understood; for example, ask you for further explanation or examples.

Worked Example for the Main activity

Topic: Migration and urbanisation

See Downloadable 3.11.

Note that the sources referenced have been created for the purpose of this activity and are not real websites.

A GLOBAL CONTRACT TO MAKE MIGRATION WORK FOR THE GOOD OF ALL

Next year, governments around the world will be preparing to sign a global contract about migration. According to a report conducted by the Worldwide Institution (2019), migration brings many benefits globally and it is time for the world to understand this. This is the first time such a contract will be agreed, and it is a way forward to make migration work for everyone, everywhere.

For the global contract to be successful, governments across the world need to recognise and emphasise the benefits of migration as migrants make massive contributions to their home country and to the country they decide to settle in. A study by the Global Work Organisation (2018) stated that migrants do thousands of jobs where there are not enough local people to do them. This boosts the economy of the country as all money earned becomes money spent. Migrants also influence global development when they send money home to their home countries. Migration also allows for richer and more varied societies. Many people love the different types of food and traditions that different nationalities bring to a country.

A global contract is needed so that governments can protect the rights of migrants, not only for the benefit of their economies, but also for the benefit of society and for the benefit of the migrants themselves. In 2018, there were over 6 million foreign-born people living in Spain, which is almost 13 per cent of the total population (Videz, 2019). Migrants living in Spain and elsewhere around the world need to feel that their welfare matters and that their rights are protected.

Urgent action is needed to safeguard the lives and human rights of all migrants, including those that are currently trapped in camps, at risk of becoming slaves, or face situations of violence, wherever they are. Global action is needed to resettle those fleeing war and conflict in their own countries. We have to take action to live in a world that celebrates the many contributions that migrants make and next year's global contract is a step in the right direction, to make migration work for us all.

References

Global Work Organisation (2018). 'A migrant workforce globally'. [Online], https://www.globalwork.org/migrants-work (Accessed 25/08/2023).

Worldwide Institution (2019). 'A global contract for migration'. [Online], https://www.worldwideinstitution.org/global-contract-for-migration (Accessed 25/08/2023).

Videz, A. (2019) 'Migrants prefer Spain as number one destination' *Spain Today* [Online], https://www.spaintoday.es/2019/migration (Accessed 28/08/2023).

Suggested answers:

1 **a** For example, 'Migration brings many benefits globally'.

b Migrants make large contributions to their home country and to the host country. They do jobs to ensure that the economy runs smoothly; they send money to their home country, which helps with the development of that country; societies are richer and more varied because of migration.

c Evidence includes facts: a report from the Worldwide Institution; a study from the Global Work Organisation and an article in *Spain Today*. Opinions come from people who love the different foods and traditions available due to migration and the author's opinion in the last paragraph of the text.

d The text presents a global perspective because the Worldwide Institution sounds like an organisation with global influence and the text talks about a global contract for migration rather than a national one. Although Spain is mentioned in the article, this is just information and not a perspective.

e An example of bias is from the Worldwide Institution as it only refers to the benefits of migration and nothing is mentioned about the drawbacks/challenges of migration.

2 The text is effective as it has reliable evidence to support the claim that migration brings many benefits, but it is not effective in that it only gives one side of the argument (the benefits of migration) and there is unsupported opinion in the last paragraph.

Independent reflection activity; Self-assessment; Issue review (approx. 15–20 mins)

Good for: Encouraging learners to consider their learning from the lesson and what skill(s) they improved, such as collaboration skills by working with a partner/ in a small group, joining in discussions etc. Learners also complete the self-assessment to set their own learning targets. They think about and shade where they think they are at this time in their learning. 'With help' refers to guidance given (pointing a learner in the right direction, although examples should still come from the learner); for example, from you, other learners, previous work done by the learner in their Learner's Skills Book. For the Issue review, learners explore the issue used in this section to develop evaluation skills. These activities can be done in class, at home or in self-study time.

Suggested examples:

78E.01 *Evaluate sources, considering the author and purpose, recognising that some sources may be more credible than others.* For example:

Evaluation: judging whether a source/argument is reliable/effective or not; checking that the author exists and looking at the purpose of the information source (to inform, entertain, persuade etc.); judging if a source contains bias and why.

Bias: can be seen as favouring a certain side; for example, a waitress in a restaurant thinking that the food there is the best in the neighbourhood or someone thinking young people today are disrespectful, unlike when they were younger.

Audience: the group of people the information source is aimed at (e.g. parents, students, sports fans).

Purpose: the reason the source was created (e.g. to inform, persuade or instruct).

78E.02 *Discuss the effectiveness of an argument, making explicit reference to its structure and use of evidence.* An argument in Cambridge Global Perspectives is made up of a claim, reasoning and evidence. Being able to identify the elements of an argument includes: claim (what the author believes), reason(s) (why the author believes this) and evidence (how the author knows this). Different types of evidence might include:

A fact: something that can be proven to be true; for example, from a report or study. Examples: migrants bring many benefits; there are 6 million immigrants in Spain.

An opinion: something that can't be proven; it's what someone thinks; for example, being able to eat different foods is the best thing about migration; immigrants create unemployment; immigrants are lazy.

Showcasing your skills: Evaluation

'Showcasing your skills' is intended to show learners (and teachers) how other learners felt at the end of the section. They have practised and developed their evaluation skills. They have learned a lot about placing their own value on (1) sources of information and (2) arguments and claims. By that, we just mean how valuable, credible, useful or well argued do learners think the arguments and sources are. Teachers are part of the journey, so you will see the response of a teacher here too.

This section includes some very new skills for learners. They may be used to saying whether they 'like' an article or argument but are probably less used to using the skills and language needed to explain why they feel as they do. We are all developing and learning all the time, and we all find value in different places. So there are no 'right answers' here for learners (or for teachers!). So long as they can justify their views, they are becoming evaluative Cambridge Global Perspectives learners. As a teacher, just remember to keep asking your learners, 'Why?', when they talk about the credibility of their sources. This will help them to deepen their understanding of evaluation and will help them to explain their evaluation better. There are a number of reflection tasks you could try. You could ask your learners to:

- Create a reflection in the form of a video blog; they could share these with the class.
- Answer questions on sticky notes that get put on the board, such as:
  - When were you the most creative, and why do you think that is?
  - What made you curious today?

Projects: If learners have had ample opportunities to practise the other skills required, they could also showcase their evaluation skills by attempting Project 8.2 or Project 8.3, available at cambridge.org/go, both of which have evaluation learning objectives.

Section 4 Reflection

Introduction

The learning objectives for reflection skills for Stage 8 are the same as those for Stage 7 and focus on the following:

- personal contribution
- teamwork
- personal viewpoints
- personal learning.

However, you might also find opportunities within these lessons to develop some of the other Cambridge Global Perspectives skills. For example, when considering ways that personal perspective on an issue can be changed as a result of exploring the causes and consequences of issues and exploring different perspectives, not only will learners be developing reflection skills, they will also be developing their research and analysis skills.

The ideas given in this Teacher's Resource are suggestions only, and the activities can be used with any of the Cambridge Global Perspectives Challenges or topics for Stages 7 to 9. Downloadables and Worked Examples are provided for many learning activities. They are linked to the topics 'Education for all', 'Change in culture and communities' and 'Law and criminality'. Reflection is a skill that can be developed via the activities that explore sustainability. Reflective learners reflect upon and care for the planet and its ever-changing needs. It is hoped that the ideas in this book will help you structure your lessons in an active learning way with input from you as the teacher to help guide and support learners to become more reflective learners.

Reflection skills overview

Learning objectives	78Rf.01 Explain personal contribution to teamwork and identify targets for improvement. 78Rf.02 Consider the benefits and challenges of teamwork experienced when working together to achieve a shared outcome. 78Rf.03 Consider ways that personal perspective on an issue may have changed as a result of conducting research or exploring different perspectives. 78Rf.04 Identify skills learned or improved during an activity and relate to personal strengths and areas for improvement.
Topic ideas	Education for all; Law and criminality; Migration and urbanisation; Climate change, energy and resources; Conflict and peace
Key points	• Understanding the difference between the terms 'evaluation' and 'reflection'. • Understanding that reflection is thinking about and considering things deeply. • Reflection is a skill that is often used with other skills, such as research (reflecting on what has been found out), evaluation (deciding whether arguments are convincing or courses of action are workable), analysis (devising courses of action to address an issue and giving reasons for the courses of action). • Personal perspective needs linking to evidence. Personal opinion is what someone thinks but there is no evidence to support this thinking. • As well as identifying personal strengths and areas for development, learners should also explain them, giving examples for their strengths and saying how they are going to improve any areas for development.

Key points	• Learners should try to explain their contributions to teamwork and how they might improve these. • Learners should try to explain how their personal perspective has changed or developed as a result of research and exploring other perspectives on an issue.
Language support	Pre-teach key vocabulary: reflective learner; evaluation; reflection; praise; criticism; feedback; interrupt; persuade; describe; explain; teamwork; benefits; challenges; contribution; support; respect; deadlines; advice; improvement; strengths; limitations; development; contributions; shared outcome; appreciated; encourage; conflict; resolved; target; compromise; influence; course of action; specific; measurable; parameters; achievable; realistic; practical; time-bound; allocate; roles; responsibilities. Also include any issue-specific vocabulary for the topics – Education for all; Law and criminality; Migration and urbanisation; Climate change, energy and resources; Conflict and peace.
Cross-skills links	**Research** 78Rs.01 Construct relevant research questions. 78Rs.02 Identify and begin to reference a range of print and multimedia sources and use them to locate relevant information and answer research questions. 78Rs.03 Select an appropriate method and conduct research to test predictions and begin to answer a research question. 78Rs.04 Select, organise and record relevant information from a range of sources and findings from primary research, using appropriate methods. **Analysis** 78A.01 Identify ideas and evidence from different perspectives within different sources, on a given issue. 78A.02 Explain how graphical or numerical data supports an argument or a perspective. 78A.03 Explain causes of a local or global issue and consequences on others. 78A.04 Suggest and justify different actions to make a positive difference to a national or global issue. **Evaluation** 78E.01 Evaluate sources, considering the author and purpose, recognising that some sources may be more credible than others. 78E.02 Discuss the effectiveness of an argument, making explicit reference to its structure and use of evidence. **Collaboration** 78Cl.01 Work positively within a team to achieve a shared outcome and improve team work, for example by contributing useful ideas, offering solutions to problems, encouraging other team members to participate and being open to others' ideas. 78Cl.02 The team assigns roles and divides tasks fairly, considering the skills of team members and the time available, resolves disagreements and works together to achieve a shared outcome. **Communication** 78Cm.01 Present information and arguments clearly with some reasoning, referencing sources where appropriate. 78Cm.02 Listen to ideas and information and offer relevant and well-judged contributions that demonstrate understanding of the issue.

Let's start thinking about reflection!

Good for: Enthusing your learners about the skill they are going to work on. Reflection is not a complex skill but learners are not often asked to do it. Here they are encouraged to pause and think about what they have learned and how their views have changed.

The questions give learners ideas about the issues they might explore as they develop their reflection skills. The first idea suggested is the Challenge 'Who am I? and the topic 'Change in culture and communities'. The second idea is based on the topic 'Education for all'. Although not precisely linked to a Challenge the downloadables provide everything your learners need to complete the activities in section 4 and become proficient at reflecting.

Activity: Look at these pages with your learners. You could begin with a quick question and answer session. Ask learners:

- What does 'reflection' mean?
- What kinds of questions could we ask?
- Where might we get our information?
- What issue shall we explore?

Ask learners to each write down one question they have about this section, e.g. on a sticky note. Collate and display their questions so that they are easy to refer to as you work through this section. In that way, learners can see their questions being answered.

Starting with reflection skills: Lesson 1

Lesson 1 focuses on understanding the difference between evaluation and reflection in Cambridge Global Perspectives lessons, and looks at identifying and explaining personal strengths and areas for development.

CAMBRIDGE STAGE 8 REFLECTION LEARNING OBJECTIVES

78Rf.01 Explain personal contribution to teamwork and identify targets for improvement

78Rf.04 Identify skills learned or improved during an activity and relate to personal strengths and areas for improvement

LEARNING GOALS

To start to:

- understand the difference between evaluation and reflection in Cambridge Global Perspectives
- identify and explain personal strengths
- identify areas for development.

How will I know if I reach my goals?

Good for: Learners to give examples of their learning from the lesson. They can complete the table at any point in the lesson but might do it at the end.

Resources needed

- Learner's Skills Book 8
- Downloadable 4.1

Prior learning (approx. 5–10 mins)

Good for: Building on previous knowledge, learning and understanding. This might be from Cambridge Primary Global Perspectives, from Cambridge Global Perspectives Stage 7, from other subject areas or from previous Cambridge Global Perspectives Stage 8 lessons.

Activity: Learners define the terms 'evaluation' and 'reflection' to establish the difference in Cambridge Global Perspectives lessons. Some might find this a challenge to start with but should be able to gain a better understanding after class discussion. Learners will develop their understanding throughout the section.

Differentiation: Learners can work in pairs for support, and whole-class discussion will give learners further ideas.

Suggested answers:

Answers will vary.

1 Evaluation in Cambridge Global Perspectives is to explore the reliability of information sources, considering their strengths and limitations according to audience and purpose, recognising that some sources may be biased. It is also to explore the effectiveness of an information source, in particular to the development of the argument in the source.

2 Reflection is to consider and think deeply about something. This section develops reflection skills about:

- personal contribution
- teamwork
- personal viewpoints
- personal learning.

4 For example, evaluation in Cambridge Global Perspectives focuses on information sources, whereas reflection focuses on my own learning and perspective.

Not issue specific.

Starter activity (approx. 10 mins)

Good for: Enabling learners to start identifying strengths and weaknesses for learning.

Activity: Learners choose their strengths (they can choose more than one). They should try to explain why they think they have these strengths. They also identify skills that need further development.

Ways of working: Individual and pair feedback.

Suggested answers: Any reasonable and relevant response; for example, H – summarising information in my own words, because I am a quick reader and can get the gist of a paragraph easily, can think about it and then write down some of the information in my own words.

Main activity (approx. 20–25 mins)

Good for: Enabling learners to work together in small groups to share information and develop reflection and communication skills.

Activity: Use one text divided into four paragraphs for the whole class (see Downloadable 4.1 and the Worked Example). Give each group one paragraph to study. (More than one small group can do the same paragraph if you have a large class of learners.) Give learners 10–15 minutes to read and discuss their paragraph, making sure that each member of the group understands it. Encourage them to look for a claim, reasoning for the claim and any supporting evidence as they make notes. They then move to new groups to tell others about their paragraph.

Differentiation: Group work as support in mixed ability groups. Choice of text (see Downloadable 4.1 and the Worked Example).

Ways of working: In small groups to start with and then move into different small groups for sharing the content of each paragraph so that all learners can access the whole text (Jigsaw activity).

Different opinions/perspectives: Encourage learners to explore the text(s), noticing the different opinions and viewpoints/perspectives, as well as forming their own opinions about what they read.

Learner response and feedback: Encourage learners to focus on the main idea(s)/key points in the text. They should pay attention to how they are behaving in the groups; refer them back to the Starter activity, which asked them to explore their personal strengths. Ask: *Are you using these strengths? Could you do more?*

Suggested answers/ideas: See the Worked Example.

Worked Example for the Main activity

Topic: Education for all

See Downloadable 4.1.

There are four clear paragraphs in the text. Give all members of each small group the same paragraph to make notes on. Give them 10–15 mins to discuss it and note the main idea/key points. Split the groups so that each new group has someone in it who has discussed each of the four paragraphs. Each member tells the other group members about their paragraph. Learners can make notes in their Learner's Skills Book during or after the discussions. Class discussion can be about the whole text.

Note that some of the sources referenced have been created for the purpose of this activity and are not real websites.

WHAT PREVENTS LEARNING GLOBALLY?

Getting an education is a basic human right, but many young people around the world are prevented from having an education for some of the following reasons:

1 One of the main reasons many children do not get an education is because they are girls. Even though there have been improvements in recent years, there are still more than 130 million girls globally (Clarke, 2019) who are not at school. There are two main reasons. The first is that schooling for girls is not as well valued as it is for boys as boys will need to earn a living to feed their families in the future, whereas girls often stay at home to look after their husbands and children. If a family can only afford to send one child to

school, then it is often the boy that gets the chance of learning. Girls are then forced to either get married or to stay at home to look after brothers and sisters and do household whilst both parents are out at work.

2 Another reason for the lack of learning is the global lack of teachers. If there is no teacher classes cannot be taught and children are sent home. It also means that class sizes can be very large and individual students do not get any attention if they have difficulties, so they fail to learn important things. Sometimes, there are not enough learning materials like textbooks or pencils, so students just sit and listen and do not get chance to take part in activities that will help them learn. There are approximately 130 million children in schools around the world who are not learning the basic skills of reading, writing or mathematics (Gitsch, 2019).

3 Children do not attend school due to poverty and the expense of school, even though the Universal Declaration of Human Rights (UN, 1948) states that all children have a right to a free basic education. School fees have been abolished in many countries and there has been an increase in the number of children attending school. However, many parents cannot afford the school uniforms, pens/pencils, books, examinations, school trips or extra lessons that are also needed (Carter, 2019). Poverty also means that many children are also so malnourished that it affects the development of their brain.

4 Whilst a lot of children around the world go to school by bus or car, others have to walk up to three hours each way to get to school. This is too much for most children, especially if they are already suffering from malnutrition, illness or a disability. So some parents keep their children at home to do the household chores whilst their parents are working (Lathe, 2019). There is also the risk of violence on such long journeys, particularly for girls, and parents are not prepared to take this risk when they can have their children at home making good use of their time.

References

Carter, S. (2019). 'Poverty affects schooling'. [Online], https://www.povertyandschooling.org (Accessed 28/08/2023).

Clarke, M. (2019). 'Gender bias – a reason for the lack of girls' education'. [Online], https://www.genderbias.org/noschooling/girls/une (Accessed 27/08/2023).

Gitsch, U. (2019). 'Poor education due to lack of qualified teachers'. [Online], https://www.lackingteachers.un (Accessed 27/08/2023).

Lathe, M. (2019) 'School is too far to walk'. [Online], https://www.schooldistance.org (Accessed 28/08/2023).

UN (1948). 'The universal declaration of human rights'. [Online], https://www.un.org/en/universal-declaration-human-rights/ (Accessed 27/08/2023).

Suggested answers:

1 **a** The text is about some of the reasons why children don't get an education globally.

b Paragraph 1: Reason for lack of education is gender bias; only boys are sent to school. Claim – Many young girls do not get an education; Reasoning – Due to gender bias; Evidence – Clarke, 2019.

Paragraph 2: Claim – A lack of learning globally; Reasoning – Lack of teachers and unqualified teachers; Evidence – Gitsch, 2019.

Paragraph 3: Claim – Children do not attend school; Reasoning – There is expense even if fees are free; Evidence – Carter, 2019.

Paragraph 4: Claim – Parents refuse to allow children to go to school; Reasoning – school is too far away; Evidence – Lathe, 2019.

2 Answers will vary; for example, 'Yes, because there were some words I didn't know and the group could explain them to me, which deepened my understanding.'

Independent reflection activity (approx. 5–10 mins)

Good for: Learners to give examples of what personal strengths they used/improved in the lesson, and to identify any areas of development and how they might improve these areas; for example, asking questions to clarify thinking a bit more or listening to the ideas of others more before interrupting. This activity can be done in class, at home or in self-study time.

Starting with reflection skills: Lesson 2

Lesson 2 focuses on working as a team towards a shared outcome, and reflecting on personal contributions to teamwork and the benefits and challenges of teamwork.

CAMBRIDGE STAGE 8 REFLECTION LEARNING OBJECTIVES

78Rf.01 Explain personal contribution to teamwork and identify targets for improvement

78Rf.02 Consider the benefits and challenges of teamwork experienced when working together to achieve a shared outcome

LEARNING GOALS

To start to:

- explain what teamwork is
- explain the benefits and challenges of teamwork
- explain personal contributions to teamwork.

How will I know if I reach my goals?

Good for: Learners to give examples of their learning from the lesson. They can complete the table at any point in the lesson but might do it at the end.

Resources needed

- Learner's Skills Book 8
- Downloadable 4.2

Prior learning (approx. 5–10 mins)

Good for: Building on previous knowledge, learning and understanding. This might be from Cambridge Primary Global Perspectives, from Cambridge Global Perspectives Stage 7, from other subject areas or from previous Cambridge Global Perspectives Stage 8 lessons.

Activity: Learners consider the abilities/strengths required for effective teamwork and put them in order with the most important first.

Differentiation: Learners work in pairs for support and share with the class.

Suggested answers: Any reasonable and relevant response. All the skills are important. The discussion about teamwork is also important.

Starter activity (approx. 5–10 mins)

Good for: Understanding what teamwork is and what it is not after discussion about the abilities/strengths team members should possess.

Activity: Ask learners to write their own definitions of what teamwork is and is not, and then share with the class to see if they agree. Learners give reasons for why they did or did not agree with their classmates; for example, 'Because most of my classmates don't think that asking for help is important and I do because it's important that every member of a group knows what they should be doing.'

Suggested answers: Any reasonable and relevant response.

Teamwork is when a group of people work together as a whole, towards a shared goal/outcome, with a positive working atmosphere, and helping and supporting each other to combine individual strengths.

Teamwork is not individuals working on their own goal/outcome and then coming together at the end or individuals imposing their own course of actions to a team issue, which conflict with the rest of the team's ideas/needs/goals.

Main activity (approx. 20–25 mins)

Good for: Getting teams to work together to discuss an issue to achieve a goal and produce a diagram of responses to a set of questions.

Activity: Learners discuss and answer the questions as a team (see Downloadable 4.2). Some questions can be for individuals and some for the whole team, but teams should work together to produce the diagram of responses. The diagram can be a mind map or a spider diagram. See the Worked Example.

Differentiation: The list of questions can have some easy questions and some that are more complex. Members of the team support each other.

Ways of working: In teams (teacher choice or friendship groups).

Different opinions/perspectives: Encourage learners to value all the viewpoints/opinions/perspectives explored.

Learner response and feedback: Learners help each other answer questions and decide what information to put in their diagram.

Suggested answers: These will vary according to the issue and questions (see the Worked Example).

Worked Example for the Main activity

Topic: Education for all

See Downloadable 4.2.

Questions about education:

1 What do you learn in lessons at school?

2 What do you learn outside of lessons at school?

3 What costs are involved with coming to school?

4 How do you get to school?

5 Why do you think it is important to have an education?

6 What do you like most about being at this school?

7 Do you feel part of the school community? Why?/Why not?

8 How would you feel if you had to leave this school?

9 Is there another school you would prefer to go to? Why?

10 Do you think learning at school is better than learning at home? Why?/Why not?

Suggested answers:

1 Learners discuss the questions and their answers as a team.

2 Learners could record their answers to the questions as a diagram, which could be a mind map. The completed diagram will record what the team think about education and learning. It's important that each diagram captures the main ideas as learners will be using these in Lesson 3 to create a presentation about school and learning.

3 Further questions might include:

- Do you think education should be free regardless of the type of school you go to?
- Do you think there should be more free study time in school?
- Do you think there should be more skills-based subjects such as Cambridge Global Perspectives in school?
- Do you think there should be more opportunities for teamwork in school?
- Which subjects do you think are going to be useful for your future?
- Do you think homework assignments are necessary for effective learning?
- Do you think learners need to be tested? Why?/ Why not?

Independent reflection activity (approx. 5–10 mins)

Good for: Encouraging learners to consider the contribution they made to teamwork, and the benefits and challenges of teamwork. Ask them to be as honest as they can.
To encourage explanation, ask learners to develop their answers by giving examples. Examples: 'I listened to others so that I could write down a correct response from the whole team.'; 'One of the challenges of teamwork is that one person sometimes dominates the discussion and this gives a false picture of what the whole team thinks. For example, because Sam shouted the loudest, his response was added to the diagram, but Mark's wasn't.'

This activity can be done in class, at home or in self-study time.

Starting with reflection skills: Lesson 3

Lesson 3 focuses on further understanding of the benefits and challenges of teamwork as teams work together on a shared outcome. It also explores contributions to teamwork and how personal perspectives might develop or change.

CAMBRIDGE STAGE 8 REFLECTION LEARNING OBJECTIVES

78Rf.01 Explain personal contribution to teamwork and identify targets for improvement

78Rf.02 Consider the benefits and challenges of teamwork experienced when working together to achieve a shared outcome

78Rf.03 Consider ways that personal perspective on an issue may have changed as a result of conducting research or exploring different perspectives

LEARNING GOALS

To start to:

- explain the benefits and challenges of teamwork
- explain personal contributions to teamwork
- explain areas for improvement in teamwork
- explore personal perspective on an issue.

How will I know if I reach my goals?

Good for: Learners to give examples of their learning from the lesson. They can complete the table at any point in the lesson but might do it at the end.

Resources needed

- Learner's Skills Book 8
- Downloadable 4.3

Prior learning (approx. 5–10 mins)

Good for: Building on previous knowledge, learning and understanding. This might be from Cambridge Primary Global Perspectives, from Cambridge Global Perspectives Stage 7, from other subject areas or from previous Cambridge Global Perspectives Stage 8 lessons.

Activity: Learners work in teams to give suitable words/phrases for each of the letters of 'teamwork' to help explain what teamwork is.

Differentiation: Learners work in teams. They discuss ideas with another team.

Suggested answers: Any reasonable and relevant response. Not issue specific.

For example:

- **T**aking turns to speak
- **E**ncouraging and motivating each other
- **A**sking for help
- **M**aking sure everyone listens to each other
- **W**orking together
- **O**rganising roles and responsibilities
- **R**especting all ideas
- **K**nowing when you are wrong.

Starter activity (approx. 10 mins)

Good for: Exploring roles and responsibilities for effective teamwork.

Activity: Learners discuss personal abilities and strengths in teams and choose who they think should be responsible for each of the teamwork tasks once they start producing their presentation in the Main activity.

Differentiation: Some learners might have more than one role depending on the size of the team. You can allow learners to decide on their roles or you can give them a role.

Suggested answers: Any reasonable and relevant response. The whole team should agree with the roles/responsibilities allocated.

Not issue specific.

Main activity (approx. 20–25 mins)

Good for: Producing a presentation as a team, delivering this presentation and gaining feedback.

Activity: Learners produce a team presentation (maximum five slides, including the title and conclusion) about the issue you are studying (information gained from answering the questions in the Main activity in Lesson 2). See Downloadable 4.3 and the Worked Example.

Differentiation: Learners work as a team, with team roles and responsibilities according to the decisions made in the Starter activity.

Ways of working: Whole-class explanation of task. In teams, which should be the same as for the Main activity in Lesson 2.

Different opinions/perspectives: Stress that the information presented should explore the views/opinions/perspectives of the whole team.

Learner response and feedback: Learners ask each other questions as they are working as a team:

- Which information should we use? Why?
- Which information should we discard? Why?
- Is the purpose of the presentation clear?
- Does the presentation have a suitable title?
- Is the content of the presentation clear?
- Do the images used make the presentation better?
- Is the content of the presentation interesting?
- Is the ... suitable for the identified audience (e.g. our peers; younger learners)?
- What's good about the ... (strengths)?
- What's not so good about the ... (limitations)?

Suggested answers:

1 Answers will vary according to the issue chosen. All teams should produce a presentation of a maximum of five slides. They will have gathered different information according to the questions given and their answers in the Main activity in Lesson 2 (see the Worked Example for the Main activity).

2 Each team evaluates another team's presentation, answering the questions a–f.

Worked Example for the Main activity

Topic: Education for all

See Downloadable 4.3.

Learners create a team presentation that includes their views about school, learning and education, according to the responses to the questions in the Main activity in Lesson 2. They present their presentation to another team for feedback.

IDEAS FOR A PRESENTATION

(Learners should keep their own notes succinct enough to fit on the individual slides.)

Slide 1: Title: Is it important to have an education?

Slide 2: What we learn – list of school subjects; list of extra-curricular activities; favourite part of being at school/in lessons

Image: Example – learners doing school subjects or extra-curricular activities.

Notes: We all like coming to this school and we feel part of the school community along with our teachers, friends and parents. In our school, we have a lot of lessons and we have a lot of important subjects such as English, Maths, Science and Cambridge Global Perspectives. We are also learning when we are not in lessons. For example, we learn how to play football, to swim and to dance. What we most like about school is that we get to explore interesting global issues and we participate in team projects that help with our collaboration and communication skills.

Slide 3: Why education is important – list of reasons

Image: Example – learners doing jobs, thinking about world issues.

Notes: Education is important because it will help you get a good job and support your family. Education gives us knowledge about the world we live in and we develop our own perspective about it and think of ways that we might be able to make the world a better place. Education helps us to form opinions and have points of view on things in life that matter.

Slide 4: Barriers to education – list of reasons

Images: Example – school uniform, books, equipment, teacher with cost or cross sign next to them.

Notes: There are many reasons some children do not go to school: it costs too much for the school uniform, books and other essential equipment, school is too far away or there is a lack of qualified teachers.

Slide 5: Conclusion

Images: Example – learners happily learning at school in teams, on computers.

Notes: Rather than learn at home, we think it's better to learn in school as our teachers are really good, we learn a lot and we get lots of opportunities to work together in teams and find out new things. We think that everyone should be given the opportunity to learn in school until they are at least 16 years old and that schools, uniforms and essential equipment should be free.

Independent reflection activity; Self-assessment; Issue review (approx. 15–20 mins)

Good for: Encouraging learners to consider their learning in lessons and answers go towards achieving the learning objectives for reflection skills.

Learners also complete the self-assessment to set their own learning targets before they move on. They think about and shade where they think they are at this time in their learning. 'With help' refers to guidance given (pointing a learner in the right direction, although examples should still come from the learner); for example, from you, other learners, previous work done by the learner in their Learner's Skills Book.

For the Issue review, learners explore the issue used in this section to develop reflection skills.

These activities can be done in class, at home or in self-study time.

Suggested examples:

78Rf.01 *Explain personal contribution to teamwork and identify targets for improvement.* Example: 'My personal contribution was making sure that everyone was working to the time limit set for producing our presentation. I also helped with the content of the presentation by giving my opinion about the importance of going to school to learn. I need to listen more to what others say as this helps my own understanding. I also need to ask more questions if I don't understand something.'

78Rf.02 *Consider the benefits and challenges of teamwork experienced when working together to achieve a shared outcome.* For example:

- Benefits of teamwork: more ideas; not struggling alone; mutual support; workload shared equally; can use individual strengths for a collective whole; some tasks can be completed faster, and so on.
- Challenges of teamwork: personality clashes; conflict over who does what; not agreeing on ideas; team members absent; team members not as committed to the team as others, and so on.

78Rf.03 *Consider ways that personal perspective on an issue may have changed as a result of conducting research or exploring different perspectives.* A personal perspective is what you think about an issue as a result of your experiences and what you learn from others and from research. Your personal perspective can change or develop as you become more informed about an issue. Example: 'I used to think that it would be great to learn at home rather than go to school, but now I think that there are more advantages to going to school as you learn other things like dance and drama.'

78Rf.04 *Identify skills learned or improved during an activity and relate to personal strengths and areas for improvement.* For example: 'A skill I have improved is evaluation as I could see strengths and a limitation of the presentation. Strengths were that the content of our presentation was clear and we mentioned all the benefits of going to school. A limitation was that we didn't really mention many of the reasons why young people around the world don't go to school.'

Developing reflection skills: Lesson 4

Lesson 4 focuses on working as a team to plan research and gain information to produce a set of questions for others to answer about the issue in Lesson 5.

CAMBRIDGE STAGE 8 REFLECTION LEARNING OBJECTIVES

78Rf.01 Explain personal contribution to teamwork and identify targets for improvement

LEARNING GOALS

To develop knowledge and understanding about:

- my contribution(s) to teamwork
- setting targets to improve my contribution(s) to teamwork.

How will I know if I reach my goals?

Good for: Learners to give examples of their learning from the lesson. They can complete the table at any point in the lesson but might do it at the end.

Resources needed

- Learner's Skills Book 8
- Downloadable 4.4

Prior learning (approx. 5–10 mins)

Good for: Building on previous knowledge, learning and understanding. This might be from Cambridge Primary Global Perspectives, from Cambridge Global Perspectives Stage 7, from other subject areas or from previous Cambridge Global Perspectives Stage 8 lessons.

Activity: Review the benefits and challenges of teamwork. Ask learners to reflect on their own opinion first and then find out what their partner thinks. After class discussion, encourage them to either keep to their original opinion in task 1 or change it – either is fine. Encourage learners to consider how they might overcome challenges as they will be working in teams in subsequent lessons; for example, value all opinions and be prepared to listen and perhaps compromise.

Differentiation: Learners can work in pairs for support and then share with another pair. Target learners for responses in class discussion.

Suggested answers: Any reasonable and relevant response.

Challenges of teamwork: personality clashes; conflict over who does what; not agreeing on ideas; team members absent; team members not as committed to the team as others and so on.

Benefits of teamwork: more ideas; not struggling alone; mutual support; workload shared equally; can use individual strengths for a collective whole; some tasks can be completed faster and so on.

Not issue specific.

Starter activity (approx. 10–15 mins)

Good for: Reviewing issue-specific vocabulary.

Activity: Learners brainstorm as many words and phrases as they can to do with the issue and can create a mind map which they add to in different colours. Suggest that learners spend 5–7 minutes working independently to leave enough time for sharing.

Ways of working: Individual, pair and class discussion.

Suggested answers: Depends on the issue.

Not issue specific, but the words/phrases will be useful for the Main activity.

Main activity (approx. 20–25 mins)

Good for: Planning to do and conducting research as part of a team.

Activity:

1 As a team, learners decide who is researching what and which websites/information sources they are going to use. For example, each member of the team might research a different country (preferably not their own) and have the same research focus for the different countries so that they can share what they have learned in subsequent lessons (see the Worked Example). This can be discussed in the planning stages in task 1. You can give them a list of websites or can direct them to different information sources such as books about the issue (e.g. different countries/nationalities). You can also encourage learners to find their own websites. Teams complete the table. There is space for five learners per team, but an optimum number is four in a team.

2 Once the team has decided who is researching what, each team member makes notes about what they want to find out (see the Worked Example for the Main activity for suggestions). For example, the whole team might want to find out the same information about different countries and then compare in Lesson 5. Next to each note, they ask a question and then have space to record an answer. They can ask as many questions as they want.

   In Lesson 5, each team will discuss their research and write questions for another team to find the answers. Each team will design a poster in Lesson 6.

Differentiation: Learners can work in pairs for support. They could use a graphic organiser to organise thoughts (see Downloadable 4.4 and the Worked Example for the Main activity).

Ways of working: Individually/in pairs to share ideas and clarify own thinking. Individual/pair research as part of a whole team project in Lessons 4–6.

Different opinions/perspectives: Learners will be finding ideas/information from different opinions/perspectives.

Learner response and feedback: Encourage learners to help and support each other in teams. They can ask questions like:

- What are you trying to find out?
- Are you looking in the right place?
- Have you tried the suggested website(s)?

- Have you found that same information somewhere else?
- Have you tried to use just one or two websites rather than lots?
- Have you noted the website address?
- Do you have a question you want an answer to?

Suggested answers: Depend on the issue chosen (see the Worked Example below).

Worked Example for the Main activity

Topic: Change in culture and communities

Sub-topic: Life in different countries

See Downloadable 4.4.

Learners can research some of the features of different countries to see how similar or different they are. Each learner in a team can choose or be given a different country; for example, Mexico.

My research is about:		Life in Mexico	
	What I want to find out about	Question(s)	Answer
1	Language(s)	• What is their national language? • How does it differ from other Spanish-speaking countries?	• Spanish • There are some differences in the vocabulary used
2	Foods	• What traditional foods do they eat? • How do you make enmoladas?	• Enmoladas, pozole, torta, tacos • There are lots of different recipes, but essentially you need mole sauce, chicken and tortillas
3	Laws	• What laws do they have? • Which is the most unusual law and why does it exist?	• You can be fined for not knowing the national anthem or not singing it correctly • Cyclists are not allowed to take their feet away from their bike pedals in case they lose control and crash
4	Sports/pastimes	• What are the most popular sports/pastimes? • How does *Lucha libre* differ from normal wrestling?	• Soccer, baseball, boxing, wrestling (*Lucha libre*) • The wrestlers wear masks
	What I want to find out about	Question(s)	Answer
5	Belief system(s)	• What belief system do they have? • How do Mexicans celebrate Christmas Eve?	• Catholic Christianity is the most dominant religion (about 83% of the total population) • From December 16 until Christmas Eve, children take part in the posada processions; typical meals include Christmas Eve salad (*ensalada de Noche Buena*), wrapped cornmeal dumplings (*tamales*) and dried salted codfish (*bacalao*)
6	Other	• What pets do Mexicans have?	• Cats and dogs: Mexico is second in the world for the number of pets kept (70% of households have a pet)

Other possible countries that might have some differences and some similarities:

- Canada
- New Zealand
- Kazakhstan
- India
- China
- Singapore.

Independent reflection activity (approx. 5–10 mins)

Good for: Encouraging learners to consider their learning from the lesson. Encourage them to reflect on the contribution(s) they made to teamwork during the lesson; for example, listening to others to decide on their research focus or agreeing on the information they were going to explore. Also encourage learners to set at least one target for improving their contribution(s) to teamwork, such as 'I will let someone finish what they are saying before I speak so I don't interrupt them.'

This activity can be done in class, at home or in self-study time.

Developing reflection skills: Lesson 5

Lesson 5 further develops work done in Lesson 4. Learners work in teams to choose questions for others to find out information in order to create a shared outcome in Lesson 6 and also to inform their own personal perspective.

CAMBRIDGE STAGE 8 REFLECTION LEARNING OBJECTIVES

78Rf.01 Explain personal contribution to teamwork and identify targets for improvement

78Rf.04 Identify skills learned or improved during an activity and relate to personal strengths and areas for improvement

LEARNING GOALS

To develop knowledge and understanding about:

- contributing to teamwork
- how learning and improving skills adds to personal strengths.

How will I know if I reach my goals?

Good for: Learners to give examples of their learning from the lesson. They can complete the table at any point in the lesson but might do it at the end.

Resources needed

Learner's Skills Book 8

Prior learning (approx. 5–10 mins)

Good for: Building on previous knowledge, learning and understanding. This might be from Cambridge Primary Global Perspectives, from Cambridge Global Perspectives Stage 7, from other subject areas or from previous Cambridge Global Perspectives Stage 8 lessons (Lesson 4).

Activity: Reflect on contributions made to teamwork in Lesson 4 and give target(s) for improving contributions to teamwork.

Differentiation: Allow learners to look back at the work done in Lesson 4. They can discuss in pairs or work individually and then share ideas with their team to see if they agree. Encourage learners to compromise to come up with a target for improving their contribution to teamwork. You can ask them to come back to this once they have seen the Starter and Main activities for the lesson.

Suggested answers: Any reasonable and relevant response.

Contributions: Listened to the opinions of others; asked the teacher questions to clarify understanding; gave personal opinions; agreed on the focus of the research; wrote questions; found and wrote answers.

Targets: Try not to dominate discussions; try not to get upset if my best question isn't used; try to agree with the majority; do my fair share of research; try to meet the time allowed for the activity.

Starter activity (approx. 10 mins)

Good for: Reviewing questions from Lesson 4 and sharing with the team to decide on the best eight questions to give to another team.

Activity: Learners review their own questions, share with a partner in their team and then share with their team. The team chooses the best eight questions to give to another team to find the answers for. Encourage teams to choose a variety of stem questions starting with 'why' and 'how', not just 'what'. See the Worked Example for the Starter activity.

Ways of working: Individual, pair and teamwork.

Suggested answers: Depend on the issue and questions from Lesson 4 (see the Worked Example below).

Worked Example for the Starter activity

Topic: Change in culture and communities

Sub-topic: Life in different countries

Example responses:

1 Individuals in a team choose their best three questions. For example:
   1 Why does the law that cyclists must not take their feet off the pedals exist?
   2 What are the most popular sports in Mexico?
   3 How do Mexicans celebrate Christmas Eve?

2 Sharing the best three questions with a partner might change the questions in task 1, maybe to reach a compromise with the partner. For example:
   1 Why is there a law that cyclists must not take their feet off the pedals?
   2 What are the most popular sports in Canada?
   3 How does *Lucha libre* differ from normal wrestling? (Partner felt this one was better.)

3 The team agrees on the best eight questions from all the team's questions.

   For example:
   1 What are the most popular sports in Mexico?
   2 What are the most popular sports in Canada?
   3 How do people in Kazakhstan celebrate Christmas?
   4 Why was chewing gum banned in Singapore?
   5 Which are the most unusual laws in Mexico?
   6 What traditional foods do they eat in China?
   7 What traditional foods do they eat in Kazakhstan?
   8 How do Mexicans celebrate Christmas?

Main activity (approx. 20–25 mins)

Good for: Doing research to answer questions about an issue.

Activity:

1 Learners work as a team to find the answers to the questions from another team. They do research and make notes and come together to share their notes. Each member of a team might do research to find the answers for one or two questions or the team might divide into two pairs so each pair works on different questions. They then share at the end of the activity.

2 Learners note any other interesting information they come across whilst researching to answer the questions.

Differentiation: Learners work in pairs to research answers to questions.

Ways of working: Individually or in pairs, and then in teams to share information gained from research (encourage teamwork by reviewing the benefits of working as a team and some of the rules: taking turns, listening to each other etc.)

Different opinions/perspectives: Learners are exploring ideas and information from different perspectives to answer the questions.

Learner response and feedback: Encourage learners to check in on each other to see how they are getting on and whether any member of the team needs support.

Suggested answers: Learners are developing their ability to answer questions to gain information about the issue to present to the whole class in Lesson 6 and form a personal perspective on the issue after reviewing the work of the whole class in Lesson 6.

Independent reflection activity (approx. 5–10 mins)

Good for: Encouraging learners to reflect on their own learning from the lesson and the skills they have used or improved in the lesson. Encourage learners to answer honestly. Learners reflect on whether the skills used are now becoming personal strengths; for example, listening to others' ideas and suggestions relates to being good at listening. They say if they improved their contributions to teamwork and, if so, how (e.g. 'by helping my partner find some of the answers to the questions') or, if not, why not (e.g. 'because my partner took charge and wouldn't let me do any research on the computer').

This activity can be done in class, at home or in self-study time.

Developing reflection skills: Lesson 6

Lesson 6 focuses on presenting information gained from research, the challenges of teamwork and how to overcome these, and looks at explaining how a personal perspective can change or develop after research.

CAMBRIDGE STAGE 8 REFLECTION LEARNING OBJECTIVES

78Rf.02 Consider the benefits and challenges of teamwork experienced when working together to achieve a shared outcome

78Rf.03 Consider ways that personal perspective on an issue may have changed as a result of conducting research or exploring different perspectives

LEARNING GOALS

To develop knowledge and understanding about:

- the challenges of teamwork and how to overcome these
- how a personal perspective can develop or change after research and considering different perspectives.

How will I know if I reach my goals?

Good for: Learners to give examples of their learning from the lesson. They can complete the table at any point in the lesson but might do it at the end.

Resources needed

- Learner's Skills Book 8
- Downloadable 4.5

Prior learning (approx. 5–10 mins)

Good for: Building on previous knowledge, learning and understanding. This might be from Cambridge Primary Global Perspectives, from Cambridge Global Perspectives Stage 7, from other subject areas or from previous Cambridge Global Perspectives Stage 8 lessons (especially lesson 5).

Activity: Review learning about perspectives by explaining what a personal perspective is and how it differs from a global or national perspective.

Differentiation: Learners can work in pairs for support and share ideas with another pair. You can refer them to Section 2 Analysis, or to the Tips on different perspectives in Lesson 3 and in this lesson in this section of their Learner's Skills Book.

Suggested answers: Any reasonable and relevant response.

A personal perspective: the view that a person has on an issue after exploring different perspectives and reflecting on the causes and consequences of an issue.

A national perspective: the view that a particular country has on an issue. This is usually explained by the laws, policies and/or speeches made by politicians of that country and might be supported by other groups within that country.

A global perspective: a view on an issue that either has global influence or takes account of the nature of the issue globally.

Starter activity (approx. 5–10 mins)

Good for: Exploring the contributions made to teamwork, and the challenges of teamwork and how to overcome these.

Activity: Learners review the work they did as a team in the Starter and Main activities in Lesson 5.

Suggested answers: Accept any relevant and reasonable response.

Contributions to teamwork: choosing three best questions; compromising with partner on three best questions; listening to the partner; listening to the group; giving an opinion with reasoning; helping to choose eight questions; resolving conflict – helping others come to a decision; recognising good questions and saying so.

Challenges: team not accepting all questions suggested; one person dominating; not all participating equally, work not evenly divided; individuals not wanting to do research on their own; taking too long to do research.

Overcoming challenges: compromising; asking for reasons; giving each person 1–2 minutes to give their opinion and reasons; having a vote and agreeing to go with the majority decision; researching in pairs; ensuring all team members have enough/the same amount to do; setting a time limit for research.

Main activity (approx. 20–25 mins)

Good for: Presenting the information found during the Main activity in Lesson 5, and gaining and giving feedback.

Activity: Each team works together to produce a poster (infographic) about the issue, using the information gained from the Main activity in Lesson 5. Encourage the members of teams to work together. For example, each team member can add two or three pieces of information to the team's poster. See Downloadable 4.5.

Differentiation: Learners work as a team supporting each other.

Ways of working: As a team so that all members of the team are familiar with all the information on their poster.

Different opinions/perspectives: The activity focuses on producing a poster of ideas and information gained from research into the issue from Lesson 5. It is likely that learners will have come across ideas from different perspectives within different information sources and they can add these to their posters.

Learner response and feedback:

1 Learners encourage each other by asking questions:
- How are you getting on?
- Is there something you're struggling with?
- How can I help?
- Is that clear?
- Do you understand that?
- How can we illustrate that?

The most popular sports in Mexico are soccer, baseball, boxing and *Lucha libre*. *Lucha libre* is wrestling, but in Mexico the wrestlers wear masks. The most popular sports in Canada are hockey, lacrosse and football.

Whereas Mexico is mostly Christian and almost 83% of people are Catholic, Kazakhstan is mostly Muslim so does not celebrate Christmas in the same way as Mexico. In Mexico, from 16 December until Christmas Eve, children take part in the *posada* processions. Mexicans typically eat Christmas Eve salad (*ensalada de Noche Buena*), wrapped cornmeal dumplings (*tamales*) and dried salted codfish (*bacalao*) on Christmas Eve. In Kazakhstan, the Kazakhs celebrate New Year like Western countries celebrate Christmas and this is on 7 January.

Chewing gum was banned in Singapore in 1992 to stop people causing problems in high-rise apartments, as vandals put chewing gum in mailboxes, inside keyholes and on lift buttons. Chewing gum stuck on the seats of public buses was also a problem with many people complaining and the costs of cleaning were high. Banning chewing gum got rid of these problems. In Mexico, you can be fined for not knowing the national anthem or not singing it correctly. Cyclists can also be fined for removing their feet from their bike pedals, but chewing gum is not banned.

2 Display the posters on the wall. Each team gives feedback on each poster, writing one highlight and one area for improvement on a sticky note. They place their sticky notes on the relevant posters. Teams then collect their own poster from the wall and review the feedback given.

Suggested answers: Answers will vary according to the information gained. See the Worked Example.

Worked Example for the Main activity

Topic: Change in culture and communities

Sub-topic: Life in different countries

See Downloadable 4.5.

1 Suggested poster based on information from Worked Examples in Lessons 4 and 5:

2 **Suggested feedback:**

Team: 4

Highlight: Includes some statistical evidence

Improvement: More information needed for why wrestlers in Mexico wear masks.

Independent reflection activity; Self-assessment; Issue review (approx. 15–20 mins)

Good for: Encouraging learners to consider any new learning and reflect on their personal perspective about the issue. Personal perspectives might be the same but stronger, or might have changed due to the evidence seen in the posters.

Learners also complete the self-assessment to set their own learning targets before they move on. They think about and shade where they think they are at this time in their learning. 'With help' refers to guidance given (pointing a learner in the right direction, although examples should still come from the learner); for example, from you, other learners, previous work done by the learner in their Learner's Skills Book.

For the Issue review, learners explore the issue used in this section to develop reflection skills.

These activities can be done in class, at home or in self-study time.

Suggested examples:

78Rf.01 *Explain personal contribution to teamwork and identify targets for improvement.* Example: 'My personal contribution was researching life in Mexico and creating some questions for others to find the answers to. I shared my research with my team, and we chose some of my questions for the final set of questions. I needed to work a bit quicker as my team were waiting for me to finish my research before we could continue with the project.'

78Rf.02 *Consider the benefits and challenges of teamwork experienced when working together to achieve a shared outcome.* For example:

- Benefits of teamwork: more ideas; not struggling alone; mutual support; workload shared equally; can use individual strengths for a collective whole; some tasks can be completed faster, and so on.
- Challenges of teamwork: personality clashes; conflict over who does what; not agreeing on ideas; team members absent; team members not as committed to the team as others, and so on.
- Overcoming challenges: compromise; ask for reasons; give each person 1–2 minutes to give their opinions and reasons; have a vote and agree to go with the majority decision; research in pairs; ensure all team members have enough/same amount to do; set a time limit for research.

78Rf.03 *Consider ways that personal perspective on an issue may have changed as a result of conducting research or exploring different perspectives.* A personal perspective is what you think about an issue as a result of your experiences and what you learn from others and from research. Your personal perspective can change or develop as you become more informed about an issue. Example: 'I used to think people in Mexico all spoke the same Spanish as in Spain. I now know from my research that Mexicans do speak Spanish but have some different words for things. However, they still say they speak "Spanish" and not "Mexican", as the word "Mexican" only refers to the people of Mexico. Knowing this has developed my perspective about how proud nationalities are of their heritage and origins, and that they don't like people assuming things that are incorrect.'

78Rf.04 *Identify skills learned or improved during an activity and relate to personal strengths and areas for improvement.* Example: 'I am getting better at research as I was able to find a lot of relevant information for my research focus and could write questions and responses for the team about my chosen country in the time limit. However, I need to ensure that I don't get distracted by other websites that come up whilst I am researching as this wastes time.'

Getting better at reflection skills: Lesson 7

Lesson 7 focuses on working as a team to discuss and plan a course of action to address an issue.

CAMBRIDGE STAGE 8 REFLECTION LEARNING OBJECTIVES

78Rf.01 Explain personal contribution to teamwork and identify targets for improvement

78Rf.04 Identify skills learned or improved during an activity and relate to personal strengths and areas for improvement

LEARNING GOALS

To get better at:

- understanding that my personal strengths can benefit teamwork
- working with others towards a shared outcome
- explaining skills used and improved.

How will I know if I reach my goals?

Good for: Learners to give examples of their learning from the lesson. They can complete the table at any point in the lesson but might do it at the end.

Resources needed

- Learner's Skills Book 8
- Downloadable 4.6

Prior learning (approx. 5–10 mins)

Good for: Building on previous knowledge, learning and understanding. This might be from Cambridge Primary Global Perspectives, from Cambridge Global Perspectives Stage 7, from other subject areas or from previous Cambridge Global Perspectives Stage 8 lessons.

Activity: Review own personal strengths.

Differentiation: Allow thinking time. Learners add other strengths after class discussion.

Suggested answers: Any reasonable and relevant examples.

1 Learners can choose more than one option but advise them that they will need to give an example for each one chosen.

3 Other possible personal strengths: good at planning, leading, working on my own, working in a team, helping others, asking others for help/support, asking 'why' and 'how' questions. They can also be examples from outside the classroom.

5 Personal strengths can make teamwork more effective as each team can allocate individual roles and responsibilities according to personal strengths.

Not issue specific.

Starter activity (approx. 10 mins)

Good for: Reviewing issues and what to consider when looking at courses of action to help resolve issues/make a positive difference to an issue.

Activity: Show picture(s) related to an issue (see the Worked Example for the Starter activity). You can show one picture to the whole class or give different pictures to different teams. Elicit the issue(s) from learners and what they know about it. Discuss steps to find a course of action to help resolve the issue/make a positive difference to the issue. Either elicit from learners without help or give them the steps to consider their importance. You can also refer them to the Tips in Section 2 Analysis, Lesson 4. Whole-class discussion to clarify thinking and gain new learning.

Suggested ideas: See the Downloadable Weblinks and Worked Example below. The issue should be the same as for the Main activity.

Worked Example for the Starter activity

Topic: Law and criminality

See Downloadable 4.6.

Ideas for pictures suggesting issues that might be resolved by certain courses of action:

- Knife crime: 'Irresponsible reporting of knife crime "alienating young people"', an article in *The Guardian*, 28 March 2017 https://www.theguardian.com/membership/2017/mar/28/irresponsible-reporting-of-knife-alienating-young-people
- Gun violence: 'Ipsos/USA today: Crime/gun violence is top concern among young people', https://www.ipsos.com/en-us/news-polls/ipsos-usa-today-poll-crime-gun-violence-top-concern-among-young-people

- Gang violence: 'Girls forced into gang violence, says Christian youth charity report', an article on Premier Christian Radio, 24 March 2014 https://premierchristian.news/en/news/article/girls-forced-into-gang-violence-says-christian-youth-charity-report
- Youth crime (vandalism): 'Why electronic surveillance monitoring may not reduce youth crime', an article in *The Conversation*, 14 June 2018 https://theconversation.com/why-electronic-surveillance-monitoring-may-not-reduce-youth-crime-97864
- Bullying: 'Is your child the bully or the bullied?', an article on *USA Today* website, 10 August 2019 https://eu.usatoday.com/story/life/2019/08/10/stop-bullying/1965145001/

Steps to developing a course of action:

- Identify the issue. (What is the issue? It is important that learners understand that it is something that can have a course of action to help resolve it/make a positive difference to it.)
- Explain the issue. (For whom is it an issue? Why is it an issue?)
- Search for and organise information. (What information do I need? Where do I get this information? Primary and/or secondary research sources?)
- Check the resources needed. (Is my course of action realistic? What do I need to implement it?)
- Check whether the course of action is SMART – **S**pecific, **M**easurable, **A**chievable, **R**ealistic and **T**ime-bound.
- Form a plan. (Who does what and when?)
- Evaluate the course of action. (Does my course of action help resolve the issue/make a positive difference to it?)

Main activity (approx. 20–25 mins)

Good for: Working in teams to discuss and plan a course of action to address an issue.

Activity: Complete the table as a team for the issue given (see the Worked Example) and decide on the best course of action ready for Lesson 8.

Differentiation: Review the Worked Example from Section 2 Analysis, Lesson 4 with the whole class. Elicit understanding about how to generate courses of action for issues. Learners work in mixed ability teams.

Ways of working: Whole class for modelling and then in teams.

Different opinions/perspectives: Encourage learners to consider the issue from different perspectives to arrive at a suitable course of action.

Learner response and feedback: Encourage learners to ask each other questions such as:

- Is this course of action specific/related to the issue?
- Is this course of action measurable? How can we tell if it works?
- Is this course of action achievable? Are we going to be able to do it?
- Is this course of action realistic (given our situation, the resources we have etc.)?
- Is this course of action achievable in the time we have?

Suggested answers/ideas: See the Worked Example.

Worked Example for the Main activity

Topic: Law and criminality

Example issue: What can we do to help reduce the amount of bullying in our community?

Possible course of action 1: Create a poster/series of posters about what bullying is and the effects of bullying. Display them around school and in the sports and community centres.

- Reasons for/against: Easy to do, can involve learners, will reach a wide audience, need to do some research about the effects, get some case studies, talk to people who have suffered from bullying, ask teacher's permission, might need to avoid being too emotional – just present facts rather than specifics.
- Other: Who to involve? How time consuming? How to get case studies? What about students' feelings and confidentiality?

Possible course of action 2: Create a presentation to present to different groups in school informing peers about bullying: what it is; reasons for it; how to spot it and what to do if bullied.

- Reasons for/against: Easy to do, learners can work as teams, will reach a wide audience of students and parents, need to do some research, need to talk to school counsellor, class teacher and headteacher.

- Other: Who to involve? Who does what? Target audience? Resources needed?

Possible course of action 3: Produce a leaflet/brochure with key information about bullying to hand out, what to do if bullied, how to spot bullying, support available with contact names and contact details etc.

- Reasons for/against: Easy to do; can be done individually or in teams; in class.
- Other: Who to involve – need permissions (class teacher and headteacher)? Who does what? Resources needed? Time frame?

Independent reflection activity (approx. 5–10 mins)

Good for: Encouraging learners to consider their learning from the lesson, specifically skills they have used and skills they still need to improve. This might be communicating (joining in discussions), reflection and evaluation (thinking about the strengths and limitations of possible courses of action etc.). Encourage learners to consider how they have used certain skills (e.g. communication skills to share ideas with their team) and why they need to improve a skill (e.g. for more effective teamwork or to feel more confident in voicing their own opinion).

This activity can be done in class, at home or in self-study time.

Getting better at reflection skills: Lesson 8

Lesson 8 continues the sequence from Lesson 7 and focuses on working in teams to plan and produce a team outcome after deciding on a course of action to help resolve an issue.

CAMBRIDGE STAGE 8 REFLECTION LEARNING OBJECTIVES

78Rf.01 Explain personal contribution to teamwork and identify targets for improvement

78Rf.04 Identify skills learned or improved during an activity and relate to personal strengths and areas for improvement

LEARNING GOALS

To get better at:

- explaining my personal contribution(s) to teamwork
- explaining the skills that I have learned or improved
- explaining areas for improvement.

How will I know if I reach my goals?

Good for: Learners to give examples of their learning from the lesson. They can complete the table at any point in the lesson but might do it at the end.

Resources needed

- Learner's Skills Book 8
- Downloadable 4.7

Prior learning (approx. 5–10 mins)

Good for: Building on previous knowledge, learning and understanding. This might be from Cambridge Primary Global Perspectives, from Cambridge Global Perspectives Stage 7, from other subject areas or from previous Cambridge Global Perspectives Stage 8 lessons (especially Lesson 7).

Activity: Review learning about courses of action from Lesson 7 and what needs considering when proposing a course of action.

Differentiation: Learners work in teams.

Suggested answers/ideas: A course of action is a plan or method for achieving a specific aim or goal and might involve producing an outcome like a video, leaflet/brochure or presentation. A course of action might also be an event like a cake sale to raise money for a particular cause. Learners need to consider:

- Is the course of action specifically/explicitly related to the issue?
- Is the course of action measurable? How can we tell if it works?
- Is the course of action achievable? Are we going to be able to do it?
- Is the course of action realistic (sensible given the situation and the resources available etc.)?
- Is the course of action achievable in the time available?

Not issue specific.

Starter activity (approx. 10 mins)

Good for: Reviewing suggestions for courses of action from Lesson 7.

Activity: Learners discuss and answer the questions about the course of action they decided on in Lesson 7. They should answer 'yes/no' and then give an explanation. They should come up with an idea for a team outcome for this course of action; for example, a poster/series of posters, a presentation, a leaflet/brochure, a video clip or podcast with a series of pictures. They should check their idea for their team outcome with you.

Suggested answers:

1. Is the course of action specific to the issue? Yes, because it focuses on helping to …
2. Is it measurable? Yes, because we can ask for feedback from … . to see if it helped …
3. Is it achievable? Yes, because we can do it in class and after school if necessary.
4. Is it realistic? Yes, because we have all the resources.
5. Can you do it in the time allowed? Yes, because we have the rest of this lesson, the next lesson and some home study time when we can meet.

Main activity (approx. 20–25 mins)

Good for: Planning and designing a team outcome in teams.

Activity:

1. Learners use a grid to create an action plan to complete their team outcome. Discuss who does what and when. See Downloadable 4.7 and the Worked Example for the Main activity for a completed plan.
2. Once they have their plan, learners can complete their team outcome. suggest that they create their outcome on a separate piece of paper. They can use some of this lesson and some of Lesson 9 to complete it.
3. Encourage learners to make amendments according to areas for improvement suggested in the Peer feedback.

Differentiation: Learners work in teams. Encourage teams to allocate tasks according to personal strengths.

Ways of working: In teams/small groups.

Different opinions/perspectives: Encourage learners to consider the audience for their team outcome as they plan and complete it.

Learner response and feedback: Encourage learners to give feedback to each other as they are completing their team outcome. Some questions to ask:

- Is that part clear?
- Do we need to add … ?
- Do you think there's too much/little information about … ?
- Would it be better to put … ?
- Is it suitable for … ?
- Have we included different perspectives?

Learners could also give peer feedback on each other's plans as they are completed as well as feedback on the final team outcome.

Suggested answers: See Downloadable 4.7 and Worked Example for the Main activity for planning to complete a leaflet to make a positive difference to the issue of bullying/help prevent bullying in school. Learners can pass their outcome to another team for peer feedback in task 3.

Worked Example for the Main activity

Topic: Law and criminality

See Downloadable 4.7.

Issue	How can we make a positive difference to the issue of bullying in school?			
Course of action	To produce a leaflet about what bullying is, how to prevent it and what to do/who to see if you are a bully or are being bullied.			
Team outcome	Leaflet with causes and effects of bullying and support for bullies and those being bullied.			
Team members	Mark, Max, Maria, Marta			
Start date	Completion date	Task (What?) Action (How?)	Person responsible	Resources needed
21/03	28/03	Reasons for bullying; interview peers and teachers; ask class teacher's permission	Mark and Max	Pen and notepad/ phone to record interviews
21/03	28/03	Effects of bullying; interview peers and teachers; ask class teacher's permission	Maria and Marta	Pen and notepad/ phone to record interviews
21/03	28/03	Support for bullies; interview teachers and school counsellor	Mark and Max	Pen and notepad/ phone to record interviews
21/03	28/03	Support for those being bullied; interview teachers and school counsellor	Maria and Marta	Pen and notepad/ phone to record interviews
28/03	04/03	Create leaflet from research on computer	Mark: introduction (purpose and audience) Max: reasons for bullying Maria: effects of bullying Marta: support and contact details	Computer, paper, printer

Independent reflection activity (approx. 5–10 mins)

Good for: Encouraging learners to consider their learning from the lesson, their individual contribution to the teamwork, what skill they learned and what skill they still need to improve. Encourage learners to reflect on how they are going to improve the skill identified, e.g. by sharing more ideas with team members.

This activity can be done in class, at home or in self-study time.

Getting better at reflection skills: Lesson 9

Lesson 9 is the last lesson in the sequence of Lessons 7–9. Learners complete their team outcome and reflect on the challenges of teamwork, how to address these challenges and their personal perspective.

CAMBRIDGE STAGE 8 REFLECTION LEARNING OBJECTIVES

78Rf.02 Consider the benefits and challenges of teamwork experienced when working together to achieve a shared outcome

78Rf.03 Consider ways that personal perspective on an issue may have changed as a result of conducting research or exploring different perspectives

LEARNING GOALS

To get better at:

- explaining the challenges of teamwork
- explaining how to overcome the challenges of teamwork
- explaining my personal perspective on an issue.

How will I know if I reach my goals?

Good for: Learners to give examples of their learning from the lesson. They can complete the table at any point in the lesson but might do it at the end.

Resources needed

Learner's Skills Book 8

Prior learning (approx. 5–10 mins)

Good for: Building on previous knowledge, learning and understanding. This might be from Cambridge Primary Global Perspectives, from Cambridge Global Perspectives Stage 7, from other subject areas or from previous Cambridge Global Perspectives Stage 8 lessons (particularly Lessons 7 and 8).

Activity: In teams, learners discuss the challenges of teamwork and, in particular, a challenge they faced in Lesson 8. They discuss and record how they overcame this challenge and any other ways of overcoming the challenges of teamwork.

Differentiation: Learners work in teams to discuss and support each other.

Suggested answers:

1 Not listening to each other, resulting in doing the wrong thing; arguing about who does what; not finishing on time/not meeting the deadline; not sharing information; no one in charge of organisation.

2 and **3** Listen to each other; take turns; plan better to meet deadlines; divide up the tasks further; support and help each other; ask questions; be more organised; have a leader; respect the team; state ideas clearly; compromise; ask your teacher etc.

Not issue specific.

Starter activity (approx. 10 mins)

Good for: Reviewing peer feedback about the team outcome.

Activity: Teams work together to review their team outcome after Peer feedback. They identify changes they need to make for their team outcome to be more effective.

Suggested answers: Specific to the team outcome created for Lessons 7–9.

Main activity (approx. 20–25 mins)

Good for: Evaluating a team outcome.

Activity: Learners work in teams. They finish their team outcome taking account of any changes identified as a result of Peer feedback. They can use the checklist in Lesson 8 to evaluate their own team outcome and, once completed, can ask another team to evaluate their team outcome. They can also use the checklist in this lesson to evaluate their team outcome from the perspective of the audience.

Differentiation: Learners work in teams.

Ways of working: Small groups to develop team-working skills.

Different opinions/perspectives: Encourage learners to evaluate their team outcome from the perspective of their target audience.

Learner response and feedback: Encourage learners to give feedback to each other using the questions from the grid in task 2 and in the Tips.

Suggested ideas: See the Worked Example below.

Worked Example for the Main activity

Topic: Law and criminality

Evaluating a team outcome, using the questions on the grid:

1 Advise looking back to see if the team outcome addresses the issue/answers the question.

2 Learners explain how the team outcome can help to resolve the issue; for example, by encouraging bullies and those being bullied to seek help.

3 Learners explain how the outcome can make a positive difference to the issue; for example, by bringing it to the attention of all concerned and by suggesting ways forward for bullies and for those being bullied.

4 Learners make a judgement based on answers to questions 1–3.

5 Learners explain how the outcome addresses both the perspectives of the bullied and the bullies.

6 Learners decide if the course of action (raising awareness and giving support by way of a leaflet) is likely to work to achieve the desired outcome. For example, will bullies and those bullied seek support as a result of the leaflet?

7 Learners might come up with other questions to evaluate their team outcome, for example, Is the content clear? Is it suitable for the age and experience of the audience? Is it helpful (ask the audience)? Will it need changing often (e.g. contact details might change)?

Independent reflection activity; Self-assessment; Issue review (approx. 15–20 mins)

Good for: Encouraging learners to consider their thoughts about what reflection is, consider how these might have changed whilst completing this section and give reasons for any change. Learners also reflect on and explain how their personal perspective about the issue studied in Lessons 7–9 has developed or changed; for example, I used to think that bullying was part of normal school life. I didn't realise the effect it had on people, sometimes for the rest of their life.

Learners also complete the self-assessment to set their own learning targets. They think about and shade where they think they are at this time in their learning. 'With help' refers to guidance given (pointing a learner in the right direction, although examples should still come from the learner); for example, from you, other learners, previous work done by the learner in their Learner's Skills Book.

For the Issue review, learners explore the issue used in this section to develop reflection skills.

These activities can be done in class, at home or in self-study time.

Suggested examples:

78Rf.01 *Explain personal contribution to teamwork and identify targets for improvement.* Example: 'My personal contribution was asking the school counsellor about the support in place in school for those being bullied; this used a personal strength, which is having confidence to speak with adults. I also created the page in the leaflet giving details of the support available in school, which used my good communication skills. I need to make sure that I listen more carefully to instruction as I was a little unclear what I was supposed to ask the school counsellor and I might have got more information if I had asked more specific questions.'

78Rf.02 *Consider the benefits and challenges of teamwork experienced when working together to achieve a shared outcome.* For example:

- Benefits of teamwork: more ideas; not struggling alone; mutual support; workload shared equally; can use individual strengths for a collective whole; some tasks can be completed faster, and so on.
- Challenges of teamwork: personality clashes; conflict over who does what; not agreeing on ideas; team members absent; team members not as committed to the team as others, and so on.
- Overcoming challenges: listen to each other; take turns; meet deadlines; divide up the tasks further; support and help each other; ask questions; be more organised; have a leader; respect the team; state ideas clearly; compromise; ask the teacher.

78Rf.03 *Consider ways that personal perspective on an issue may have changed as a result of conducting research or exploring different perspectives.* A personal perspective is what you think about an issue as a result of your experiences and what you learn from others and from research. Your personal perspective can change or develop as you become more informed about an issue. Example: 'I used to think that bullying was part of normal school life. I didn't realise the awful effects it had on people, sometimes for the rest of their life. My personal perspective has changed as a result of the research I did into the effects of being bullied.'

78Rf.04 *Identify skills learned or improved during an activity and relate to personal strengths and areas for improvement.* Example: 'I am getting better at reflecting on my personal perspective due to being asked to consider if my opinion about bullying had changed or not. It had and I could say why. I must get better at evaluating by not only saying what's good about something but also pointing out areas for improvement. I will try to do this the next time we give feedback on each other's work.'

Showcasing your skills: Reflection

Good for: Showing learners how others felt at the end of this section after practising and developing their reflection skills. Your learners have learned a lot about their own changing perspectives. They may have even learned, for the first time, that their perspectives are important.

This section requires levels of insight and honesty into learners' own performances (as part of their team) and into their own opinions. It is important for them to make taking notes about these views, and the changes in what they think and know, habitual.

Activity: This is an opportunity for learners to reflect on elements of their work that they are particularly pleased with. Read through and discuss the reflections with your class. There are a number of reflection tasks you could try. You could ask your learners to:

- 'Reflect and sketch': Learners could use pictures, numbers and symbols (but no words) to illustrate what they have done well in this section.
- 'Exit tickets': This activity can kick-start reflective thinking. Ask learners to write down a few sentences to summarise their successes in this section. They should add them to a box when the lesson ends.

Projects: If learners have had ample opportunities to practise the other skills required, they could also showcase their reflection skills by attempting Project 8.2 or Project 8.3, available at cambridge.org/go, both of which have reflection learning objectives.

Section 5 Collaboration

Introduction

The learning objectives for collaboration skills for Stage 8 are the same as those for Stage 7 and focus on the following:

- cooperation and interdependence
- engaging in teamwork.

However, you might also find opportunities within these lessons to develop some of the other Cambridge Global Perspectives skills. For example, when completing teamwork, not only will learners be developing collaboration skills, it is likely that they will also be developing their reflection skills.

The ideas given in this Teacher's Resource are suggestions only, and the activities can be used with any of the Cambridge Global Perspectives Challenges or topics for Stages 7 to 9. Downloadables and Worked Examples are provided for many learning activities. They are linked to the topics 'Climate change, energy and resources' and 'Law and criminality'. It is hoped that the ideas in this book will help you structure your lessons in an active learning way with input from you as the teacher to help guide and support learners to become more collaborative learners.

Collaboration skills overview

Learning objectives	78Cl.01 Work positively within a team to achieve a shared outcome and improve team work, for example by contributing useful ideas, offering solutions to problems, encouraging other team members to participate and being open to others' ideas. 78Cl.02 The team assigns roles and divides tasks fairly, considering the skills of team members and the time available, resolves disagreements and works together to achieve a shared outcome.
Topic ideas	Climate change, energy and resources; Development, trade and aid; Law and criminality
Key points	• Understanding the terms 'claim', 'reasoning', 'evidence', 'fact', 'opinion' and 'bias'. • Collaboration is about working together as a team towards a shared outcome and not simply sitting in a group and working independently. • Understanding that individual strengths and characteristics lead to effective teamwork. • Knowing that effective teamwork relies on the participation and contributions of the whole team. • Knowing some strategies to avoid/resolve conflict for effective teamwork as conflict in teams is normal. • Feedback is important in developing learning and skills.
Language support	Pre-teach key vocabulary: collaboration; claim; reasoning; evidence; fact; opinion; bias; relevant; compromise; shared outcome; argument; presentation; perspective; supported; structure; conflict; resolve; valid; combined; critical; feedback; highlights; areas for improvement. Also include any issue-specific vocabulary for the topics – Climate change, energy and resources; Development, trade and aid; Law and criminality

Cross-skills links	Research 78Rs.01 Construct relevant research questions. 78Rs.02 Identify and begin to reference a range of print and multimedia sources and use them to locate relevant information and answer research questions. 78Rs.03 Select an appropriate method and conduct research to test predictions and begin to answer a research question. 78Rs.04 Select, organise and record relevant information from a range of sources and findings from primary research, using appropriate methods. Analysis 78A.01 Identify ideas and evidence from different perspectives within different sources, on a given issue. 78A.02 Explain how graphical or numerical data supports an argument or a perspective. 78A.03 Explain causes of a local or global issue and consequences on others. 78A.04 Suggest and justify different actions to make a positive difference to a national or global issue. Evaluation 78E.01 Evaluate sources, considering the author and purpose, recognising that some sources may be more credible than others. 78E.02 Discuss the effectiveness of an argument, making explicit reference to its structure and use of evidence. Reflection 78Rf.01 Explain personal contribution to teamwork and identify targets for improvement. 78Rf.02 Consider the benefits and challenges of teamwork experienced when working together to achieve a shared outcome. 78Rf.03 Consider ways that personal perspective on an issue may have changed as a result of conducting research or exploring different perspectives. 78Rf.04 Identify skills learned or improved during an activity and relate to personal strengths and areas for improvement. Communication 78Cm.01 Present information and arguments clearly with some reasoning, referencing sources where appropriate. 78Cm.02 Listen to ideas and information and offer relevant and well-judged contributions that demonstrate understanding of the issue.

Let's start thinking about collaboration!

Good for: Enthusing your learners about the skill they are going to work on. Collaboration is all about working together as a team. There are lots of ways learners can do this. In the early stages, they may be excited to work with their friends, but they may struggle to organise themselves in ways that are effective and fair. Or they may be disappointed that their group doesn't include their friends. Similar problems of organisation and fairness may arise!

The questions give learners ideas about the issues they might explore as they develop their evaluation skills. The first idea suggested is the Challenge 'What everyone needs: How is aid money spent?' and the topic 'Development, trade and aid'. Both the Challenge and the issue focus on the skill of collaboration. The second idea is based on the topic 'Law and criminality'. Although not linked to specific Challenges, the downloadables provide everything your learners need to complete the activities in section 5 and become proficient collaborators.

Activity: Look at these pages with your learners. You could begin with a quick question and answer session. Ask learners:

- What does 'collaboration' mean?
- What kinds of questions could we ask?
- Where might we get our information?
- What issue shall we explore?

Ask learners to each write down one question they have about this section, e.g. on a sticky note. Collate and display their questions so that they are easy to refer to as you work through this section. In that way, learners can see their questions being answered.

Starting with collaboration skills: Lesson 1

Lesson 1 focuses on explaining what the term 'collaboration' means, giving examples of collaboration in Cambridge Global Perspectives lessons and exploring the characteristics that team members need for effective collaboration.

CAMBRIDGE STAGE 8 COLLABORATION LEARNING OBJECTIVES

78Cl.01 Work positively within a team to achieve a shared outcome and improve team work, for example by contributing useful ideas, offering solutions to problems, encouraging other team members to participate and being open to others' ideas

78Cl.02 The team assigns roles and divides tasks fairly, considering the skills of team members and the time available, resolves disagreements and works together to achieve a shared outcome

LEARNING GOALS

To start to:

- explain the term 'collaboration'
- explain how to collaborate in Cambridge Global Perspectives lessons
- explain the characteristics that team members need for effective collaboration.

How will I know if I reach my goals?

Good for: Learners to give examples of their learning from the lesson. They can complete the table at any point in the lesson but might do it at the end.

Resources needed

- Learner's Skills Book 8
- Downloadable 5.1

Prior learning (approx. 5–10 mins)

Good for: Building on previous knowledge, learning and understanding. This might be from Cambridge Primary Global Perspectives, from Cambridge Global Perspectives Stage 7, from other subject areas or from previous Cambridge Global Perspectives Stage 8 lessons.

Activity: Learners reflect on what the term 'collaboration' means and give examples of ways they collaborate in Cambridge Global Perspectives lessons.

Differentiation: Learners work in pairs for support or can work individually for challenge.

Suggested answers/ideas: Answers will vary. Collaboration is working with others towards a shared outcome. Examples in Cambridge Global Perspectives lessons include team projects, working towards and producing a shared outcome such as a presentation, video clip, podcast, poster and so on.

Not issue specific.

Starter activity (approx. 10 mins)

Good for: Enabling learners to identify and explain the type of characteristics needed for effective teamwork.

Activity: Learners decide which characteristics are important for a team to have when organising a charity event. They should try to explain why they think the team should have these characteristics.

Ways of working: Individual and pair feedback.

Suggested answers: Answers will vary. Any reasonable and relevant response. Encourage learners to say why these characteristics are important/necessary or not. For example, after they have discussed with their partner, they might have changed their view and agree with their partner that sharing good ideas, listening to others and being organised are the three most important characteristic as, without these, an event is unlikely to happen. Learners will probably identify A, B, C, D, E, H, I and L as important because they all help with effective teamwork. F, G, J and K are not helpful for effective teamwork.

Main activity (approx. 20–25 mins)

Good for: Enabling learners to work together in small groups to gain and share information and develop collaboration skills.

Activity:

1 Give learners a text to read or read through a text with learners and ask them to answer the questions individually or in pairs (see Downloadable 5.1 and the Worked Example).

3 Give each team a different question (see the Worked Example for ideas). Each team discusses their question to complete each of the K, W and H parts of the chart. Encourage learners to be specific (e.g. website addresses for the 'how' part rather than just 'internet') and to write three bullet points for each section of the table.

Water – why worry?

'Water is running out,' say Friends of the Planet. We need to act now if there is to be enough water for future generations.

71% of Earth is covered in water, so why should we be so worried about saving it? There are many reasons:

- Only 3% of water on Earth is fresh water. Of this, only 0.5% is safe drinking water, according to the United Nations. The other 2.5% of fresh water is inaccessible – in ice caps, glaciers, the atmosphere, the soil or under Earth's surface – or is too polluted for human consumption.

So what can you do?

You can …

1 Save about 6 litres of water a minute just by turning off the tap whilst brushing your teeth.

2 Get someone to fix those leaking taps. For every leaky tap, about 60 litres of water gets drained away every week.

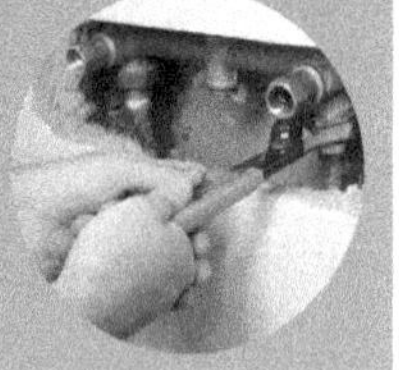

3 Keep your showers short and save water. Every minute you spend in the shower can use up to 17 litres of water.

- The human race cannot exist without water. Every person on Earth needs at least 20–50 litres of clean, safe water a day for drinking, cooking and keeping themselves clean.

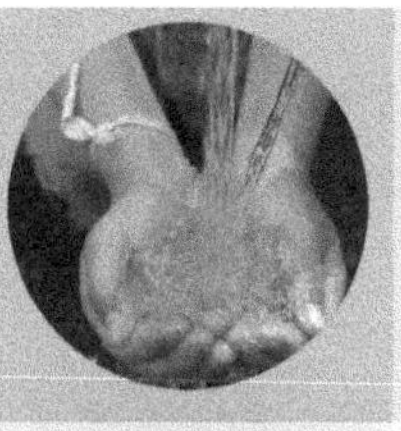

- Water is essential for food production. Without water, there is no means of feeding livestock or watering crops and, therefore, providing food for the ever-increasing population. It takes 5000–20 000 litres of water to produce 1kg of meat and 500–4000 litres of water to produce 1kg of wheat.

4 Use rainwater to water your plants. Get a water butt to collect rainwater so you can save up to 5000 litres of water a year. Plants don't need fresh, clean, drinking water.

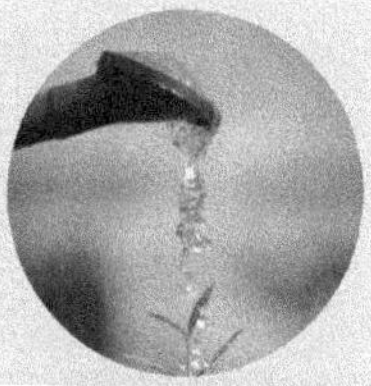

5 Eat less meat and dairy. Producing these uses a lot of water. Reducing your consumption of them not only helps conserve water, you'll also be helping to protect the climate as meat and dairy production causes global warming.

Friends of the Planet, 2020

Differentiation: Mixed ability group work as support. Choice of text (see Downloadable 5.1 and the Worked Example). Refer learners to the Tips about claims, reasoning, evidence and bias.

Ways of working: Individually or in pairs for support and then in small groups/teams.

Different opinions/perspectives: Encourage learners to consider the different opinions/viewpoints/perspectives explored in the text, as well as forming their own opinion about what they see.

Learner response and feedback: Encourage learners to focus on the issue/key points (claim, reasoning, evidence, bias) in the text.

Suggested answers/ideas: See the Worked Example for the Main activity.

Worked Example for the Main activity

Topic: Climate change, energy and resources

See Downloadable 5.1.

Question ideas for team discussion:

- Should governments restrict the amount of water people use?
- Is lack of access to safe, clean drinking water a global issue?
- Can an individual do anything about water shortages?
- Is water scarcity a national issue?
- Does water scarcity impact global society?
- Does climate change impact water availability?

Suggested answers/ideas

1 **a** The text is about issues to do with water: lack of access to safe, clean drinking water, disease by drinking unsanitary water supplies, water shortages etc.

b Example claims: 'Water is running out'; 'We need to act now if there is to be enough water for future generations'; 'The human race cannot exist without water'; 'Water is essential for food production'.

c Example reasoning: We need water because each one of us 'needs at least 20–50 litres of clean, safe water a day for drinking, cooking and keeping themselves clean.'

d Example evidence: 'Friends of the Planet'; 'Only 3% of water on Earth is fresh water. Of this, only 0.5% is safe, drinking water, according to the United Nations. The other 2.5% of fresh water is inaccessible.'; 'It takes 5000–20 000 litres of water to produce 1kg of meat and 500–4000 litres of water to produce 1kg of wheat.'

e Bias: Yes, as the source is Friends of the Planet, an organisation concerned about the planet wanting to make people aware of what they can do to save water.

Independent reflection activity (approx. 5–10 mins)

Good for: Learners to give examples of how they might have participated in teamwork; for example, by discussing the main ideas in the text; by contributing claims, reasoning, evidence or examples of bias to the discussion about the text; by participating in discussion about the question given; by completing the KWH chart. Encourage learners to also give examples of how they could improve their participation in teamwork.

This activity can be done in class, at home or in self-study time.

Starting with collaboration skills: Lesson 2

Lesson 2 focuses on using information gained in Lesson 1 to plan and present arguments to develop a certain perspective and reflecting on the strengths individual team members brought to the teamwork.

CAMBRIDGE STAGE 8 COLLABORATION LEARNING OBJECTIVES

78CI.01 Work positively within a team to achieve a shared outcome and improve team work, for example by contributing useful ideas, offering solutions to problems, encouraging other team members to participate and being open to others' ideas

78CI.02 The team assigns roles and divides tasks fairly, considering the skills of team members and the time available, resolves disagreements and works together to achieve a shared outcome

LEARNING GOALS

To start to:

- explain the strengths of individual team members
- share relevant ideas with team members
- work with a team to plan and produce a shared outcome.

How will I know if I reach my goals?

Good for: Learners to give examples of their learning from the lesson. They can complete the table at any point in the lesson but might do it at the end.

Resources needed

- Learner's Skills Book 8
- Downloadable 5.2

Prior learning (approx. 5–10 mins)

Good for: Building on previous knowledge, learning and understanding. This might be from Cambridge Primary Global Perspectives, from Cambridge Global Perspectives Stage 7, from other subject areas or from previous Cambridge Global Perspectives Stage 8 lessons (especially Lesson 1).

Activity: Learners identify the strengths that different members of their team possess.

Differentiation: Learners work in teams.

Suggested answers/ideas: Any reasonable and relevant response. Different teams will have different strengths/characteristics. The aim of the activity is to get learners thinking about the strengths in their team.

Starter activity (approx. 5–10 mins)

Good for: Reviewing words/phrases relevant to the issue and related question. The question can be the one from the Main activity in Lesson 1 or a new question related to the issue. Learners will prepare arguments for a presentation based on this question in the Main activity.

Activity: Learners brainstorm relevant words/phrases to prepare a response to the question in readiness for the Main activity.

Suggested answers: Any reasonable and relevant response, depending on the question (see the Worked Example below for question ideas).

Worked Example for the Starter activity

Topic: Climate change, energy and resources

Question ideas:

- Should governments restrict the amount of water people use?
- Is lack of access to safe, clean drinking water a global issue?
- Can an individual do anything about water shortages?
- Is water scarcity a national issue?
- Does water scarcity impact global society?
- Does climate change impact water availability?
- Are humans responsible for biodiversity and ecosystem loss?
- Does water scarcity impact biodiversity and ecosystem loss?
- Is the protection of the Amazon rainforest a global issue?
- Is climate change responsible for biodiversity and ecosystem loss?

Main activity (approx. 20–25 mins)

Good for: Getting teams to work together to come up with arguments from a certain perspective for a research question and to produce a presentation.

Activity: See Downloadable 5.2. Teams need to decide which perspective they are presenting and relate their arguments to this perspective. Learners can do research, discuss their arguments and choose up to five arguments/points/claims. They should justify their claims with reasoning and support their claims with evidence. They then create their presentation, using the checklist provided in task 2 to check their work.

Differentiation: Team members support each other.

Ways of working: In teams/small groups.

Different opinions/perspectives: Encourage learners to value all the viewpoints/opinions/perspectives explored.

Learner response and feedback: Learners help each other prepare arguments for the perspective chosen.

Suggested answers: These will vary according to the question and perspective chosen (see the Worked Example below).

Worked Example for the Main activity

Topic: Climate change, energy and resources

See Downloadable 5.2.

Question ideas: As for the Worked Example for the Starter activity. All these questions can be explored from the YES/NO perspective to allow learners to produce arguments for each.

Note that the sources referenced have been created for the purpose of this activity and are not real websites.

Our question: Are humans responsible for biodiversity and ecosystem loss?	
Our perspective: Yes, humans are responsible for biodiversity and ecosystem loss.	
Arguments	
1	Loss of wildlife habitats is the biggest threat to the ecosystem. Urban development caused by humans creates changes to natural areas, which cause loss of vegetable species and therefore animal extinction. Source: Bartlett (2019). 'Causes of biodiversity and ecosystem loss'. [Online], https://www.lossofwildlife.com/science/ (Accessed 05/09/2023).
2	Introduction of genetically modified organisms and exotic species causes biodiversity and ecosystem loss. This can lead to an imbalance in the ecological system with loss of existing/native species, and this can allow in pathogens that destroy species. Source: Green (2019). 'Invasive species are a threat to biodiversity'. [Online], https://www.invasivespecies.co.uk/threat/biodiversity (Accessed 05/09/2023).
3	Overexploitation of resources is a major threat to wildlife. Overexploiting a species, such as fish, can have detrimental effects on the ecosystem as some fish are top predators and their disappearance changes the ecosystem. Overfishing with trawler nets also impacts on the oceans as they destroy habitats. Source: Winkler (2019). 'How overfishing destroys the ecosystem'. [Online], https://www.overfishing.com/trawlernets (Accessed 06/09/2023).
4	Climate change is threatening the ecosystem. Climate change causes the planet to warm up quickly, which could harm many species and cause species extinction as species struggle to survive in new climatic conditions. Source: James (2019). 'Climate change causes species extinction'. [Online], https://www.climatechange.org/speciesextinction/ (Accessed 06/09/2023).
5	Pollution harms the ecosystem. All pollution affects the survival of species, particularly air pollution as it robs species of oxygen. Source: Cotter (2019). 'Pollution and species survival'. [Online], https://www.pollution.org/global/wildlifethreat/ (Accessed 06/9/2023).

Independent reflection activity (approx. 5–10 mins)

Good for: Encouraging learners to consider the strengths they brought to the team (e.g. organising who does what) and areas they need to improve on to be an effective member (e.g. trying not to dominate discussions).

This activity can be done in class, at home or in self-study time.

Starting with collaboration skills: Lesson 3

Lesson 3 focuses on presenting the perspectives and arguments from Lesson 2 and reflecting on the strengths of team members.

CAMBRIDGE STAGE 8 COLLABORATION LEARNING OBJECTIVES

78Cl.01 Work positively within a team to achieve a shared outcome and improve team work, for example by contributing useful ideas, offering solutions to problems, encouraging other team members to participate and being open to others' ideas

78Cl.02 The team assigns roles and divides tasks fairly, considering the skills of team members and the time available, resolves disagreements and works together to achieve a shared outcome

LEARNING GOALS

To start to:

- explain the strengths of individual team members
- work with a team to review and evaluate a shared outcome.

How will I know if I reach my goals?

Good for: Learners to give examples of their learning from the lesson. They can complete the table at any point in the lesson but might do it at the end.

Resources needed

- Learner's Skills Book 8
- Downloadable 5.3

Prior learning (approx. 5–10 mins)

Good for: Building on previous knowledge, learning and understanding. This might be from Cambridge Primary Global Perspectives, from Cambridge Global Perspectives Stage 7, from other subject areas or from previous Cambridge Global Perspectives Stage 8 lessons (especially Lesson 2).

Activity: Learners put the criteria for presenting an argument in a presentation in order from most to least important. They can use this as a checklist for their own presentation in the Starter activity.

Differentiation: Learners work in pairs/teams. Discuss responses in class.

Suggested answers/ideas: Any reasonable and relevant response. There may be some disagreement, which is fine, and some of the criteria might be equally as important as others. The main thing is the discussion and the thinking that the activity generates.

Not issue specific.

Starter activity (approx. 10 mins)

Good for: Reviewing the presentation of arguments from Lesson 2.

Activity: Learners review their presentation, making any changes according to the criteria rating from the Prior learning activity. They could also use the questions in the Main activity as a checklist.

Differentiation: Learners are working in teams.

Suggested answers: Will vary.

Main activity (approx. 20–25 mins)

Good for: Judging the quality of another team's presentation and arguments.

Activity: One team presents to another team and each team completes the grid to give feedback (see Downloadable 5.3 and the Worked Example).

Differentiation: Learners work in teams to discuss and give feedback on another team's presentation.

Ways of working: In teams/small groups.

Different opinions/perspectives: Stress that the feedback given is the opinion of the team. There is space in the grid for the evaluating team to give peer feedback and for the presenting team to record teacher feedback, self-assessment and targets for development.

Learner response and feedback: Whilst they work as a team, learners ask each other questions as given on the grid.

Suggested answers: Will vary according to presentations and feedback (see downloadable 5.3 and the Worked Example).

Worked Example for the Main activity

Topic: Climate change, energy and resources

See Downloadable 5.3.

Team: Jack's team

Question: Are humans responsible for biodiversity and ecosystem loss?

Perspective: Yes, humans are responsible for biodiversity and ecosystem loss.

	Opinion	Comment
Was there a range of visuals (text, images)?	😀	Well-chosen visuals
Was the type of font and size suitable for the audience?	😀	Yes, easy to read
Was there a clear structure (beginning, middle and end)?	🙂	Conclusion missing
Was the content relevant?	😀	Yes, very
Did the content answer the question?	😐	Not really, as there was no conclusion
Were the arguments supported with evidence?	🙂	Some but not all points had evidence
Did the presenters make eye contact with the audience?	😀	Yes
Did they speak clearly?	😀	Yes
Were all members of the team actively involved?	🙂	Jack did more than the others and Maria did very little

Peer feedback comments:

Highlight(s): Engaging presentation with lots of ideas relevant to the issue.

Area(s) for development: Needs a conclusion to answer the question and would benefit from further evidence to support points made.

Teacher feedback comments: Agree with peer feedback

Self-assessment comments: Agree with peer feedback

Targets for development:

1 Add a conclusion
2 Answer the question
3 Include at least one piece of evidence for each point.

Independent reflection activity; Self-assessment; Issue review (approx. 15–20 mins)

Good for: Encouraging learners to think about the strengths and skills used this lesson. Encourage learners to give an example in support of each strength and skill used; for example, 'collaboration' and 'worked effectively with team members to give feedback from the whole team'. Also, encourage learners to identify the skills each team member still needs to work on.

Learners also complete the self-assessment to set their own learning targets before they move on. They think about and shade where they think they are at this time in their learning. 'With help' refers to guidance given (pointing a learner in the right direction, although examples should still come from the learner); for example, from you, other learners, previous work done by the learner in their Learner's Skills Book.

For the Issue review, learners explore the issue used in this section to develop collaboration skills.

These activities can be done in class, at home or in self-study time.

Suggested examples:

78Cl.01 *Work positively within a team to achieve a shared outcome and improve team work, for example by contributing useful ideas, offering solutions to problems, encouraging other team members to participate and being open to others' ideas.* Example: 'Including the facts from sources was my idea and they were all included in our final presentation to add evidence to the points made. There was a disagreement about which was the biggest threat to biodiversity and ecosystem loss, so we decided to look for the information in three different sources and this resolved the disagreement.'

78Cl.02 *The team assigns roles and divides tasks fairly, considering the skills of team members and the time available, resolves disagreements and works together to achieve a shared outcome.* Example: 'Collaboration in Cambridge Global Perspectives is working together to achieve a shared outcome like a presentation. I am good at listening to others. This helped when I made my presentation page as I knew to add reasoning and evidence to support the claims I made.'

Developing collaboration skills: Lesson 4

Lesson 4 focuses on developing an understanding about how to resolve conflict during teamwork as learners work towards a shared outcome.

CAMBRIDGE STAGE 8 COLLABORATION LEARNING OBJECTIVES

78Cl.01 Work positively within a team to achieve a shared outcome and improve team work, for example by contributing useful ideas, offering solutions to problems, encouraging other team members to participate and being open to others' ideas

78Cl.02 The team assigns roles and divides tasks fairly, considering the skills of team members and the time available, resolves disagreements and works together to achieve a shared outcome

LEARNING GOALS

To develop knowledge and understanding about:

- resolving conflict during teamwork
- collaboration to achieve shared outcomes.

How will I know if I reach my goals?

Good for: Learners to give examples of their learning from the lesson. They can complete the table at any point in the lesson but might do it at the end.

Resources needed

- Learner's Skills Book 8
- Downloadables 5.4, 5.5 and 5.6

Prior learning (approx. 5–10 mins)

Good for: Building on previous knowledge, learning and understanding. This might be from Cambridge Primary Global Perspectives, from Cambridge Global Perspectives Stage 7, from other subject areas or from previous Cambridge Global Perspectives Stage 8 lessons.

Activity: Learners consider their learning from Lesson 3 and discuss it with their team.

Differentiation: Learners can look back at their Independent reflection, Self-assessment and Learning targets from Lesson 3.

Suggested answers/ideas: Any reasonable and relevant response. Encourage learners to respond honestly and to look back through Lessons 1–3 to see if they are developing their collaboration skills.

3 Suggest that, in the Action column, each learner writes one goal that they can achieve this lesson. They should come back to this goal in the Independent reflection activity to reflect on their achievement of this goal.

Not issue specific.

Starter activity (approx. 10 mins)

Good for: Reviewing issue-specific vocabulary.

Activity: Learners give ideas and thoughts to answer the questions you provide (see the Worked Example for the Starter activity).

Ways of working: Individual/pair and class discussion.

Suggested answers/ideas: Depends on the issue (see the Worked Example below).

Worked Example for the Starter activity

Topic: Law and criminality

Sub-topic: Youth crime

See Downloadable 5.4.

Example questions:

1. Do you think youth crime is a major issue in global society today?
2. What sort of crimes do young people commit?
3. Is youth crime a big issue in … (insert country)?
4. Why do you think youth crime is a big issue in … (insert country)?
5. What do you think might deter young people from committing crimes?
6. What do you think can be done about youth crime in … (insert country)?

Suggested answers:

1. Yes, as we hear about it a lot in the news from all over the world.
2. Answers will vary; for example, robbery, burglary, vandalism, trashing/throwing litter in the street, violence against another person, fraud.
3. Answers will vary depending on country.
4. Answers will vary; for example, young people have become disillusioned due to cuts in services that affect them (e.g. after-school clubs and activities, community services such as youth clubs and local leisure facilities), the increasing cost of living and living in disadvantaged areas.
5. Answers will vary; for example, providing more activities for young people to participate in after school, ensuring that young people are receiving a relevant and useful education – including learning about social responsibility, involving community law enforcement officers and parents in talks and activities in the local community.
6. Answers will vary; for example, training and education programmes, proper support and guidance for families from affected communities, tackling the issue of gangs.

Main activity (approx. 20–25 mins)

Good for: Working in pairs and in teams to write questions to gain information about an issue.

Activity: Learners work in pairs to formulate questions for a specific purpose (see Downloadables 5.5 and 5.6 and the Worked Example). They complete the table with their questions. They then discuss the questions as a team with another pair and produce the five best questions. As a class, all the questions can be discussed and the best five questions chosen. Remind learners of question starters (What? Where? When? Who? Why? How?)

Differentiation: Learners can work in pairs for support before sharing with their team. Some further research might be needed to come up with questions.

Ways of working: Individually/pairs and in teams.

Different opinions/perspectives: Learners will be formulating questions to gain information to start to develop a local perspective about an issue.

Learner response and feedback: Encourage learners to help and support each other in teams. They can ask questions such as:

- What are you trying to find out?
- Do you think they will know the answer to that?
- Do you think there is an answer to that?
- Does that question help us find out … ?
- Is that question too difficult?
- Does that question require a fact/opinion as the answer?

Suggested answers/ideas: Depends on the issue scenario chosen (see the Worked Example below).

Worked Example for the Main activity

Topic: Law and criminality

Sub-topic: The litter problem

See Downloadables 5.5 and 5.6.

Scenario: Interviewing community leaders or local community officer (it might be a video interview or could be face-to-face) about littering in the community to raise awareness of the problems of littering, reduce the amount of litter/rubbish in the area and pledge not to drop litter/rubbish (to be developed in Lesson 5).

Interview questions:

- Is litter/rubbish a big problem in the community?
- How much litter/rubbish is dropped on average per day/per week/per month?
- Where do people mostly drop their litter/rubbish?
- Why do you think young people drop litter/rubbish?
- What is the main source of litter/rubbish?
- What happens to dropped litter/rubbish?
- How can we reduce the amount of litter/rubbish that people drop?

Suggested answers: Answers will vary. Questions can be given to the community leaders/officer beforehand to give enough time for learners to process the answers ready for Lesson 5.

Independent reflection activity (approx. 5–10 mins)

Good for: Encouraging learners to refer back to their Prior learning to see if they have achieved their goal to improve their collaboration skills. They also identify any conflict whilst working in teams to produce questions and say how this conflict was resolved. For example, not listening to the ideas of others can create conflict as people don't feel that their ideas are being heard. A way to resolve this is to listen and make brief notes as each person speaks.

This activity can be done in class, at home or in self-study time.

Developing collaboration skills: Lesson 5

Lesson 5 follows on from Lesson 4. Learners use the information they have gained to create a shared outcome.

CAMBRIDGE STAGE 8 COLLABORATION LEARNING OBJECTIVES

78Cl.01 Work positively within a team to achieve a shared outcome and improve team work, for example by contributing useful ideas, offering solutions to problems, encouraging other team members to participate and being open to others' ideas

LEARNING GOALS

To develop knowledge and understanding about:

- collaborating to produce shared outcomes
- contributing ideas to shared outcomes.

How will I know if I reach my goals?

Good for: Learners to give examples of their learning from the lesson. They can complete the table at any point in the lesson but might do it at the end.

Resources needed

- Learner's Skills Book 8
- Downloadable 5.7

Prior learning (approx. 5–10 mins)

Good for: Building on previous knowledge, learning and understanding. This might be from Cambridge Primary Global Perspectives, from Cambridge Global Perspectives Stage 7, from other subject areas or from previous Cambridge Global Perspectives Stage 8 lessons (especially Lesson 4).

Activity: Review learning about what a shared outcome is and examples of a shared outcome.

Differentiation: Learners can work in pairs and share with another pair (their team).

Suggested answers: Any reasonable and relevant response.

1 **a** A shared outcome is a product produced by a team to meet a specific aim or purpose. It is then presented to a specific audience/group of people.

b Ideas: brochure, leaflet, presentation, charity awareness event, poem, song, story, pledge (see the Worked Example for the Main activity), awareness campaign, video clip, podcast/audio recording, board game etc.

Starter activity (approx. 10 mins)

Good for: Reviewing information gained from Lesson 4 in preparation for creating the team outcome.

Activity: Learners answer questions about the information they gained in Lesson 4.

Ways of working: Individual, pair and whole-class discussion.

Suggested answers: Depends on issue and information gained.

Main activity (approx. 20–25 mins)

Good for: Creating a shared outcome to address a local issue.

Activity: Learners work in teams to create a first draft of their shared outcome (see Downloadable 5.7 and the Worked Example). They can share their first draft in Lesson 6 for feedback before finalising their outcome.

Differentiation: Learners work in teams to create a shared outcome. Different teams can produce different outcomes. Learners can refer to the answers to their questions in the Starter activity. Encourage them to share the workload; for example, one pair might need to do some further research whilst another pair starts to write sentences.

Ways of working: In teams/small groups.

Different opinions/perspectives: Learners are creating an outcome using information gained from a local perspective.

Learner response and feedback: Encourage learners to discuss their progress.

Suggested ideas: Teams can produce any outcome, but it should contribute to the issue they are investigating, for example, to raise awareness about the issue; to promote … ; to take action in support of … (see the Worked Example for an idea).

Worked Example for the Main activity

Topic: Law and criminality

See Downloadable 5.7.

Issue: Litter
Shared outcome: Pledge to not drop litter
Aim: To take action to help stop litter/rubbish dropping in our community

First draft of shared outcome

Nearly half the population (about 48%) admit to dropping litter/rubbish.

This term, we, ___________________________, pledge to do the following things to help reduce the amount of litter dropped. We will also encourage our families to help too.

1 ....

2 ....

3 ....

4 ....

5 ....

Here are some suggestions for action we can take.

No Food Waste

- Give a presentation to our peers in school about the litter issue(problem) and not dropping litter/rubbish.
- Tell our families about the issue(problem)s created by dropping litter/rubbish.
- Take any litter/rubbish home with us.
- Take a cloth bag to the shop to avoid buying a plastic carrier bag.
- Take lunch to school in a reusable container.
- Tell people we see in the street to pick up any litter/rubbish they throw.
- Help mum/dad take all the rubbish to the recycling.
- Keep our street clean by going out once a week to pick up any litter.
- Only eat somewhere that has a bin to put any litter/rubbish in after eating.
- Put litter in our pocket until we see a litter/rubbish bin.
- Participate in the community clean-up day.
- Post on social media about the issue(problem)s of littering.
- Campaign to have more litter bins in the community.
- Produce a poster to put up around school reminding everyone to put litter/rubbish in the bin.
- Learn more about the issue(problem)s of littering and how to prevent it.

We are Champions at not dropping litter/rubbish.

We pledge to do at least five of these this term ☐
GOLD No Food Waste Champions

We pledge to do at least three of these this term ☐
SILVER No Food Waste Champions

We pledge to do at least one of these this term ☐
BRONZE No Food Waste Champions

Signed: .... Date: ....

Independent reflection activity (approx. 5–10 mins)

Good for: Encouraging learners to reflect on their contributions to teamwork by asking them for their best idea and how they have used communication skills this lesson; for example, by sharing some relevant ideas to add to their shared outcome.

This activity can be done in class, at home or in self-study time.

Developing collaboration skills: Lesson 6

Lesson 6 follows on from Lesson 5 and focuses on completing shared outcomes after feedback.

CAMBRIDGE STAGE 8 COLLABORATION LEARNING OBJECTIVES

78CI.01 Work positively within a team to achieve a shared outcome and improve team work, for example by contributing useful ideas, offering solutions to problems, encouraging other team members to participate and being open to others' ideas

LEARNING GOALS

To develop knowledge and understanding about:

- collaborating to produce shared outcomes
- how feedback can improve shared outcomes.

How will I know if I reach my goals?

Good for: Learners to give examples of their learning from the lesson. They can complete the table at any point in the lesson but might do it at the end.

Resources needed

- Learner's Skills Book 8
- Downloadable 5.8

Prior learning (approx. 5–10 mins)

Good for: Building on previous knowledge, learning and understanding. This might be from Cambridge Primary Global Perspectives, from Cambridge Global Perspectives Stage 7, from other subject areas or from previous Cambridge Global Perspectives Stage 8 lessons (especially Lessons 4 and 5).

Activity: Review learning about the importance of giving and receiving feedback.

Differentiation: Learners can work in pairs for support and share ideas with another pair.

Suggested answers/ideas: Any reasonable and relevant response. Feedback gives learners clear guidance on how to improve their learning. Feedback also helps learners understand the skill being developed and the issue taught. It provides learners with the necessary information to improve their learning towards achieving learning objectives.

Starter activity (approx. 10–15 mins)

Good for: Developing understanding about how to give both positive and helpful feedback on each other's work.

Activity: Learners look at the example shared outcome document (see Downloadable 5.8 and the Worked Example) and decide on two highlights and one area for improvement. An authentic piece of learner work might be used. Learners then give and receive feedback on their draft outcome from Lesson 5. Teams will then incorporate this feedback into the final version of their shared outcome in the Main activity.

Ways of working: Team and whole-class discussion.

Suggested answers/ideas: Depends on the work given (see Downloadable 5.8 and the Worked Example below, with useful descriptors for giving feedback).

Worked Example for the Starter activity

Topic: Law and criminality

Sub-topic: Littering

See Downloadable 5.8.

Example shared outcome document for feedback:

Aim: To encourage others to take action to reduce the amount of litter/rubbish dropped in our community
OUR PLEDGE TO TAKE ACTION TO REDUCE THE AMOUNT OF LITTER IN OUR COMMUNITY
Everyone drops litter. This term, we, ________________, promise to help. We will also tell our families about what we're 1 .... 2 .... 3 .... Ideas … No litter • Put litter in our pocket until we see a litter/rubbish bin. • Participate in the community clean-up day. • Post on social media about the dangers of littering. We are Champions at not dropping litter. We pledge to do at least five of these this term ☐ GOLD No Food Waste Champion We pledge to do at least three of these this term ☐ SILVER No Food Waste Champion We pledge to do at least one of these this term ☐ BRONZE No Food Waste Champion Names: ....

Constructive feedback:

Kind Use kind words and be positive.	Specific and detailed Give an exact idea of where and how the work can be improved.	Helpful Give suggestions for improvements linked to the learning objective/goal.
Examples:		
You include issue-specific words and phrases well. There are some great suggestions, which I've highlighted. I love how you have given some really good suggestions for action.	In the first part, you could have included … You need evidence to support your claim. What facts did you find out? This idea is powerful because …	Perhaps next time, you could try … Have you looked at the language support sheet to help with … ? Make sure you proofread to check you have included everything.

Suggested answers:

1 Highlights: Clear aim; clear title; outcome suitable for the aim; some good suggestions for actions; 'Champions at not dropping litter' is a great label.

2 Areas for improvement: Need more suggestions to choose from; sentence starting 'Everyone drops litter' is a claim but is not supported by evidence and is vague and incorrect; sentence starting 'We will also tell our families about what we're,' is unfinished; sentence starting 'Ideas' is too short and needs something adding, for example, 'Ideas for action'.

Discussion about feedback: Stress to learners that feedback should be kind, specific and detailed, and helpful. You can refer learners to the table at the bottom of Downloadable 5.8 to help them to give constructive feedback.

Main activity (approx. 20–25 mins)

Good for: Giving feedback and finishing shared outcome after feedback.

Activity: This leads on from the Starter activity where learners recap on the value of judging work and giving feedback. Firstly, they share their outcome with another team and give feedback. Teams then incorporate this feedback into the final version of their shared outcome. They share their final outcome with another team and give feedback. Highlights can be in one colour and areas for improvement in another. It's always a good idea to encourage more highlights than areas of improvement. Ask learners to refer to the learning objectives/goals when judging the shared outcome.

Differentiation: Learners work in teams to give feedback and improve shared outcome.

Ways of working: In teams/small groups.

Different opinions/perspectives: Remind learners that giving feedback generally means that someone will be looking at the work from a different perspective, perhaps as the user of the outcome or as the audience if the outcome has to be watched or listened to.

Learner response and feedback: Learners are giving feedback to each other.

Suggested answers: Feedback will vary. See ideas for giving feedback in the Worked Example for the Starter activity.

Independent reflection activity; Self-assessment; Issue review (approx. 15–20 mins)

Good for: Encouraging learners to consider what they used to think teamwork was and how their thinking might have developed. Encourage learners to give an example from any of Lessons 1–6.

Learners also complete the self-assessment to set their own learning targets before they move on. They think about and shade where they think they are at this time in their learning. 'With help' refers to guidance given (pointing a learner in the right direction, although examples should still come from the learner); for example, from you, other learners, previous work done by the learner in their Learner's Skills Book.

For the Issue review, learners explore the issue used in this section to develop collaboration skills.

These activities can be done in class, at home or in self-study time.

Suggested examples:

78Cl.01 *Work positively within a team to achieve a shared outcome and improve team work, for example by contributing useful ideas, offering solutions to problems, encouraging other team members to participate and being open to others' ideas.* Example: 'Some of the suggestions were my idea, which meant that we used the information gained from the interview in our outcome. There was a bit of conflict as we were all talking at once, so I suggested we take it in turns. This helped when we made our outcome better after the feedback.'

78Cl.02 *The team assigns roles and divides tasks fairly, considering the skills of team members and the time available, resolves disagreements and works together to achieve a shared outcome.* Example: 'I am good at organising who does what. This helped when we completed our pledge as we managed to meet the deadline set.'

Getting better at collaboration skills: Lesson 7

Lesson 7 focuses on reflecting on and evaluating teamwork.

CAMBRIDGE STAGE 8 COLLABORATION LEARNING OBJECTIVES

78Cl.01 Work positively within a team to achieve a shared outcome and improve team work, for example by contributing useful ideas, offering solutions to problems, encouraging other team members to participate and being open to others' ideas

78Cl.02 The team assigns roles and divides tasks fairly, considering the skills of team members and the time available, resolves disagreements and works together to achieve a shared outcome

LEARNING GOALS

To get better at:

- understanding what effective teamwork is
- reflecting on roles and responsibilities during teamwork
- evaluating teamwork.

How will I know if I reach my goals?

Good for: Learners to give examples of their learning from the lesson. They can complete the table at any point in the lesson but might do it at the end.

Resources needed

- Learner's Skills Book 8
- Downloadable 5.9

Prior learning (approx. 5–10 mins)

Good for: Building on previous knowledge, learning and understanding. This might be from Cambridge Primary Global Perspectives, from Cambridge Global Perspectives Stage 7, from other subject areas or from previous Cambridge Global Perspectives Stage 8 lessons (especially Lessons 3–6).

Activity: Review all the skills used during teamwork. Encourage learners to give examples from Lessons 3–6.

Differentiation: Allow thinking time. Learners list all the skills they have used during the teamwork. You can start them off: for example, listening, writing (communication skills) to share ideas to create the shared outcome.

Suggested answers: Any reasonable and relevant examples.

Research: asking/writing questions, looking for information, organising and recording information.

Analysis: exploring causes and consequences, gaining ideas from different perspectives, supporting shared outcome with evidence, completing shared outcome, identifying course of action.

Evaluation: judging which sources to use to provide relevant information, evaluating teamwork (strengths and limitations of the team and own work processes).

Reflection: reflecting on effectiveness of teamwork and own contribution to teamwork, identifying skills learned and how perspective on the issue changed/developed.

Communication: listening, reading, writing, speaking, producing shared outcome.

Collaboration: working in a team, taking turns, listening to others, sharing ideas, and so on.

Not issue specific.

Starter activity (approx. 10 mins)

Good for: Reviewing what effective teamwork looks like.

Activity: Ask learners to predict what might be included in a document about effective teamwork. Then give learners a text (poster/infographic) about effective teamwork (see Downloadable 5.9 and the Worked Example for the Starter activity). You could ask them to produce something similar based on the title, but that will take longer.

Not issue specific.

Worked Example for the Starter activity

See Downloadable 5.9.

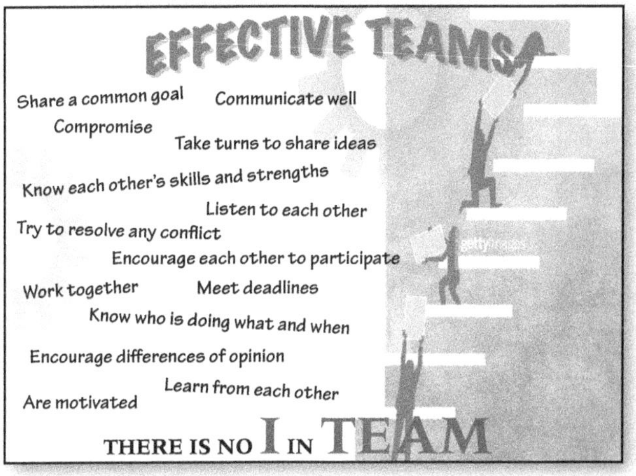

Suggested answers:

1 1 Listen to each other.
2 Try to resolve conflict.
3 Meet deadlines set.

3 1 I tried to do this when we were planning our outcome so I could write down all the ideas.
2 There was some disagreement about how we should present our ideas, so I suggested a compromise and that resolved the conflict.
3 I ensured that we kept to the time frame for each part of the task so that we could meet the deadline set.

4 Ineffective teamwork is just considering yourself and not the team. Ideas include the opposite of those on the poster.

Main activity (approx. 20–25 mins)

Good for: Working in teams to reflect on their own teamwork during Lessons 3–6 and on the production of their shared outcome.

Activity: Discuss and complete the tables as a team.

Differentiation: Learners work in teams to review how they worked together as a team.

Ways of working: In teams/small groups.

Different opinions/perspectives: Encourage learners to be honest and give their own opinions.

Learner response and feedback: Encourage learners to ask each other questions such as:

- When did you participate?
- How often did you participate?
- What did you say?
- Which idea was yours?
- Did you keep the team on task? How?
- Did you help to resolve conflict? How?
- What feedback did you give to improve our shared outcome?
- Did you help to review our shared outcome? How?

Suggested answers: Answers will vary according to teams.

Independent reflection activity; Self-assessment; Issue review (approx. 15–20 mins)

Good for: Encouraging learners to consider the skill(s) they have improved this lesson and which one(s) still need improving; for example, joining in discussions, reflecting on work produced to evaluate it by giving and receiving feedback on strengths and areas for improvement, and so on.

Learners also complete the self-assessment to set their own learning targets. They think about and shade where they think they are at this time in their learning. 'With help' refers to guidance given (pointing a learner in the right direction, although examples should still come from the learner); for example, from you, other learners, previous work done by the learner in their Learner's Skills Book.

There is no Issue review for this section as learners have been focusing on the skill of collaboration.

These activities can be done in class, at home or in self-study time.

Suggested examples:

78Cl.01 *Work positively within a team to achieve a shared outcome and improve team work, for example by contributing useful ideas, offering solutions to problems, encouraging other team members to participate and being open to others' ideas.* Example: 'Some of the suggestions on our pledge were my idea. Other suggestions came from Hans. I encouraged him to share his ideas as we had discussed them, but he hadn't shared them with the whole team.'

78Cl.02 *The team assigns roles and divides tasks fairly, considering the skills of team members and the time available, resolves disagreements and works together to achieve a shared outcome.* Example: 'I was good at organising who did what and I noticed how good Marta was at dividing the tasks so that everyone was involved.'

Showcasing your skills: Collaboration

Good for: Showing learners how others felt at the end of this section after practising and developing their collaboration skills. Learners have learned a lot about their own ability to organise themselves and their group members. Collaboration takes a lot of organisation and maturity, so don't be discouraged if they are not as effective in group tasks as they could be at this point!

As the teacher, you are very welcome to support them with their organisation. Feel free to give them guidance and structure where needed. As they become better at this important life skill, you can slowly withdraw this scaffolded support so they can make their own plans and their own decisions.

Teachers are part of the journey, but are also on their own journey. You may find that the teacher on this 'Showcasing your skills' page had similar problems to your own.

The key here is for learners to become better and better at collaborating with others. Encourage your learners to reflect at the end of their group task in the same way as the learners on this page do. In this way, your learners can improve.

Activity: This is an opportunity for learners to reflect on elements of their work in this section that they are particularly pleased with. Read through and discuss the reflections with your class. There are a number of reflection tasks you could try, for example:

- 'Two stars and a wish' means 'Two things I am pleased with and one thing I want to improve on'. Ask your learners to write their own 'two stars and a wish' on a sticky note and stick it on the board.
- Ask each learner to cut out two speech bubbles. On the first one, they write 'What went well'. On the second they write 'Even better if'. Create a class display of speech bubbles.

Projects: If learners have had ample opportunities to practise the other skills required, they could also showcase their collaboration skills by attempting Project 8.1, available at cambridge.org/go, which has collaboration learning objectives.

Section 6 Communication

Introduction

The learning objectives for communication skills for Stage 8 are the same as those for Stage 7 and focus on the following:

- communicating information
- listening and responding.

However, you might also find opportunities within these lessons to develop some of the other Cambridge Global Perspectives skills. For example, when identifying ideas and evidence from different perspectives within different sources and recording these ideas in their own words, not only will learners be developing communication skills, it is likely that they will also be developing their analysis skills.

The ideas given in this Teacher's Resource are suggestions only, and the activities can be used with any of the Cambridge Global Perspectives Challenges or topics for Stages 7 to 9. Downloadables and Worked Examples are provided for many learning activities. They are linked to the topic 'Climate change, energy and resources'. It is hoped that the ideas in this book will help you structure your lessons in an active learning way with input from you as the teacher to help guide and support learners to become more communicative learners.

Communication skills overview

Learning objectives	78Cm.01 Present information and arguments clearly with some reasoning, referencing sources where appropriate. 78Cm.02 Listen to ideas and information and offer relevant and well-judged contributions that demonstrate understanding of the issue.
Topic ideas	Change in culture and communities; Climate change, energy and resources; Migration and urbanisation; Law and criminality; Digital world; Education for all
Key points	• Structure helps with the organisation of ideas and allows for easy reading. • In Cambridge Global Perspectives, paragraphs need a claim, reasoning and evidence. • Understanding that communication is about being able to present ideas in own words, and not simply copying and pasting someone else's ideas. • Credit should be given to all sources of information referred to in the text by using a reference list. • Written work needs a logical structure with an introduction, main points and conclusion. • Transition words like 'finally', 'to sum up' and 'to conclude' are useful to introduce a conclusion. • Transition words like 'such as', 'like' and 'for instance' are useful when referring to evidence. • Knowing that there is a difference between listening and hearing and that it is important to show people that you are actively listening. • Understanding that listening is just as important as speaking. • Appreciating the importance of feedback to improve work and develop communication skills.

Language support	Pre-teach key vocabulary: communication; feature; argument; paragraph; structure; beginning; middle; end; introduction; claim; conclusion; reasoning; supporting evidence; logical; sum up; heading/title; reference; citation; critical; feedback; highlights; areas for improvement; transition words; verbal and non-verbal feedback; paraphrasing; transition words like 'therefore', 'however', 'in addition'; cross-referencing; active listening; passive listening. Also include any issue-specific vocabulary for the topics – Change in culture and communities; Climate change, energy and resources; Migration and urbanisation; Law and criminality; Digital world; Education for all
Cross-skills links	**Research** 78Rs.01 Construct relevant research questions. 78Rs.02 Identify and begin to reference a range of print and multimedia sources and use them to locate relevant information and answer research questions. 78Rs.03 Select an appropriate method and conduct research to test predictions and begin to answer a research question. 78Rs.04 Select, organise and record relevant information from a range of sources and findings from primary research, using appropriate methods. **Analysis** 78A.01 Identify ideas and evidence from different perspectives within different sources, on a given issue. 78A.02 Explain how graphical or numerical data supports an argument or a perspective. 78A.03 Explain causes of a local or global issue and consequences on others. 78A.04 Suggest and justify different actions to make a positive difference to a national or global issue. **Evaluation** 78E.02 Discuss the effectiveness of an argument, making explicit reference to its structure and use of evidence. **Reflection** 78Rf.01 Explain personal contribution to teamwork and identify targets for improvement. 78Rf.02 Consider the benefits and challenges of teamwork experienced when working together to achieve a shared outcome. 78Rf.03 Consider ways that personal perspective on an issue may have changed as a result of conducting research or exploring different perspectives. 78Rf.04 Identify skills learned or improved during an activity and relate to personal strengths and areas for improvement. **Collaboration** 78Cl.01 Work positively within a team to achieve a shared outcome and improve team work, for example by contributing useful ideas, offering solutions to problems, encouraging other team members to participate and being open to others' ideas. 78Cl.02 The team assigns roles and divides tasks fairly, considering the skills of team members and the time available, resolves disagreements and works together to achieve a shared outcome.

Let's start thinking about communication!

Good for: Enthusing your learners about the skill they are going to work on. Learners can look at some ideas on what 'communication' means and read some tips to get them thinking about how they might start to organise the information they wish to communicate.

The questions give learners ideas about the issues they might explore as they develop their communication skills. The first idea suggested is the Challenge 'How can we use resources more sustainably?' and the topic 'Climate change, energy and resources'. The Challenge and the issue focus on the skill of communication. The second teaching idea is based on the topic 'Climate change, energy and resources'. It isn't linked to a specific Challenge, but the downloadables provide everything your learners need to complete the activities in section 6 and become proficient at communication.

Activity: Look at these pages with your learners. You could begin with a quick question and answer session. Ask learners:

- What does 'communication' mean?
- What kinds of questions could we ask?
- Where might we get our information?
- What issue shall we explore?

Ask learners to each write down one question they have about this section, e.g. on a sticky note. Collate and display their questions so that they are easy to refer to as you work through this section. In that way, learners can see their questions being answered.

Starting with communication skills: Lesson 1

Lesson 1 focuses on explaining the term 'communication', giving examples of communication in Cambridge Global Perspectives lessons and exploring how texts are structured.

CAMBRIDGE STAGE 8 COMMUNICATION LEARNING OBJECTIVES

78Cm.01 Present information and arguments clearly with some reasoning, referencing sources where appropriate

LEARNING GOALS

To start to:

- explain the term 'communication'
- give examples of communication in Cambridge Global Perspectives lessons
- explain how to structure a text.

How will I know if I reach my goals?

Good for: Learners to give examples of their learning from the lesson. They can complete the table at any point in the lesson but might do it at the end.

Resources needed

- Learner's Skills Book 8
- Downloadable 6.1

Prior learning (approx. 5–10 mins)

Good for: Building on previous knowledge, learning and understanding. This might be from Cambridge Primary Global Perspectives, from Cambridge Global Perspectives Stage 7, from other subject areas or from previous Cambridge Global Perspectives Stage 8 lessons.

Activity: Learners work with a partner to explain the term 'communication' and give examples of how learners communicate in Cambridge Global Perspectives lessons.

Differentiation: Learners work in pairs and as a class to share their ideas. Give a time limit. The idea is to get learners thinking about what the skill of communication involves and how they communicate.

Suggested answers/ideas: Answers will vary. Communication is a way of transferring information from one place to another, either by using spoken or written texts or by non-verbal means such as pictures and diagrams. Examples in Cambridge Global Perspectives include reading texts (articles, poems, posters), listening to texts (songs, podcasts, video clips), writing texts (summaries, paragraphs, arguments), discussing ideas (debates, conversations, feedback for improvement).

Not issue specific.

Starter activity (approx. 10–15 mins)

Good for: Enabling learners to start exploring text structure.

Activity:

1. Learners decide which features are the most and least important in structuring text. For challenge, they should try to explain why they think these features are important.
2. Learners add a further feature (e.g. there's a conclusion, the content is clear, claims are justified with reasoning, the arguments are supported with evidence, credit to someone else's work is given in the body of the text (cited) as well as in the reference list).
3. Learners discuss why it's important that texts have structure. Encourage learners to think about why some texts might be easier to read/follow than others.
4. Stress the importance of using their own words as this helps learners clarify their own understanding. Ask them to avoid just writing a list and, instead, to explain their features; for example, 'You need to start with the claims you want to make, ensuring that they are clear, have reasoning to justify them and evidence to support them.'

Ways of working: In pairs and whole-class discussion.

Suggested answers:

1. Answers/choices will vary. Any reasonable and relevant response. All the features are important.
2. Reasons include: 'Without the title, it's not clear what the text will be about'; 'If there is no conclusion, we don't know what the author thinks or what the answer to the question is'; 'Without paragraphs, a text is difficult to follow'.
3. Answers will vary; for example, 'It's important that texts have structure so we can follow the author's train of thought.'
4. Answers will vary; for example, 'Create a list of points (claims) with justifications (reasoning) and evidence; organise these points so that the structure is logical; create a paragraph for each point to keep the ideas together; use transition words like 'therefore', 'however', 'in addition' to help the flow; use headings to help the reader know what each section/paragraph is about; write a conclusion to sum up the key points/answer the question'.

Main activity (approx. 20–25 mins)

Good for: Enabling learners to work together in small groups to explore the features of a text.

Activity: Show learners a text (see Downloadable 6.1 and the Worked Example) and ask them to answer the questions.

Differentiation: Work in mixed ability groups as support. Choice of text (see Downloadable 6.1 and the Worked Example). Refer learners to the Tips about texts and text structure.

Ways of working: In teams/small groups.

Different opinions/perspectives: Encourage learners to consider the perspective that the ideas and evidence in the text come from, as well as forming their own opinion about what they read.

Learner response and feedback: Encourage learners to focus on answering the questions and giving examples.

Suggested answers/ideas: See the Worked Example.

Worked Example for the Main activity

Topic: Climate change, energy and resources

See Downloadable 6.1.

Any of the 17 UN Sustainable Goals for Development would be good to use for this activity. The boxed text is based on Sustainable Development Goal 11: Sustainable cities and communities.

Note that the sources referenced have been created for the purpose of this activity and are not real websites.

IS IT POSSIBLE TO HAVE SAFE, INCLUSIVE, SUSTAINABLE CITIES?

Introduction

Cities are great places to live. Cities are centres of science and technology. Ideas for business and society are developed in cities. Cultural diversity is in abundance in cities; for example, in theatres, restaurants and concert halls. Cities have helped people advance both socially and economically (Grey, 2018). More than half the world's population now lives in a city (Worldwide Institution, 2007) and this is on the increase, so cities need to be safe, inclusive and sustainable. But can they be?

Furthermore, the number of people living in cities is set to increase to five billion in approximately ten years – by the year 2030. Therefore, it is important that cities can cope with this population increase, that people who live in cities feel safe and included, and that city living is sustainable. For, as well as being beneficial for business and society, city living also brings challenges.

One of the biggest challenges in cities is inequality as more than a billion people live in slums around the world, and this is on the increase. It is not unusual to see a wealthy area of a city surrounded by a slum, bringing into sharp focus the difference between the 'haves' and the 'have nots'. In fact, in some cities, the gap between rich and poor is overwhelming. It is common to see homeless people lining up for food brought by volunteers outside some of the world's wealthiest stores and restaurants.

Another challenge in cities is the level of global carbon emissions. Cities are responsible for approximately 70 per cent of global carbon emissions (Bart, 2019). The main polluters are vehicles, even though some cities have banned private cars from the city centre, which has helped with pollution and congestion. Encouraging the use of public transport has to be a priority to reduce the use of private vehicles and therefore reduce pollution from this source, states Grey (2018).

Conclusion

If more and more people are choosing to live in cities, then something needs to be done to ensure that there is enough safe, affordable housing so that people can have a decent standard of living where their health is not at risk. City councils need to manage the waste produced by households and ensure a clean environment with green spaces. Governments need to prioritise cities so that people can prosper and live healthy lives. If they do this, then it is possible to have sustainable cities.

References

Bart (2019). 'Reducing pollution through the use of public transport'. [Online], https://www.sustainabledevelopmentgoals.com/cities (Accessed 10/09/2023).

Grey (2018). 'Benefits of cities'. [Online], https://www.cities.org/benefits/globally (Accessed 11/09/2023).

https://www.worldwideinstitution.org/cities-population

Suggested answers:

1 **a** Cities are popular places for people to live so it's important to have safe and sustainable cities.

b There are five paragraphs:

1. Introduction: Cities are great places to live. The number of people living in cities is increasing and they need to be safe and sustainable – links to the title.
2. It is important that people feel safe and included, and that city living is sustainable as more and more people are now living in cities.
3. There are challenges, and one of the biggest is inequality: 1 billion people live in slums and there is a rich/poor divide in many cities.
4. A further challenge is global carbon emissions causing pollution.
5. Conclusion: sums up ideas. Something needs doing to make sure there is affordable housing, cities are safe and people can have a decent, healthy standard of living.

c Yes. The end of paragraph 2 suggests 'challenges' and paragraph 3 talks about inequality as one of the challenges of cities; paragraph 4 follows this by suggesting pollution as a further challenge.

d Yes, the conclusion does sum up the content of the text; however, it also brings up new points, so point this out to learners. The conclusion could be stronger.

e Yes

f There is a reference list. It is mostly accurate but one of the references is just the website address. The author, date, title of the article and date the website was accessed need including.

g Answers will vary. Spellings are correct.

h Generally, the text is well-structured, but point out the problem with the conclusion and remind learners that all claims need reasoning to justify them and evidence to support them. The sub-headings for the introduction and conclusion help with the structure.

Independent reflection activity (approx. 5–10 mins)

Good for: Learners to reflect on what they learned about text structure that they had not thought about before; for example, that a paragraph is made up of a claim, reasoning for the claim and supporting evidence; a text is structured when it has a beginning, middle and end; a conclusion sums up points made in the rest of the text. Encourage learners to reflect on the skill(s) they have used this lesson, for example, research skills to answer questions about the text.

This activity can be done in class, at home or in self-study time.

Starting with communication skills: Lesson 2

Lesson 2 focuses on the features that help to make up a well-structured argument to enable learners to start creating their own well-structured arguments.

CAMBRIDGE STAGE 8 COMMUNICATION LEARNING OBJECTIVES

78Cm.01 Present information and arguments clearly with some reasoning, referencing sources where appropriate

78Cm.02 Listen to ideas and information and offer relevant and well-judged contributions that demonstrate understanding of the issue

LEARNING GOALS

To start to:

- explain what helps to make a well-structured argument
- create a well-structured argument with a claim, reasoning and supporting evidence
- contribute ideas to show understanding of an issue.

How will I know if I reach my goals?

Good for: Learners to give examples of their learning from the lesson. They can complete the table at any point in the lesson but might do it at the end.

Resources needed

- Learner's Skills Book 8
- Downloadable 6.2

Prior learning (approx. 5–10 mins)

Good for: Building on previous knowledge, learning and understanding. This might be from Cambridge Primary Global Perspectives, from Cambridge Global Perspectives Stage 7, from other subject areas or from previous Cambridge Global Perspectives Stage 8 lessons.

Activity: Learners discuss the features, tick the ones they think make up a well-structured argument and say why they think these features are important.

Differentiation: Learners can look back to the work done in the last lesson and refer to the Tips in Lessons 1 and 2.

Suggested answers/ideas: All the features contribute to a well-structured argument. A reference list is necessary for the supporting evidence. Perspectives are necessary, but the argument may be from only one perspective. A conclusion is necessary to sum up the key ideas and give personal perspective after research in Cambridge Global Perspectives. The main outcome of the activity is that learners understand, through discussion, the features and their importance in constructing an argument, which they will be doing in subsequent lessons.

Starter activity (approx. 5–10 mins)

Good for: Stating claims about an issue.

Activity:

1 Give learners various issues. You can use two or three different issues so that learners can work in pairs to come up with claims and then find another pair that has produced claims for the same issue (see the Worked Example for the Starter activity for suggestions). Ask learners to discuss their issue in pairs and to come up with three related claims.

2 Learners then find another pair with the same issue and discuss the claims (six in total). As a group, they choose one claim to create an argument in the Main activity.

Suggested answers: Any reasonable and relevant response. You can list all the claims on the board as you elicit them from learners at the end of task 1.

Worked Example for the Starter activity

Topic: Climate change, energy and resources

Choice of sub-topics (taken from the UN Sustainable Development Goals):

1 No Poverty

2 Zero Hunger

3 Good Health and Well-being

4 Quality Education

5 Gender Equality

6 Clean Water and Sanitation

7 Affordable and Clean Energy.

You can use two or three of these goals or any of the other UN Sustainable Development Goals. Elicit from learners what a claim is (an assertion that something is true) and stress that the claims learners come up with should allow them to research for reasoning for the claim and evidence to support the claim.

Example claims for the goals listed:

1 Social protection for all children is essential for reducing poverty.

2 There should be an end to world food hunger.

3 Good health should be available to all.

4 Everyone should have access to free primary education.

5 We must empower all girls and women.

6 Clean, safe drinking water is a right for everyone.

7 Energy sources will soon run out if they are not renewable.

Main activity (approx. 20–25 mins)

Good for: Starting to write a structured argument in pairs.

Activity: Each small group choses one claim in the Starter activity. In small groups, learners now do research and complete the table with ideas for the introduction, middle and conclusion of an argument about their claim. They should give reasoning for their claim and find some evidence to support their claim and each further point they make in the middle section of their argument see Downloadable 6.2 and the Worked Example for the Main activity.

Differentiation: Team members support each other.

Ways of working: In fours.

Different opinions/perspectives: Encourage learners to value all the viewpoints/opinions/perspectives explored and consider the perspective their argument is coming from.

Learner response and feedback: Learners help each other create their notes for the introduction, middle and conclusion.

Suggested answers: These will vary according to the claim (see the Worked Example for the Main activity).

Worked Example for the Main activity

Topic: Climate change, energy and resources

See Downloadable 6.2.

Claim ideas: See the Worked Example for the Starter activity. All these claims lend themselves to an argument with an introduction, middle and conclusion.

Suggested answer:

Claim: There should be an end to world food hunger.	
Introduction	• Currently, about 850 million people around the world go to bed hungry. Many of these are children. • World food hunger is not due to a shortage of food. • Everybody needs to recognise that there is a problem and start doing something to help.
Middle	• In some countries, lack of adequate nutrition is responsible for 45% of deaths in children under the age of 5 years. Evidence from the World Health Authority. • There could be enough food in the world, but we would need to stop food going to waste through poor storage or address the lack of transport to get it to where it is most needed. Evidence from a reputable and reliable newspaper. • People can help by petitioning governments to help stop world food hunger. Evidence from an international aid magazine.
Conclusion	• We have seen from … that food hunger exists globally today. Particularly, children are suffering from malnutrition in some parts of the world and many don't live past the age of 5 years old due to nutrition-related illnesses. • This crisis is only going to get worse unless we all do something about it such as … as suggested by …

Independent reflection activity (approx. 5–10 mins)

Good for: Encouraging learners to consider how they learned best in the lesson; for example, by explaining something to someone else and how they helped someone else to learn. Encourage learners to reflect on the skill(s) they have used this lesson; for example, research skills to search for reasoning and evidence to support a claim.

This activity can be done in class, at home or in self-study time.

Starting with communication skills: Lesson 3

Lesson 3 focuses on creating the arguments from the notes made in Lesson 2.

CAMBRIDGE STAGE 8 COMMUNICATION LEARNING OBJECTIVES

78Cm.01 Present information and arguments clearly with some reasoning, referencing sources where appropriate

78Cm.02 Listen to ideas and information and offer relevant and well-judged contributions that demonstrate understanding of the issue

LEARNING GOALS

To start to:

- explain the features that help to create a well-structured argument
- create a well-structured argument with a claim, reasoning and supporting evidence
- give and receive feedback to improve an argument.

How will I know if I reach my goals?

Good for: Learners to give examples of their learning from the lesson. They can complete the table at any point in the lesson but might do it at the end.

Resources needed

- Learner's Skills Book 8
- Downloadable 6.3

Prior learning (approx. 5–10 mins)

Good for: Building on previous knowledge, learning and understanding. This might be from Cambridge Primary Global Perspectives, from Cambridge Global Perspectives Stage 7, from other subject areas or from previous Cambridge Global Perspectives Stage 8 lessons (especially Lessons 1 and 2).

Activity: Learners write down three features of a well-structured argument. After class discussion, they can add a further two features.

Differentiation: Learners work in pairs. Discuss responses in class.

Suggested answers: Any reasonable and relevant response. Ideas covered in Lesson 2: introduction, middle, conclusion, supporting evidence, reference list, title/heading, punctuation, correct spelling, issue-specific words/phrases, paragraphs etc.

Not issue specific.

Starter activity (approx. 10 mins)

Good for: Reviewing notes made in the Main activity in Lesson 2.

Activity: Learners review their notes. They can add to them if they want to (perhaps after homework to do further research). The same groups of four (from Lesson 2 and this activity) will work together to write their argument in the Main activity.

Differentiation: Learners work in pairs and in small groups/teams.

Suggested answers: Will vary according to the claim chosen/given.

Main activity (approx. 20–25 mins)

Good for: Working as a team to create an argument to read aloud or record as a podcast.

Activity:

1 and 2 Notes are used to write a final draft of the argument related to the claim. (See Downloadable 6.3 and the Worked Example.)

3 Learners complete a self-assessment on their argument using the table.

4 Learners give feedback to another team.

Differentiation: Learners work in teams to write the script. Each team member can be allocated a different part of the script; for example, one team member does the introduction, another the conclusion and the others the points in the middle. The team meets to share and amend their part before a final review once it's all put together.

Ways of working: In teams/small groups.

Different opinions/perspectives: Stress that the argument produced is the opinion/perspective of the team based on the research done and the different perspectives explored. Also encourage learners to look at different perspectives of the ideas they include in their argument; for example, the perspective of a non-governmental organisation might be different to that of a sponsored company or that given on a government website.

Learner response and feedback: Learners ask each other questions as they are working as a team according to the checklist in task 3.

Suggested answers: Will vary according to the claim and information gained by learners (see Downloadable 6.3 for an example of a good script and the Worked Example below).

Worked Example for the Main activity

Topic: Climate change, energy and resources

See Downloadable 6.3.

Claim: There should be an end to world food hunger.

Note that the sources referenced have been created for the purpose of this activity and are not real websites.

TITLE: CAN THERE BE AN END TO WORLD HUNGER?

Introduction

This report will explore the issue of world hunger, its causes and consequences, and present a global and national perspective on the issue of world hunger. The report will present evidence to help reach an answer to the question, 'Can there be an end to world hunger?' The claims we will explore are that, currently, about 850 million people around the world go to bed hungry and many of these are children. It has been said that world food hunger is not due to a shortage of food and that everybody needs to recognise that there is a problem and start doing something to help.

Causes and consequences

Some of the main causes of world hunger are poverty (as people simply can't afford to eat and rely on food banks for some of their nutritional needs), food shortages, climate change, war and conflict, and food waste. However, opinion is divided about which is the major cause of world hunger. The consequences of insufficient food are a lack of adequate nutrition, chronic diseases and, of course, death from malnutrition. In some countries, lack of adequate nutrition is responsible for 45 per cent of deaths in children under the age of 5 years (Global Health Society, 2018).

Perspectives

According to a report issued by the Worldwide Institution (2018), the world produces enough food to feed the 7.5 billion people that inhabit it and yet one in nine people globally go hungry every day. The Worldwide Institution is a global organisation with global influence, so therefore presents a global perspective. It argues that food hunger is a global issue and more needs doing quickly if the Sustainable Development Goal of Zero Hunger is to be reached by the year 2030. This perspective is supported by many governments around the world, and other global organisations and charities (Fry, 2018).

Whilst some claim that food hunger is due to a shortage of food (Barker, 2018), others insist that this is not the case (Greene, 2019). According to Greene (2019), reporting in a well-known British newspaper, there could be enough food in the world, but we need to put an end to the amount of food waste, either from poor storage or lack of transport to get it to where it is most needed or by educating people about the importance of not wasting food. Greene supports his views by stating that in the UK, many people are unaware that the choices they make impact others globally. Portion sizes are too large, which means that food is wasted in restaurants. Food is thrown out once it gets past its sell-by date and people allow food to rot in the bottom of their fridge.

To help raise awareness about and stop the issue of world hunger, people in the UK can be more careful and not waste food, restaurants can serve smaller portions and supermarkets can ensure that they don't waste food by throwing it away, instead giving it to food banks and charities that help feed the needy.

Conclusion

We have seen from the Global Health Society that food hunger exists globally today and is the leading cause of malnutrition and death of children in some countries, many of who don't live past the age of 5 years old due to nutrition-related illnesses. The main cause of world food hunger is not food shortages, so it is important that people think about what they are eating and throwing away and try to reduce the amount of food they are wasting to help others. Our own perspective about this issue has changed as we thought at first that world food hunger was just about there not being enough food in the world. Now, we know that this isn't the case and we were shocked by the research we did for our national perspective, particularly as the report we used was written by an expert (Greene) in a well-respected national newspaper. We will try to ensure that our families and friends know not to waste food so that we know we are helping in some small but active way to resolve the issue of world food hunger.

References

Barker (2018), 'There's not enough food for everyone'. [Online], https://www.notenoughfood.org/world (Accessed 19/09/2023).

Fry (2018), 'We need to do more towards meeting Sustainable Goal 2'. [Online], https://www.sustainablegoals.com/zerohunger/ (Accessed 20/09/2023).

Greene (2019), 'Education needed in Great Britain'. [Online], https://www.greatbritain.co.uk/education/food/guardian/ (Accessed 20/09/2023).

Worldwide Institution (2018), 'There is enough food for everyone'. [Online], https://www.worldwideinstitution.org/food-for-everyone (Accessed 19/09/2023).

Global Health Society (2018), 'World food hunger'. [Online], https://www.globalhealthsociety.org/world-food-hunger (Accessed 18/09/20202319).

This text is an exemplar that you may wish to share with the learners after they have written their own script. Stress that learners are not expected to have written a perfect text. The checklist is a good way of reviewing their own work and the work of others. The learning is in the review of the text and the discussion, which will help learners create and improve their own structured arguments.

Suggested answers:

Claim: There should be an end to world food hunger			
Title: Can there be an end to world hunger?			
Is there …?	**Yes**	**No**	**Notes**
an introduction (including title)	✓		Clear title and clear introduction about what the report will cover
a conclusion (including personal perspective)	✓		Sums up – no new material apart from a personal perspective which is linked to the national perspective
a middle with claims	✓		Section on perspectives – claims include: 'food hunger is due to a shortage of food'; 'there could be enough food in the world, but we need to put an end to the amount of food waste'; 'portion sizes too large'
reasoning to justify the claims in the middle	✓		Wasting through 'poor storage or lack of transport to get it where it is most needed'; 'food is wasted in restaurants'; 'food rotting in people's fridges'
supporting evidence for the claims in the middle	✓		Greene (2019) – newspaper article for the national perspective; Worldwide Institution (global perspective)
a reference list	✓		Accurate – author/organisation, date, title, website address and date accessed
transition words/phrases (e.g. therefore, so, in summary)	✓		'yet', 'so', 'we have seen', 'now'
accurate spelling	✓		
relevant issue-specific words and phrases	✓		World food hunger; causes; consequences; shortage; waste; etc.
punctuation	✓		
paragraphs	✓		
different perspectives	✓		Global and national – some contrast
a logical structure	✓		Each point follows the next with transition words linking and making it easy to read

Independent reflection activity; Self-assessment; Issue review (approx. 15–20 mins)

Good for: Encouraging learners to think about the skills they improved this lesson and those that still need improving. Encourage learners to give an example in support of the skill improved; for example, for collaboration, 'shared relevant ideas with team members'; for evaluation, 'be able to give examples to highlight some of the strengths'.

Learners also complete the self-assessment to set their own learning targets before they move on. They think about and shade where they think they are at this time in their learning. 'With help' refers to guidance given (pointing a learner in the right direction, although examples should still come from the learner); for example, from you, other learners, previous work done by the learner in their Learner's Skills Book.

For the Issue review, learners explore the issue used in this section to develop communication skills.

These activities can be done in class, at home or in self-study time.

Suggested examples:

78Cm.01 *Present information and arguments clearly with some reasoning, referencing sources where appropriate.* Example: 'Communication is a way of transferring information from one place to another, either by using spoken or written texts or by non-verbal means such as pictures and diagrams. I am good at knowing some of the features of a well-structured argument, such as an introduction, a middle with claims, reasoning and supporting evidence, and a conclusion.'

78Cm.02 *Listen to ideas and information and offer relevant and well-judged contributions that demonstrate understanding of the issue.* Example 'I was able to share my ideas about food being wasted by supermarkets.'

Developing communication skills: Lesson 4

Lesson 4 focuses on listening to each other's arguments and giving feedback to improve the arguments.

CAMBRIDGE STAGE 8 COMMUNICATION LEARNING OBJECTIVES

78Cm.02 Listen to ideas and information and offer relevant and well-judged contributions that demonstrate understanding of the issue

LEARNING GOALS

To develop knowledge and understanding about:

- the importance of feedback
- listening to and recording ideas and information gained from others.

How will I know if I reach my goals?

Good for: Learners to give examples of their learning from the lesson. They can complete the table at any point in the lesson but might do it at the end.

Resources needed

- Learner's Skills Book 8
- Downloadables 6.3 and 6.4

Prior learning (approx. 5–10 mins)

Good for: Building on previous knowledge, learning and understanding. This might be from Cambridge Primary Global Perspectives, from Cambridge Global Perspectives Stage 7, from other subject areas or from previous Cambridge Global Perspectives Stage 8 lessons (Lessons 2 and 3).

Activity: Learners discuss with their team the importance of giving and receiving feedback.

Differentiation: Learners can look back at their Main activity, Independent reflection activity, Self-assessment and development targets from Lesson 3.

Suggested answers/ideas: Any reasonable and relevant response.

1 Feedback is important as it allows you to improve work and to develop skills further. It helps you know what you are doing well and what you need to improve on. It can be encouraging and motivating and allow you to achieve your learning goals.

2 You need to remember to always start with the positive, to be prepared to give an example for any points you make that will help improve someone else's work, to always give more positives than negatives, and to remember that good feedback is not personal – it's about the work produced.

Not issue specific.

Starter activity (approx. 10 mins)

Good for: Improving work after feedback.

Activity: Learners review the feedback on their argument from Lesson 3 and make changes to make the argument better according to the checklist.

Ways of working: In teams/small groups.

Suggested answers/ideas: Depends on the argument created in Lesson 3.

Main activity (approx. 20–25 mins)

Good for: Listening to and evaluating another team's argument.

Activity: Learners listen to each other's arguments – either read or played as a podcast. They complete the table with their observations and notes (notes can include the content of the argument, depending on the statement/claim chosen). They can then review the completed table and discuss with each other in order to give overall feedback on highlights (stars) and areas for improvement (wishes).

Differentiation: Learners work in teams, sharing ideas and feedback with each other.

Ways of working: In teams/small groups.

Different opinions/perspectives: Learners are asked about whether the argument has different perspectives in it. Encourage learners to state what these are.

Learner response and feedback: Encourage learners to help and support each other in teams. They can ask questions linked to the criteria in the checklist.

Suggested answers: Depends on the arguments presented (see Download 6.4 for an example script and the Worked Example for the Main activity).

Worked Example for the Main activity

Topic: Climate change, energy and resources

See Downloadable 6.4.

Claim: Everyone should have access to affordable and reliable energy.

Note that some of the sources referenced have been created for the purpose of this activity and are not real websites.

TITLE: IS IT POSSIBLE FOR EVERYONE TO HAVE ACCESS TO AFFORDABLE AND RELIABLE ENERGY?

Introduction

This report is about having affordable and reliable energy, and the reasons why this is important. It will explore a global and a national perspective about the issue of having affordable and reliable energy. It will present evidence to help reach an answer to the question, 'Is it possible for everyone to have access to affordable and reliable energy?' The claims we will explore are that, currently, not everyone in the world has access to electricity, many people don't have adequate cooking facilities and there is still limited use of renewable energy in many parts of the world.

It is important that everyone has access to affordable and reliable energy because, without it, our safety and security are threatened. Energy is needed for education, the production of food, as a source of heat, for healthcare systems and many other services that we sometimes take for granted, like entertainment.

However, not everyone has access to electricity in the world, due to unequal provision. According to the Worldwide Institution (2019), approximately 16 per cent of the world's population (1.2 billion people) have little or no access to electricity, which is unacceptable. Another interesting fact is that more than 80 per cent of those with inadequate energy supplies live in rural areas. Lack of energy means that people around the world, particularly those in rural areas, find it difficult to break out of the cycle of poverty they are in.

Many people don't have adequate cooking facilities, so they use wood stoves for cooking and heating their homes. Using a wood stove to cook can result in high levels of air pollution from wood smoke. This increases the risk of disease, as does not being able to cook many foods. Global Health Society (2019), which is another global organisation, states that is simply unacceptable that more than 3 billion people globally still breathe in deadly smoke on a daily basis just by using stoves in their homes.

Whilst some countries have a high usage of renewable energies like solar and wind power, use of these renewable energies is still limited in many parts of the world.

Some places, like we do here in … generate all their electricity using renewable energy because the government is committed to slowing down climate change and ensuring that energy is available once fossil fuels run out. Our government is proud to boast that we produce most of our energy from geothermal, solar and wind sources (Wikipedia, 2018).

Conclusion

We think that not having access to affordable and reliable energy sources is a big global issue. We all need to be more aware of how much energy we are using, and governments should do more to ensure that we have renewable energy so that we don't run out of energy sources in the future.

References

Worldwide Institution (2019), 'Access to energy is unequal'. [Online], https://www.worldwideinstitution.org/energy/x3044696j884786e (Accessed 20/09/2019).

https://www.globalhealthsociety.org/deadly-smoke-stoves

https://www.wikipedia.org/wiki/Renewableenergy

This text is an exemplar that you may wish to share with the learners. Stress that this text is far from perfect (e.g. there could be more transition words) and learners should look at the strengths and the areas that need developing. You might at this stage like to ask learners to compare the Example scripts provided in Downloadables 6.3 and 6.4. The learning is in the review of the texts and the discussion, which will help learners create and improve their own structured arguments.

Suggested answers:

1

Claim: Everyone should have access to affordable and reliable energy			
Title: Is it possible for everyone to have access to affordable and reliable energy?			
Is/are there …?	Yes	No	Notes
an introduction (including title)	✓		Clear title and clear introduction about what the report will cover
a conclusion (including personal perspective)	✓		Gives personal perspective but is not linked to the evidence presented and doesn't actually answer the question
a middle with claims	✓		There are no sub-headings but there are claims, which include: 'It is important that everyone has access to affordable and reliable energy'; 'Many people don't have adequate cooking facilities, so they use wood stoves for cooking and heating their homes'; 'use of these renewable energies is still limited'
reasoning to justify the claims in the middle	✓		'because without it our safety and security are threatened'; 'Lack of energy means people around the world find it difficult to break out of the cycle of poverty they are in'; 'This increases the risk of disease, as does not being able to cook many foods'
supporting evidence for the claims in the middle	✓		Worldwide Institution (reliable, global perspective); Global Health Society (reliable, global perspective); Wikipedia (unreliable, national perspective and could have been mentioned in the conclusion to change/develop personal perspective)
transition words/phrases (e.g. 'therefore', 'so', 'in summary')	✓		However; Another; so; this; whilst (compares)
relevant issue-specific words and phrases	✓		Renewable energy; electricity; access; solar; wind; etc. could add more, e.g. To conclude …
different perspectives	✓		Global and national – some contrast
a logical structure	✓		Each point follows the next with transition words linking and making it fairly easy to read

Claim: Everyone should have access to affordable and reliable energy	
Title: Is it possible for everyone to have access to affordable and reliable energy?	
Team: A	
☆	The argument has a logical structure and is linked with some transition words.
☆	The claims in the argument are justified with reasoning and supported by evidence.
☆	The conclusion would be better if it was linked to the evidence and answered the title question.

Independent reflection activity (approx. 5–10 mins)

Good for: Encouraging learners to identify the part of the lesson that helped them to learn the best; for example, listening to the arguments of another team to help them identify what a logical structure is. Encourage learners to be in honest in their ratings for the effort they made in the lesson and to give at least one reason for their rating.

This activity can be done in class, at home or in self-study time.

Developing communication skills: Lesson 5

Lesson 5 focuses on presenting information clearly and actively listening to show understanding.

CAMBRIDGE STAGE 8 COMMUNICATION LEARNING OBJECTIVES

78Cm.01 Present information and arguments clearly with some reasoning, referencing sources where appropriate

78Cm.02 Listen to ideas and information and offer relevant and well-judged contributions that demonstrate understanding of the issue

LEARNING GOALS

To develop knowledge and understanding about:

- presenting information clearly
- recording information accurately
- listening actively to increase understanding.

How will I know if I reach my goals?

Good for: Learners to give examples of their learning from the lesson. They can complete the table at any point in the lesson but might do it at the end.

Resources needed

- Learner's Skills Book 8
- Pictures for the Starter activity
- Downloadable 6.5

Prior learning (approx. 5–10 mins)

Good for: Building on previous knowledge, learning and understanding. This might be from Cambridge Primary Global Perspectives, from Cambridge Global Perspectives Stage 7, from other subject areas or from previous Cambridge Global Perspectives Stage 8 lessons.

Activity: Learners consider how they can tell when someone is listening actively.

Differentiation: Learners work in pairs for support and to clarify own thinking.

Suggested answers: Any reasonable and relevant response. Active listening is fully concentrating on what is being said rather than just passively hearing. It involves paraphrasing to show understanding and giving verbal feedback such as affirmations like 'I see', 'I know' and 'I understand', and non-verbal feedback such as nodding, leaning forward and making eye contact.

Starter activity (approx. 10 mins)

Good for: Presenting information clearly so that the partner understands what's in the picture/what the picture is about.

Activity: Give each pair two different pictures; one each. Working in turn, and without showing their partner, learners describe the content of their picture (see the Worked Example below) to their partner, who tries to either sketch the picture or to write down the details of the picture by listening carefully but without seeing the picture.

Ways of working: Individual and pairs.

Suggested answers/ideas: Depends on the issue and pictures given (see the Worked Example for the Starter activity for ideas). Class discussion about the importance of speaking clearly when presenting/describing, but also about actively listening to help understanding. Encourage learners to ask questions and use affirmations as well as non-verbal gestures to show active listening. Learners may have found the activity challenging because they got distracted and missed some details, or they are not used to listening for specific details or the person describing the picture didn't speak clearly.

Worked Example for the Starter activity

Topic: Climate change, energy and resources

Pictures can relate to the 17 UN Sustainable Development Goals.

1 No Poverty
2 Zero Hunger
3 Good Health and Well-being
4 Quality Education
5 Gender Equality
6 Clean Water and Sanitation
7 Affordable and Clean Energy
8 Decent Work and Economic Growth
9 Industry, Innovation and Infrastructure
10 Reduced Inequalities
11 Sustainable Cities and Communities
12 Responsible Consumption and Production
13 Climate Action
14 Life Below Water
15 Life on Land
16 Peace, Justice and Strong Institutions
17 Partnerships

Suggested answers/ideas: Learners can sketch or write the details of the picture as their partner describes it. You might ask learners to find their own picture about the issue and then do this activity, but it will take longer.

Main activity (approx. 20–25 mins)

Good for: Developing listening skills and gaining key information.

Activity: Learners watch or listen to three video/audio clips to identify the main message of each clip and any further information provided (see Downloadable 6.5 and the Worked Example for the Main activity for ideas).

Differentiation: Learners can discuss in pairs after each clip. A Language Support handout might be useful for some learners.

Ways of working: Individual/pairs and whole-class discussion.

Different opinions/perspectives: Encourage learners to try to identify the perspective from which the ideas in the clips come and to record this in the 'other information' column.

Learner response and feedback: Encourage learners to discuss their ideas between clips.

Suggested answers/ideas: Depends on the clips (see the Worked Example for ideas). Sharing and listening to the ideas of others helps for gaining further information and perhaps a different perspective and to clarify own thinking.

Worked Example for the Main activity

Topic: Climate change, energy and resources

See Downloadable 6.5 for three possible video clips.

	Main message	Other information
1	Things that you can do to be more sustainable – a chef shares what she does.	She tries to make climate conscious choices: asks guests to bring own containers for leftovers, never lets food go to waste, shops at farmers markets for seasonal produce, uses cloth bags and avoids plastic, eats a more plant-based diet (personal perspective).
2	Gender equality matters. Women and girls make up half the world's population and half the world's potential.	Raising women's participation in the workforce boosts the economy. Investing in women's health leads to higher standards of living. Provide women with equal access to education, healthcare and opportunities in politics. Get rid of violence towards women (global perspective).
3	Biodiversity is the way we connect with plant and wildlife. Without these connections, we wouldn't have food.	Bees and other pollinators are dying. Biodiversity is being lost. Only nine crops account for 66% of total crop production. Forests are shrinking. As forests disappear, so do plants, insects and animals. 26% of livestock breeds risk extinction. 33% of fish stocks are overfished. Act by buying local and seasonal (global perspective).

Video clip ideas: (Please check that these videos are suitable for your learners.)

- 'ActNow Climate Campaign – Chef Grace Ramirez' from Sustainable Development Goals page on United Nations website (https://www.un.org/sustainabledevelopment/blog/2019/07/green-life-hacks-with-chef-grace-ramirez/)
- 'Gender Equality: Sustainable Goal 5' from Sustainable Development Goals page on United Nations website (https://www.un.org/sustainabledevelopment/blog/2019/03/gender-equality-sustainable-development-goal-5/)
- 'Without biodiversity we wouldn't have the food we eat today! But it's disappearing before our eyes' from Sustainable Development Goals page on United Nations website (https://www.un.org/sustainabledevelopment/blog/2019/02/without-biodiversity-we-wouldnt-have-the-food-we-eat-today-but-its-disappearing-before-our-eyes/)

Independent reflection activity (approx. 5–10 mins)

Good for: Encouraging learners to reflect on how they know they have been actively listening; for example, by gaining further knowledge and understanding about the issue. Encourage learners to reflect on other skills (research, analysis, evaluation, reflection, collaboration) they have used this lesson as well as communication skills (e.g. collaboration skills as they worked with a partner).

This activity can be done in class, at home or in self-study time.

Developing communication skills: Lesson 6

Lesson 6 focuses on listening to gain further information about the issue to produce a shared outcome in Lesson 7.

CAMBRIDGE STAGE 8 COMMUNICATION LEARNING OBJECTIVES

78Cm.01 Present information and arguments clearly with some reasoning, referencing sources where appropriate

78Cm.02 Listen to ideas and information and offer relevant and well-judged contributions that demonstrate understanding of the issue

LEARNING GOALS

To develop knowledge and understanding about:

- presenting information clearly and with some reasoning
- improving listening skills to gain information.

How will I know if I reach my goals?

Good for: Learners to give examples of their learning from the lesson. They can complete the table at any point in the lesson but might do it at the end.

Resources needed

- Learner's Skills Book 8
- Downloadable 6.6

Prior learning (approx. 5–10 mins)

Good for: Building on previous knowledge, learning and understanding. This might be from Cambridge Primary Global Perspectives, from Cambridge Global Perspectives Stage 7, from other subject areas or from previous Cambridge Global Perspectives Stage 8 lessons (e.g. Lesson 5).

Activity: Review learning about giving and receiving feedback.

Differentiation: Learners can work in pairs for support.

Suggested answers: Any reasonable and relevant response.

- Giving feedback helps others to improve their work or develop a skills.
- Receiving feedback helps us identify the highlights in our work and areas that might need improving.
- When giving feedback, we should remember to start with the positive and focus on the quality of the work produced.
- When receiving feedback, we should remember to be thankful and know that feedback can allow us to produce better quality work.

Starter activity (approx. 5–10 mins)

Good for: Developing active listening skills.

Activity: Read out the statements to the class (see Downloadable 6.6 and the Worked Example) and ask learners to decide whether the statement is true or false. They will be able to check their answers in the Main activity. In this activity, the aim is not about stating correctly if the statement is right or wrong, it is about ensuring that learners understand the statement.

Ways of working: Individual work.

Suggested answers/ideas: Depends on the statements given (see the Worked Example).

Worked Example for the Starter activity

Topic: Climate change, energy and resources

See Downloadable 6.6.

Statement ideas:

1 Sustainability is something from the environment that people use.

2 Oil is a natural resource.

3 Riding a bicycle is not sustainable.

4 'No Poverty' is Sustainable Development Goal 3.

5 Since 2000, 15.6 million children have died of measles.

6 There are 17 Sustainable Development Goals in total.

7 Globally, more than 3 billion people depend on marine and coastal biodiversity for their livelihoods.

8 Globally, about 26 million children do not currently attend school.

9 Women earn 12.5 per cent more than men in 40 out of the 45 countries that provide data.

10 More than 80 per cent of all land-dwelling species of animals, plants and insects rely on forests for their natural habitat.

Suggested answers:

1 False – it's the avoidance of the depletion of natural resources in order to maintain an ecological balance

2 True

3 False – no resources are used in riding a bicycle, apart from people peddling

4 False – it is Sustainable Development Goal 1

5 False – 15.6 million deaths have been prevented by vaccines

6 True

7 True

8 False – more than 265 million children are currently out of school

9 False – the opposite is true: women earn less

10 True

Explain that learners will clarify their own responses with research in the Main activity.

Main activity (approx. 20–25 mins)

Good for: Researching to clarify understanding of an issue.

Activity: This leads on from the Starter activity and learners will need a list of the original statements from Downloadable 6.6 or can write down the original statements in the starter activity. Learners work in pairs to find a source of information that supports (or corrects) their true/false responses to each statement. If the statement is false, learners correct it with a true statement. Pairs also create five new statements (recording the answers separately) to ask another pair if they are true or false.

Differentiation: Learners work in pairs to share ideas and then in fours to answer each other's extra five statements.

Ways of working: In pairs and then fours.

Different opinions/perspectives: Remind learners to check the type of website and which perspective the ideas come from, although they should be cross-referencing and checking and will write mostly factual statements.

Learner response and feedback: Learners can give each other feedback to check the quality of the statements:

- Is the statement relevant to the issue?
- Is the statement clear?
- Is there a definite true/false answer?
- If the answer is false, do we know the true answer?
- Do we have a mixture of true and false statements?

Suggested answers: Learners answers will vary (see the Worked Example for the Starter activity for answers to the first ten questions).

Independent reflection activity; Self-assessment; Issue review (approx. 15–20 mins)

Good for: Encouraging learners to consider what they used to think about the issue and how their thinking might have developed/changed. This encourages personal perspective and how it is influenced by research and other perspectives. Learners also complete the self-assessment to set their own learning targets before they move on. They think about and shade where they think they are at this time in their learning. 'With help' refers to guidance given (pointing a learner in the right direction, although examples should still come from the learner); for example, from you, other learners, previous work done by the learner in their Learner's Skills Book.

For the Issue review, learners explore the issue used in this section to develop communication skills.

These activities can be done in class, at home or in self-study time.

Suggested examples:

78Cm.01 *Present information and arguments clearly with some reasoning, referencing sources where appropriate.* Example: 'Communication is a way of transferring information from one place to another, either by using spoken or written texts or by non-verbal means such as pictures and diagrams.' Feedback is important as it helps to develop skills and improve work. Any reasonable response from Lessons 1–6 showing reasoning; for example, 'It's important to use renewable sources of energy for sustainability because natural sources like oil will eventually run out.'

78Cm.02 *Listen to ideas and information and offer relevant and well-judged contributions that demonstrate understanding of the issue.* Any reasonable response from Lessons 1–6. Example: 'I was able to identify which statements were true and which were false, and help others correct the false ones by asking them questions like "Does it sound likely?"'

Getting better at communication skills: Lesson 7

Lesson 7 focuses on presenting information learned from research in Lessons 1–6.

CAMBRIDGE STAGE 8 COMMUNICATION LEARNING OBJECTIVES

78Cm.01 Present information and arguments clearly with some reasoning, referencing sources where appropriate

78Cm.02 Listen to ideas and information and offer relevant and well-judged contributions that demonstrate understanding of the issue

LEARNING GOALS

To get better at:

- presenting information with reasoning
- sharing ideas with others.

How will I know if I reach my goals?

Good for: Learners to give examples of their learning from the lesson. They can complete the table at any point in the lesson but might do it at the end.

Resources needed

- Learner's Skills Book 8
- Teacher's own pictures for Starter activity
- Downloadable 6.7

Prior learning (approx. 5–10 mins)

Good for: Building on previous knowledge, learning and understanding. This might be from Cambridge Primary Global Perspectives, from Cambridge Global Perspectives Stage 7, from other subject areas or from previous Cambridge Global Perspectives Stage 8 lessons (i.e. Lessons 1–6).

Activity: Review all the skills used during their Cambridge Global Perspectives lessons. Encourage learners to give examples for the different skills.

Differentiation: Allow thinking time. Learners list all the skills they have used during Global Perspectives lessons. You can start them off – research, communication, listening, writing (communication skills). Set a time limit as there will be a lot.

Suggested answers: Any reasonable and relevant examples.

Research: asking/writing questions, looking for information, organising and recording information.

Analysis: exploring causes and consequences, gaining ideas from different perspectives, supporting shared outcome with evidence, complete shared outcome, identifying course of action.

Evaluation: judging which sources to use to provide relevant information, evaluating strengths and limitations of the team and own work processes within teamwork.

Reflection: Reflecting on effectiveness of teamwork, own contribution to teamwork, identify skills learned and how perspective on the issue changed/developed.

Communication: listening, reading, writing, speaking, producing shared outcome.

Collaboration: working in a team, taking turns, listening to others, sharing ideas etc.

Not issue specific.

Starter activity (approx. 10 mins)

Good for: Reviewing learning about the issue ready to create a poem/song/rap (in the Main activity) to get an important message across.

Activity: Show one (or more) pictures (see the Worked Example for ideas) and ask learners to say what each picture is about. This can be done orally or written. Learners also think about what other information they want to know related to the picture. Encourage them to ask questions and come up with at least three questions. Questions can be discussed in class. Learners then do some research to record what they have learned in response to their questions.

Suggested answers/ideas: See the Worked Example below.

Worked Example for the Starter activity

Topic: Climate change, energy and resources

Picture and question ideas: Any pictures to relate to the 17 UN Sustainable Development Goals.

1. No Poverty
2. Zero Hunger
3. Good Health and Well-being
4. Quality Education
5. Gender Equality
6. Clean Water and Sanitation
7. Affordable and Clean Energy
8. Decent Work and Economic Growth
9. Industry, Innovation and Infrastructure
10. Reduced Inequalities
11. Sustainable Cities and Communities
12. Responsible Consumption and Production
13. Climate Action
14. Life Below Water
15. Life on Land
16. Peace, Justice and Strong Institutions
17. Partnerships

Suggested questions:

UN Sustainable Goal 1: How many people globally are still classed as living in poverty? Where is poverty at is worst? Who does poverty affect the most? What are the causes of poverty? What are the consequences of poverty? What does the UN hope to achieve by 2030?

UN Sustainable Goal 3: What is the life expectancy in different parts of the world? Why is life expectancy different depending on where you live? What are the main causes of disease? What can be done to prevent these diseases? What do vaccinations do? What does the UN hope to achieve by 2030?

UN Sustainable Goal 6: Why don't people globally have access to clean, affordable water? What are the consequences of not having access to clean, affordable water? How do people gain access to water? Does this differ depending on where you live? Why can't we use water from oceans for drinking and cooking? What does the UN hope to achieve by 2030?

Main activity (approx. 20–25 mins)

Good for: Working in pairs/small groups to create a poem/song/rap based on the information learned about the issue. The aim is to make people aware of the situation and perhaps suggest courses of action to help resolve or make a positive difference to the situation.

Activity: Learners write a poem/song or rap (see the Worked Example for the Main activity) to raise awareness about making the world a more sustainable place. They write down the references of the sources they used to create their poem/song/rap.

Differentiation: Learners work in pairs/small groups to support and share ideas. Use a Language Support handout if appropriate. You might want to give an example poem/song/rap to start with (see the Worked Example for the Main activity).

Ways of working: In pairs/small groups.

Different opinions/perspectives: Encourage learners to consider the perspective their poem/song/rap is coming from.

Learner response and feedback: Encourage learners to ask each other questions such as:

- What are we trying to say?
- Is the message relevant to the issue?
- Does the message make people aware of the issue?
- Do we give a reason why someone should do this?
- Do we give a clear course(s) of action that people can take?
- Is the message clear?
- Is the message short and to the point?

Also encourage groups to give feedback on other groups' ideas. The best poems/songs/raps can be put onto paper/card and displayed around the school.

Suggested answers: Answers will vary according to groups (see the Worked Example below for ideas).

Worked Example for the Main activity

Topic: Climate change, energy and resources

See Downloadable 6.7.

Poem/song/rap ideas: Search for websites using search terms 'Sustainability songs' and 'Sustainability poems'

MY ODE TO THE WORLD

Sustainability – what does it mean?
Recycling, reusing, being green.
Buying local produce and locally made goods.
Protecting species by saving forests and woods.
Avoid single-use plastics – water bottles and shopping bags.
Instead of paper tissues, choose cloth washrags.
Rather than cars, choose to go on foot or ride your bike.
There's nothing better than a good hike!
Save water for future generations – instead of a bath, take a shower.
Petition governments to provide renewable power.
Wind, water and solar are all better than oil.
Sustainability – that's our goal.

Reference

UN (n.d.), 'Take Action for the Sustainable Development Goals'. [Online], https://www.un.org/sustainabledevelopment/sustainable-development-goals/ (Accessed 07/07/2022).

Independent reflection activity; Self-assessment; Issue review (approx. 15–20 mins)

Good for: Encouraging learners to consider the skills they have improved this lesson and how they improved this skill; for example, this might be communicating – sharing ideas and joining in discussions; evaluation – judging the best poem/song/rap, giving feedback for improvements etc.

Learners also complete the self-assessment to set their own learning targets. They think about and shade where they think they are at this time in their learning. 'With help' refers to guidance given (pointing a learner in the right direction, although examples should still come from the learner); for example, from you, other learners, previous work done by the learner in their Learner's Skills Book.

For the Issue review, learners explore the issue used in this section to develop communication skills.

These activities can be done in class, at home or in self-study time.

Suggested examples:

78Cm.01 *Present information and arguments clearly with some reasoning, referencing sources where appropriate.* Examples: 'Communication is a way of transferring information from one place to another, either by using spoken or written texts or by non-verbal means such as pictures and diagrams'; 'I can present information clearly; for example, "Avoid using single-use plastic, use cloth bags".'

78Cm.02 *Listen to ideas and information and offer relevant and well-judged contributions that demonstrate understanding of the issue.* Example: 'I was able to add two lines to our song, which suggested action and included a reason for this action.'

Showcasing your skills: Communication

Good for: Showing learners how others felt at the end of this section after practising and developing their communication skills. Learners have learned a lot about their ability to organise their written and spoken ideas. These reflections from learners will show them that the skills they find difficult are difficult for others too. But they can do it!

Communication is the skill of organising what we say and write so that it makes sense. This always seems easy until we try to teach someone to do it. There are lots of ways we can support learners, e.g. writing frames, using headings and subheadings. As you will have done in 'Section 5: Collaboration', you are very welcome to support learners with their organisation. Feel free to give them guidance and structure where needed. As they become better at this important life skill, you can slowly withdraw your support so they can organise their own work. But it will take them time (and it will require your patience and support).

The key here is for learners to become better and better at communicating their ideas with others. We all know how important this skill is, especially in our increasingly complex digital world, where messages are so easily miscommunicated.

Activity: This is an opportunity for your learners to reflect on elements of their work in this section that they are particularly pleased with. Read through and discuss the reflections with your class. Then do one of these reflection tasks:

- Ask learners a question, e.g. 'What surprised you today, and why?' or 'What's the most important thing you learned today?' Ask learners to write their answers on sticky notes and stick them on the board.
- 'Two stars and a wish' means 'Two things I am pleased with and one thing I want to improve on'. Ask your learners to write their own 'two stars and a wish' on a sticky note and stick it on the board.

Projects: If learners have had ample opportunities to practise the other skills required, they could also showcase their communication skills by attempting Project 8.2 or Project 8.3, available at cambridge.org/go, both of which have communication learning objectives.

[redacted]

> Acknowledgements

The authors and publishers acknowledge the following sources of copyright material and are grateful for the permissions granted. While every effort has been made, it has not always been possible to identify the sources of all the material used, or to trace all copyright holders. If any omissions are brought to our notice, we will be happy to include the appropriate acknowledgements on reprinting.

Thanks to the following for permission to reproduce images:

Cover Radoslav Zilinsky/GI; *Downloadables* **1.9** xPACIFICA/ GI; Zhihao/ GI; **2.1** Gary John Norman/ GI; Tim Grist Photography/ GI; Hans Georg Roth/ GI; We Are/ GI; Jonathan Knowles/ GI; Fcafotodigital/ GI; **2.6** Westend61/ GI; Xrrr/ GI; Jamie Grill/ GI; **4.5** Ethan Miller/ GI; Leonardo Alvarez Hernandez/ GI; Nuccio DiNuzzo/ GI; **5.1** Reda&Co/ GI; Godong/ GI; AFP/ GI; Westend61/ GI; Pastorscott/ GI; Onoky - Fabrice Lerouge/ GI; Thomas Trutschel/ GI; Roberto Machado Noa/ GI

Key GI = Getty Images

Thanks to the following contributors:
Dawn Harris, author of the downloadable projects.